Richie McCaw

THE OPEN SIDE

Richie McCaw

THE OPEN SIDE

with Greg McGee

Hodder Moa

Front endpaper: The Hakataramea Valley, looking north-west from the Hunter Hills towards the Kirklistons. The farm where Richie grew up is just beyond the hills in the foreground, running up to the irrigation pond. *Sarah Rowland*
Back endpaper: When the whole nation smiled. Eden Park, 23 October 2011. *Getty*

Photo credits
Getty: 6–7, 15, 16, 19, 23, 26, 27, 30, 31, 33, 35, 38, 51, 54, 56, 61, 63, 73 (left and right), 75, 82, 83, 85, 89, 93, 95, 97, 99, 105 (bottom), 106, 109, 111, 113, 121, 123, 131, 134, 135, 137, 140, 141, 143, 144, 146, 149, 150, 153, 154, 157, 161 (left and right), 167, 173, 178, 179, 181, 183, 184, 187, 190 (left and right), 193, 194, 197, 200, 202, 204, 206, 209, 212, 213, 215, 218, 219, 220, 223, 224, 226, 227, 230, 231, 232, 233, 234, 238, 242, 243, 245, 246, 247, 248 (left and right), 249, 252, 256, 259, 261.
Photosport: 64, 76, 80, 91, 94, 116, 132, 151, 170, 177, 189, 211, 216, 239, 258 (bottom).
Rugby Images: 2–3, 87, 98, 129, 162, 165, 175, 188, 192, 217, 228, 235, 237, 240, 258 (top).
McCaw Family Collection: 11, 14, 42, 45, 47 (top and bottom), 49, 66, 67 (top and bottom), 69, 126.
Richie McCaw: 38, 39, 43, 105 (top), 117, 119, 164, 198, 262, 263.
John McCaw: 122, 195, 199.
Sarah Rowland: 12, 264.
Hodder Moa: 13.
Martin Hunter: 41.
Barney McCone: 46.
Paul Daly Photography: 101.
Fairfax Media: 260.

National Library of New Zealand Cataloguing-in-Publication Data
McGee, Greg, 1950-
Richie McCaw : the open side / Greg McGee.
Includes index.
ISBN 978-1-86971-276-1
1. McCaw, Richie, 1980-—Career in sport. 2. Rugby Union football players—New Zealand—Biography. I. McCaw, Richie, 1980- II. Title.
796.333092—dc 23

A Hodder Moa Book
Published in 2012 by Hachette New Zealand Ltd
4 Whetu Place, Mairangi Bay
Auckland, New Zealand
www.hachette.co.nz

Reprinted 2012 (twice)

Designed and produced by Hachette New Zealand Ltd
Printed by Everbest Printing Co. Ltd., China
Front cover photo: Getty

For Mum and Dad and my sister Jo. Your love and
support have helped me every step of the way. And to all
my other family and friends, a very big thank you.

Contents

Writer's note

One of the first things Richie said to me when I saw him in late December 2011, a couple of months after the Rugby World Cup final, was 'I feel like I've been in a tunnel for four years and just got out.'

The image of him I'd been carrying was from moments after the whistle blew in the final: that battered, bloodied warrior at the end of his tether, not so much on his last legs, but, as we now know, on his last leg, and looking a decade older than his 30 years.

Two months later, the young man who opened the door of his townhouse in Christchurch was scarcely recognisable as the same man, despite the moon boot. He looked radiant. He looked like a man with the sun on his face.

I'd come down to Christchurch to ask a question, before anything was signed and sealed. I wanted to ask him face to face with no agents or publishers around if he was doing the book out of a sense of obligation or pressure, because if he was, I doubted that I'd get the access or material the book would need. I should have known better. Richie doesn't commit to anything lightly, and after about two minutes, I knew it was a question I'd never have to ask.

What was supposed to be a half-hour chat turned into an animated two-hour exchange about what we were going to do, how we were going to attack it. His opening statement suggested a way forward: that we go back into that four-year tunnel and discover what it took to find the light. From there, we would spin backwards at opportune times to defining events and people in Richie's life.

As we did that, I came to see Richard Hugh McCaw as an increasingly rare alchemy of old-school and contemporary. His origins are as rural and tough as any All Black icons of the past, yet he's also a boarding school and university-educated urbanite. He's technologically extremely adept, runs everything off his smart phone, but would as soon eat his own entrails as tweet. He's the consummate professional yet essentially plays for the love of the game. He's driven by an elemental fierce joy for the conflict, yet has sought out an understanding of the psychological underpinnings of behaviour and motivation. He trusts his instincts and what he knows, but is hungry to learn what he doesn't know. And perhaps the biggest paradox in his life these days: he now occupies a hugely public position in the nation's psyche, yet is a man who likes to keep a substantial part of himself to himself.

He shares some characteristics it seems, with all champions. Dominic Lawson of *The Independent* was thinking of Roger Federer — who, more than most champions, gives an impression of languid grace and effortless genius — when he wrote: 'A proper investigation of the careers of the supreme achievers, whether in sport or other fields, reveals that they are based above all on monomaniacal diligence and concentration. Constant struggle, in other words. Seen in this light, we might define genius as talent multiplied by effort.'

I would hesitate to call Richie monomaniacal, given his many other interests and pursuits, but my hope is that no one who reads this book should be left in any doubt about what it took for him to do what he did.

Greg McGee
July 2012

G.A.B.

I was 12 years old when my father told me I'd enjoy my rugby more if I got fitter. That was how he put it. I was a big kid, and he could have said I might make a better player for losing some weight, or that I might be selected for better teams. Instead, he said I'd *enjoy* it more.

That stuck; I don't know why.

The County Council had left markers in blue paint on the verge of the loop road and I worked out these markers were 500 metres apart, so I tried to run five markers one way and back three or four times a week. Three kilometres, four kilometres, five. Right through late summer, as the sun burnt the valley brown, I jogged down our shingle driveway after school, past the sheep yards and on to the loop road.

I'd turn left and head up towards the Kirkliston Range, past my grandfather's farm, to where the road turned north and linked back to the main road running up the valley towards Cattle Creek. On either side, grazing and cropping flats rose to high-country tussock, where there'd be snow on the tops through to October most years. Familiar sentinels watched over me: the Kirklistons in front of me, Mount Domett and Te Kohurau to the south, the Hunter Hills running up towards Mount Menzies to the north, where the road petered out and our river began. The Hakataramea River ran down through our valley and fed into the Waitaki. At the confluence, there was a one-way wooden bridge across to Kurow, a little two-pub town on the road that connected the Mackenzie Country basin to Oamaru on the east coast. These were the boundaries of the world I knew.

A year later, my world expanded when I became a boarder at Otago Boys' High School in Dunedin. When they left me there, Mum and Dad told me this was a big opportunity that I had to make the most of. I put myself up for every sport that came along and worked so hard at my studies through the years that some of my mates from the First XV and First XI felt I was overdoing it, in danger of becoming a geek.

That didn't worry me. What worried me more was letting myself down.

Spaghetti Junction, Haka Valley style.

In our end-of-year exams for sixth-form maths, I got 99.4 per cent. I missed one bloody mark. The very last question on the paper. I can still remember what I missed and how I missed it — it was the only one I didn't check. There was a diagram of a circle, with a hexagon inside it. I had to work out how much of the circle was left if you removed the hexagon. I worked out the radius and tangents, made the calculations and wrote it down. I forgot to multiply it by six.

If I hadn't known the answer, I could accept that. I could forget it.

The reason I still remember every detail of it is because I did know it, but lost concentration.

The following year, my world enlarged again, when I was selected for the New Zealand Under 19 trials. We had one camp in Wellington before Christmas and one after, and we'd been given a programme for the summer to get fit for the trials in late January.

After I got home from the first training camp, my Mum's brother, John 'Bigsy' McLay, and his family met us in Timaru for a family lunch prior to Christmas. Uncle Bigsy had been a really good rugby player who'd been selected for the New Zealand Colts and New Zealand Universities. He hadn't quite reached his potential due to injuries from a car accident, but he'd still played around 100 games for Mid Canterbury, many of them alongside Mum's other brother, Peter. Uncle Bigsy was someone in the family who knew a bit about rugby and was a mentor, interested in strategy and motivation.

There were a few of us sitting around McDonald's waiting for our orders — my folks, my sister Joanna, my aunty and cousins. I was sitting next to Uncle Bigsy and showed him the book I'd been given, with the training programme in it.

He scrutinised it carefully. 'You want to be in the New Zealand Under 19s,' he said. 'Do you want to be an All Black?'

'Oh yeah.'

He took out a pen, smoothed a table napkin. 'Let's map out how you become an All Black.'

I was a bit fazed, felt lucky to be given a trial for the Under 19s, thought I was only there because our school First XV had had a great year. But with his encouragement, I told him that this coming year, when I was embarking on a Bachelor of Agricultural Science degree at Lincoln University in Christchurch, I wanted to make the New Zealand Under 19s, then the Canterbury Under 19s, then next year the New Zealand Colts.

Uncle Bigsy on the charge for Mid Canterbury, 1982.

Uncle Bigsy wrote it all down, kept prompting me. 'Then what?'

I listed the Canterbury Under 21s, the Canterbury team, and he insisted I put a target year beside each of the teams that I needed to make. We worked out that after the 2003 Rugby World Cup there'd be a bit of a clean-out in the All Blacks and there'd be guys going overseas, so I might make the Crusaders then and maybe the All Blacks after that, maybe 2004.

'All Blacks 2004,' wrote Uncle Bigsy.

I was keeping my voice down, aware that this was all pie in the sky given that I hadn't yet made a national age-group team, but Uncle Bigsy wasn't finished. 'You don't just want to be an All Black,' he said, 'you want to be a great All Black.'

What could I say? Who wouldn't? So I nodded, and he wrote that down too, then pushed the napkin over and gave me the pen. 'Sign it,' he said. 'Sign it *Great All Black*.'

I was hoping no one could overhear him — Dad had already taken himself outside for a walk. I looked at the list Uncle Bigsy had constructed. It was a stairway to rugby heaven all right, but looked more like fantasy than a legitimate aspiration for someone like me. 'Sign it,' he said.

I couldn't bring myself to write the words Great All Black, so I wrote down *G.A.B.*

'Put that up somewhere,' he said.

I quickly stuck it in my pocket.

Aged 12, on top of the Kirklistons. Behind me, Lake Aviemore looking towards Otematata.

Back home on the farm there was a cupboard up high, so I pinned it in the back there, where I could be sure no one else could see it.

I had no idea what the reality of becoming a *G.A.B.* might be, and despite Uncle Bigsy's enthusiasm, I can't say I ever really expected to find out. But the pictures I had in my head were amazing, of scoring fabulous tries in the black jersey and silver fern in front of huge roaring crowds at exotic places I'd read about, Eden Park, Ellis Park, Twickenham, Cardiff Arms Park . . .

The wrong picture

I'm not superstitious, but the portents aren't that flash. We're in the wrong dressing room. The team we always beat should be in this one. The words *Undeb Rygbi Cymru* are plastered on the wall above our cubicles over the symbol of Welsh rugby, a stylised scarlet-jerseyed player springing out of a yellow coronet, flanked by what look like scarlet claws. We've never lost at this stadium, which is the same as saying the Welsh have never won against us. But this week, we're not playing Wales, we're playing France. France is the host nation of the 2007 Rugby World Cup, but here we are playing them in a quarter-final in Cardiff.

It's all wrong. We feel like we've stepped out of the tournament temporarily for this game. If we win it, we get back to Paris next week for the real thing. If we lose, we're on a plane home. That's not a thought I want in my head. But we've lost the toss for our usual dressing room, lost the toss for our usual hotel in Cardiff, lost the toss for our black strip and lost the toss for kick-off . . .

We thought there might be an upside to playing France in Cardiff rather than in front of their own at Paris or Marseilles, but before the game, we can hear the crowd above us singing, and it isn't 'Bread of Heaven' or 'God Defend New Zealand'. They've closed the roof on Millennium, and when we line up for the anthems and they launch into 'La Marseillaise', most of the crowd, it seems, join in, and the atmosphere is as charged as anything I've heard from a Welsh crowd.

The haka confirms France are well and truly up for the game. They stand right in front of us, Caveman Sebastien Chabal, all flowing black locks, beard and eyebrows, giving us the evil eye.

I've seen it all before in his TV ads: he's usually a fitful presence in a game as an undersized lock or ungainly loosie, which is probably why he's on the bench. But the way all his team-mates eyeball us like that . . . We go into the huddle before the kick-off thinking, *Uh oh, they're here to play.*

That isn't always the case: we whacked this team 47–3 in Lyon last year, and followed that up with 23–11 in Paris, where, even though they got a lot closer to

Uh oh, they're here to play . . . Les Tricolores accept our challenge before kick-off in the 2007 World Cup quarter-final.

us, they hadn't played that impressively. But they're host nation for this RWC and they've been humiliated by Argentina in pool play, which is why they, rather than Argentina, are here playing us in Cardiff. They're desperate. This is their last chance at redemption.

Desperate winner-take-all knockouts between the All Blacks and France at the World Cup aren't new. We beat France to take the very first Webb Ellis Cup in '87, but that's ancient history: the most recent clash wasn't such a happy ending. In the semi-final at Twickenham in 1999, the All Blacks led 17–10 at halftime, then went out to 24–10 early in the second half. France had looked dead and buried, but had come back to mow the All Blacks down and win 43–31.

I'd heard that '99 match described by some people as the greatest in RWC history, but none of those people were All Blacks. Byron Kelleher and Anton Oliver, beside me in the huddle, had played that day.

Plenty more of us were in Sydney in 2003, when Australia beat us in the semi-final, and George Gregan had yelled into Byron's ear: 'Four more years, boys! Four more years!'

We've served our four-year sentence. Our time is up.

The first half goes to plan in most respects, and yet . . . That Welsh symbol looming over us at halftime isn't the only strangeness. I say something to assistant coach Steve Hansen that I can't remember saying, but that he remembers, because he's never heard me say anything like it before. *I can't get into this game. Don't know why, but I can't seem to catch hold of it.*

That'd be a worry for Steve, because that's my job as openside flanker, not to mention captain. Be all over the game. Control the breakdowns, impose myself on their ball, slow it, read the ref, do whatever it takes to get into their heads. At my best, I live in that split second of time and space at the breakdown, a collision zone where 100-plus-kilogram bodies are hurtling from diverse points of the compass towards a small ovoid focus. Success or failure can be measured in microseconds. Openside flankers live or die in those slivers of time.

But the French have picked a team to kick the ball at us, and that's what they do through the first half. Their fullback Damien Traille makes their intentions known by drop-kicking for goal from a good attacking position after just six minutes — he misses, but everything we throw at them comes back to us in the air. For the first 10 minutes we get suckered into this aerial ping-pong, kicking long but keeping it in play, hoping they'll run it back at us so we can attack the tackled ball in the breakdown. But there's nothing to attack; they won't bring the ball back to contact, and keep hoisting bombs.

We don't get a chance to counter until the 10-minute mark, when fullback Leon MacDonald takes a high ball, steps the chasers and initiates our first counter. We're finally able to stretch them left and right and hit them with multiple phases for a full two minutes, which culminates in Luke McAlister stepping inside Yannick Jauzion, offloading to centre Mils Muliaina, who's dragged down short. Fabien Pelous, one of two French players who'd also been there in '99, gives away a desperation penalty in front of their posts. Dan Carter slots it: 3–nil.

A couple of minutes later at a French lineout, Ali Williams slaps it out of Imanol Harinordoquy's hands. The blond Basque has come on for Serge Betsen, who was KO'd after five minutes. To my mind that makes their loosies a much more potent mix, as Harinordoquy goes to No. 8 and gives them another big option at lineout, Julien Bonnaire switches to the bindside and, crucially, forces Thierry Dusautoir to play openside.

The only similarities between Betsen and Dusautoir are that they're both black and both brave. Betsen's a classic fetcher, but Dusautoir is bigger, faster and completely indomitable. He can fetch, carry, dominate the tackle and clean out. And, worryingly, I've never seen a bead of sweat on the man.

Luke breaks the French line again from that turnover. I'm clear inside him, but he doesn't see me, flips it back to Byron and Ali goes over in the corner. Replays show that despite Ali's celebrations, his size 14s are well out. Ali's notoriously optimistic — part of his charm — but the first bad picture pops into my mind and probably the minds of several other players: of Mils seeming to score early in the Sydney semi-final in 2003, but being disallowed for the same reason. It didn't seem that important at the time: we thought we had Australia on the rack, just as I think we've got France on the rack here.

From the defensive lineout, France kicks out, Sitiveni Sivivatu takes a quick throw and Leon sets up the counter. From the ruck, Dan drifts wide and puts Luke through a hole inside David Marty and outside Jauzion. Dusautoir is sweeping, but can't nail him. Luke straightens and this time finds Jerry Collins on his inside. When Jerry's run down two metres out, he palms it up to Luke who goes over. I flop on the ball to make sure it's grounded, but Luke has got it down under pressure. Dan converts: 10–nil after 18 minutes. We've had the ball for the last eight minutes, played the game our way and got the points on the board to prove it. *So much for bad pictures.*

The next 20, however, don't quite go to plan.

Referee Wayne Barnes calls a marginal forward pass on Dan when he wraps around Carl Hayman. Then we wheel the French scrum, but Barnes won't give us the put-in we've earned. Then we fluff a bomb — Byron tracks back and gets in Leon's way. The crowd noise must have drowned Leon's call.

From the scrum, Harinordoquy breaks right and Jerry gets trapped in their side of the ruck. Seems like a harsh call from Barnes, but he's at least being consistent, nailing Pelous for the same thing, and me too, early in the game. Lionel Beauxis misses the shot, and Dan tries a fiddly drop-out that almost gets us into trouble, but at 30 minutes gone, 10 to go, our game is still tracking well.

But right on 30, Jerry's carrying the ball up when Dusautoir hits him so hard with his shoulder and head that it charlies Jerry's quad and cripples him for the rest of the game. As some compensation, we get a penalty from Barnes for offside at the ensuing ruck, and Dan nails it: 13–nil.

Luke doesn't need me to help him score.

The last 10 minutes are wobbly. Anton makes a wild tip from the restart, Byron scrambles, and Joe Rokocoko clears. Then Traille kicks it dead and I sense French heads dropping. Shortly after, Dan attacks wide on the French 22, and we might have them if we're able to recycle. But Dusautoir wins the turnover — another big play from him — and France runs at us for the first time. Mils stops Marty in his tracks, but Barnes gets a heads-up from assistant referee Jonathan Kaplan who reckons his tackle was high. Barnes also thinks Rodney So'oialo was late on the other side.

There's nothing much in either, but Barnes insists I give the team a general warning. That's frustrating, but I figure that if Barnes and Kaplan are going to be officious, that's okay, as long as what goes around comes around.

The French penalty gives them an attacking lineout which Ali takes away from them. By the time Byron hooks it out, though, we're back to square one. This time, the French secure the ball, set up a big drive in the middle, then come roaring back on the switch. Our tight forwards defend well on the blind, but Keith Robinson gets trapped in the ruck and is pinged by Barnes. *Fair enough.*

Jean-Baptiste Elissalde misses the kick from close in and just to the right of the sticks, and I think, *That's it.* France has had a good period on attack, but we've shipped no points and halftime is only three minutes away. French heads *should* be dropping: they've got nothing for their endeavour.

Instead, we're the ones who have a brain-fade. Maybe it's these last three minutes that put the wrong pictures in Byron's head, and make him say what he says at halftime.

Dan drops out long, Traille kicks high, and it's back to aimless aerial ping-pong until we get messy and disorganised behind a defensive ruck. Dusautoir — who else? — charges down Byron's kick, Harinordoquy chases and sets up a great attacking ruck. France have numbers right, set up another ruck, then swing back left, only to blow an overlap with a shocker of a pass to left winger, Cedric Heymans. We manage to turn the ball over, but again we're disorganised. Byron throws a long pass to Leon, but he has no space and has to take it into contact.

We only just manage to recycle in front of our own posts, but we're holding on, with halftime looming, when Dan decides on a delicate wipers kick 10 metres out from our own line. We've been encouraged by the coaches to stay positive and not get too conservative under RWC pressure, but that's just about a step too far. Siti's standing wide, manages to take the ball under pressure, still five metres short of our own 22. I get over him, bridge long enough for Mils at halfback to clear it to Jerry, an unlikely first-five, who has clearly had a gutsful of this carry-on and boots it into touch.

I look at the clock: 39.11. Less than a minute to go. *Safe.* I know the coaches will be out of their chairs and heading down to the dressing room. We've had 10 minutes of bad options, no options, and a drop in energy and concentration.

We need to get to that wrong dressing room and regroup.

Last play. Jerome Thion drives from the lineout on halfway, and Ali gets penalised on the wrong side of the maul when Barnes tells him to get out and he can't. Thion has torn Ali's headgear off trying to hold him in there, and throws it on the ground in triumph. Beauxis kicks from over 40 metres out. The ball crosses the bar at exactly 40 minutes and 30 seconds.

We've given the French a sniff.

Under the Welsh logo, Ted — coach Graham Henry — and assistants Shag and Smithy — Steve Hansen and Wayne Smith — talk about composure, and about the positives. We're 13–3 up. Our scrum is dominant, our restarts are pretty secure, and our lineout is as good as it's been in my six years with the All Blacks. So much so that we're encouraged to kick it out and attack the French lineout instead of kicking to keep it in play.

The only other change we make is to narrow the attack a little. We want to commit them to the tackle closer to the set-piece, try to get our forwards hitting a narrower target, get us over the gain-line and create more space out wide for our quick guys.

Otherwise, Ted wants us to play our game, impose ourselves on the game, take that eight minutes between 10 and 18 where we scored one try and could have had two others, and extend that template across the second half. We're playing the game at France's tempo, he says. We've got to change that, lift it to a pace and intensity that they can't live with, that no one else in world rugby has the skill-set or fitness to live with. Lift the game to an altitude where they can't breathe.

That's our game. That's what we resolve to do. Impose our style. Keep the ball, hurt them, don't let them breathe, be relentless, take their resolve away from them, find out whether they really want to be out there with us for every second of these last 40 minutes, being stretched, compressed, shunted, battered, pummelled, having their lungs seared, their bodies bruised, their confidence overrun with rats of doubt in the face of our indomitable desire to beat them. Find out whether they just want to compete with us, or whether they really believe they can beat us.

There's a huge difference, and the last 20 minutes always reveals the truth. If somewhere deep in their souls they have a sliver of doubt about what they're doing, we will find it in that last 20 and enlarge it into a black hole that will swallow them.

In the collision combat that is international rugby, we know this works for us. It has given us a whitewash over the Lions in 2005, three successive Tri Nations championships, a mortgage on the Bledisloe Cup and the number-one ranking in the world. It's why we're favourites for this RWC. But history shows it doesn't always work. Other All Black teams have gone into the Cup as favourites, with much the same game plan, and lost.

France seems to be the All Blacks' greatest fear, our *bête noir*. Not always. Not even often. Just when it counts, like '99. I'd watched that game on television. One moment in particular stays with me. France have conjured a try out of nothing and taken the lead for the first time in the game. The All Blacks are standing under their posts waiting for the conversion. They've stopped talking. No one is saying a word. At one point the camera zooms in on Jeff Wilson, the All Black winger. I can't put my finger on exactly what that expression is on Goldie's face, but he looks frozen, bewildered at the turn of events. They all do.

That isn't something I want to think about. Bad pictures don't help the confidence. Bugger 1999. We have our plan. We have to get out there and climb into them.

But those pictures are stronger in some of us than I'd imagined, lying in wait under the surface. In the lull as we wait for the call to start the second half, Byron shouts, 'Come on guys, this is starting to feel like '99!'

What the hell does he mean by that?

If I'd known what he was going to say, I'd have told him to shut up, but who knew what Byron was going to say, ever? He's a quick, brave, cheeky, feisty little guy, ideal halfback personality, but a man who never leaves a thought unsaid. No doubt he's trying to gee us up.

The thought crosses my mind, as it must do for others in the team: *What has Byron seen that reminds him of '99, f'godsakes?*

No point in asking, no time. Trainer Graham Lowe is at the door, time to go. Forty minutes to kill or be killed.

As if to make amends, Byron scuttles away on the blind off a pass from Rodney after Carl gets his right shoulder up in the scrum. Byron flicks it to Luke, but Joe's too flat and the pass from Luke goes out. Ali takes another lineout against the throw, and we crunch it up. We keep possession for over three minutes, but the French defence is consistent and brutal and we're going nowhere. When we try to recycle under pressure on halfway, a stray French boot flays through the back of our ruck and hoofs the ball on the fly.

Their left winger, Heymans, wins the race for the ball, but Rodney makes a desperation tackle five metres from the line and somehow we get the turnover. Mils plays halfback, kicks it upfield, but not out. Harinordoquy takes it on the 10-metre mark, brings it up towards the 22 and spreads it wide. Vincent Clerc tries a grubber and it bounces off Leon into touch, 10 metres out from our line.

This isn't the plan.

From the attacking lineout, we're under the hammer. Thion sets up a rolling maul which we push sideways towards the posts. The inevitable happens as it crabs across: one of our players gets caught in Wayne Barnes' sacred ground on their side of the maul. Barnes shows no mercy, calls the penalty against Rodney and plays advantage. Elissalde flicks it to Beauxis who nudges a little kick behind our goal-line.

As Leon and Byron smash heads diving in to cover it, Luke holds his ground on the turn, his opposite Jauzion runs into him and does a big sideways dive, all flailing arms and French expletives: 9.9 for execution, at least in Barnes' opinion, and he's the only judge.

You could say that Jauzion saw Beauxis' kick was covered and did what he had to do. Cynical but clinical. You could say that Luke was too naive: that he shouldn't have taken the risk of holding his line and presenting his shoulder to Jauzion. Whatever, it's Luke who's penalised for a cynical foul and gets 10 minutes in the bin.

We've had virtually all the pill in the five minutes since halftime and made almost all the play, but have posted no points and now we've shipped a penalty and a yellow card.

Standing under the posts as Beauxis formalises the penalty for 13 to 6, I'm trying to collect myself and keep the bad pictures at bay. It's not the pictures from '99 that I'm getting but more graphic and recent ones from June of this year, when we played Australia at Melbourne. We'd been lethargic after halftime, couldn't get our physical edge, but still had the game won until Carl Hayman was sin-binned. It turned the game. In that 10 minutes, Australia scored the winning try.

For most of the next 10 minutes, we play some of our best rugby of the game, keeping the ball close, long sequences of pick-and-gos, hurling ourselves at the desperate French, who need to get their hands on the ball to exploit their numerical superiority. They can't. Metre by desperate metre, we punch the ball up, using our bodies as fists, looking for an opening. It's the trench warfare of modern rugby, not pretty, but for us it has a brutal logic: it's low risk and hard to stop, legally.

At one stage, we camp 10 metres out from the French line. We go through 13 phases. Seventeen phases. Anton finally hits through a hole, goes five metres. We pile in behind him and I think we're going to crack them, even with 14 men. On the twentieth phase, just two metres out, I'm screaming at Barnes about the French

Wayne Barnes shows no mercy. Luke gets sin-binned.

standing offside, when Woody — Tony Woodcock — throws a wild pass to Rodney on the short blind. Rodney has no chance of holding it and knocks on.

Scrum France, but we've used up five minutes of the 10. Chris Jack comes on to replace Keith Robinson, new legs, a planned change.

Barnes finds his whistle, penalises us for an early engagement. Beauxis peels off a good touch, five metres on their side of halfway. Ali puts huge pressure on Harinordoquy at the lineout, forces him to knock on.

Caveman Chabal comes on for Pelous and Dimitri Szarzewski for Raphael Ibanez, but the two replacements don't help their scrum, which collapses under big pressure from Carl, Anton and Tony. No penalty for us, so Rodney takes it off the back into contact, and we're back into pick-and-gos, keeping it close, using up the clock. Seven phases later, Dan tries a drop-kick from our 10-metre mark. I guess it makes sense in the general scheme of things — if he gets it, it's a bonus; if he misses, the restart eats up time. It's wide. We turn, get ready for the restart, drop our guard.

The French finally have the ball: they realise their 10 minutes of having an extra man is almost up, they've got to do something. We're not as vigilant as we should be and when they take a quick 22 drop-out, they retrieve it and pile into a ruck on our 10-metre mark, go left, then come back right and make big progress, breaking down to our line. We stop them two metres out, then Elissalde finds Clerc cutting in from his right wing, but Jacko — Chris Jack — and I hit him. They recycle, keep going left, and are stopped on the far side by Dan and Jerry. I have time to think — *What's Dan doing out there?*

When the French come back right, Jacko and I drop Szarzewski, but when they go right again, it's a numbers game that simply can't add up for us. They have seven out there against four. It's Dusautoir — of course — who surges through Leon's tackle to score, but it could just as easily have been any of the three outside him.

The French go off. Dusautoir is mobbed by his team-mates. He looks as unruffled and unreadable as ever. He's made all the big plays to get them back in the game, and I still can't see a bead of sweat on his face.

It's 54 minutes 30 seconds. Just 30 seconds before Luke comes back on. We've held them out for nine minutes 30 seconds.

Beauxis pulls the conversion, but it hits the far post and bounces back in. *Bounce of the ball; we need it.* That locks the game up at 13 all — unlucky for some. But that's not what I'm thinking. *The worst has happened and we're still all square.*

Twenty-five minutes to go. That leaves an awful lot of game still out there to be played. The last quarter is where we really ask the tough questions.

When we get back to halfway, Dan's on one leg, and I realise why he was hanging out there on the sideline, with crippled Jerry. He was waiting to go off. We weren't one man down for that last French surge, we were two, or three, counting Jerry, which helps explains the numbers the French had.

Dan limps off, replaced by Nick Evans. It's musical chairs. Byron's done his utmost to stop the bad pictures developing, but now he's gone too, for Brendon Leonard. Anton's gone for Andrew Hore, and Luke comes back on.

We regroup, back to a full complement, but Leon tries to push a pass in midfield, knock on, French scrum. In the back of my mind, I'm remembering how well we did with a really narrow focus, even one man down. We put in a huge shunt, the French scrum collapses and Barnes finally gives us something: the put-in, not a penalty.

Shortly after, I'm stunned by a trailing boot when I'm on the ground after a pick-and-go. It might have been friendly fire. For a second or two, I'm not getting any pictures, just a blank screen, but I go through the motions as we put together more pick-and-gos, make some progress, then get stalled by the French.

Twenty to go. Jacko makes real inroads, until the Caveman dives off his feet over to our side, handles the ball on the ground. Barnes is right there, puts his hand on Woody's rump, yelling, 'Don't stop the ball!' — presumably to the French. The strict referee of the ruck seems to have lost his zeal to penalise. I'm hoping it's a temporary aberration.

I hand off to Rodney, who takes it up a metre, but the French are right up on us — they have to be riding the offside line — and it's almost static just outside the French 22.

From there, we go left, Luke cuts inside, and Szarzewski plays the ball on his knees, but loses it and we go left again. Mils ducks under two backs, but the Caveman goes in and wins — legitimately this time — a turnover, but then flops over to our side of the ruck. Barnes whistles for a scrum, which I think is at least some consolation, until he gives the put-in to France.

The changes of personnel to the French and All Black packs haven't changed the scrums: we're dominant and put Harinordoquy under huge pressure at the back. As the French pack go backwards, he tries to pick it out of the tangle of sliding boots and is nailed by Jerry. Barnes blows it up, sticks his arm up and I'm thinking it's our penalty until I see he's pointing at Jerry for detaching early.

Back to a defensive lineout on our 10-metre mark. Ali steals it again. Nick Evans to Luke on the cut, I take it off Luke and get a couple of metres. We go short blind where quick passes from Jerry and Rodney put Siti away. They only just scrag him, but Jerry takes it on, then Horey — Andrew Hore — and we're really making inroads, getting in behind them, forcing them to scramble, as Siti and Nick and Rodney come back left down the blind. Rodney sets it up 20 metres out. I take it round the side, get snotted by Bonnaire, but Brendon dabs right, makes ground, and we pour on to it 15 metres out.

We set up another series of brutal pick-and-gos. Crunch the bastards. It's like lateral pile driving with a human drill. If we can't do it by metres, we'll do it by centimetres, doesn't matter. I keep telling myself that if we're hurting, the French must be in agony. Ali makes two metres, Horey makes three. Jacko only makes a pace, but by then we're a metre from their line. Brendon flicks it blind to Rodney, who puts his head down and bulldozes through Thion to the line. Ali and Woody are on top of him: we know he's made it, but Barnes is unsighted and asks for a replay.

There's a long wait. Must be close . . . But it's given. Try.

The last 10 minutes is *always* ours. We've pulled so many games out of the fire over the past couple of seasons. Though not at Melbourne back in June. *Get that picture out of your head. Stay in the present.*

Luke is lining up the conversion, 15 metres to the left of the posts, bread and butter. He pushes it to the right.

It's 18–13 to us. We're back. We've taken the momentum away from them — I can actually feel that as Cedric Heymans drops a bomb from Nick, and we get an attacking scrum. *They're gone.* The crowd have stopped singing 'Allez Les Bleus'.

One more score of any description and we're home.

From the scrum, Nick clean breaks the French line, accelerating inside Beauxis and outside Elissalde who gets a hand on his waist-band and drags him down. We're

Rodney scores, with a bit of help from Ali and Woody.

in behind them, got them at sixes and sevens. All we have to do is hold on to the ball and good things will happen. But Nick goes for a miracle pass to Mils as he's tackled and loses it forward.

Scrum France. Once again, we destroy the French scrum, pour over Harinordoquy, pull him backwards towards his own line. He's lying full-length on his back, being dragged along the ground, holding on to the ball in a moving ruck. I'm a metre away watching this, screaming at Barnes — *Ref!* — who does nothing. Then he tells Horey to go back.

Beauxis thumps it to halfway, Leon passes infield to Joe, who brings it back strongly to contact, then throws another wild pass in the tackle. Forward. Jesus wept.

We had them. Two bad passes we didn't need to make.

We keep having to go back to the well, the French scrum, but this time it holds. There's still confusion at the back between Harinordoquy and Elissalde, which draws Brendon in to them, which means that when Harinordoquy manages to throw it wide to Traille coming from fullback, there's no sweeper and the French suddenly have numbers on a wide blind. Traille sees it, plays it perfectly, punches between Luke and Siti, makes the half-break and forces me to commit to the tackle. As I drag him down, he offloads to Frederic Michalak on his outside. The pass *has* to be forward — my head is on Traille's left shoulder, he can't pass it through me. Traille throws the pass two metres short of halfway and Michalak takes it on the halfway line. As I hit the ground I see assistant referee Jonathan Kaplan right in

This can't be happening! Yannick Jauzion scores.

line. Barnes is back behind us and might have been obscured, but Kaplan, so keen to assert himself in the first half, says nothing. By the time I look back up, I see the end of a brilliant French move — Jauzion diving across the line for the try.

This can't be happening! They'd been on the rack, mixed up behind a retreating scrum on their own 10-metre line, and seconds later they're 60 metres downfield, scoring.

We're tied, 18 points each.

We stand under the posts. Disbelief has been replaced by a really bad picture. I suddenly understand the expression I saw on Jeff Wilson's face in '99. Bewilderment, disbelief, yes, all there. But something else. *Fear.*

What we went through after Sydney in 2003 surges back, the recriminations, the anguish, the anger. Bad pictures from the past fomenting fear of the future. The headlines, the national grief, the disappointment of my parents and my sister somewhere up there in the crowd, among thousands of Kiwis who have flown across the world on package tours to support us here and next week in the semi in Paris, and in the final. I look at the eyes around me and can see they're not here, they're watching the same reels. I'm standing right in front of them and they can't see me. I don't understand what's happening, but instinctively I know I have to somehow get my mind back to the here and now in Cardiff.

Someone is standing right in front of me. Physio Pete Gallagher. Repeating messages from the coaches. There's still time. *Got that.* Retain possession. *Got that.* Play at the right end of the field. *Got that.* Don't forget the drop-kick option. *What?*

Going to sleep after Dan's speculative drop-kick has cost us seven points already, whereas our applied pressure after that through 26 phases got us Rodney's try and a conversion we should have had. And there's something else. There's no drop-kick in our play-book. I know that Byron and Dan discussed it at training, but they're gone, Nick Evans is gone, and Aaron Mauger, who slotted a crucial drop for the Crusaders in a Super 14 final and might have been able to make that call, is sitting in the stand. A drop-kick has never been part of our plan. We've never practised setting up for it. If I suddenly tell the guys we're playing for the drop-kick, what does that tell them about the plan? The word that springs to mind is 'panic'.

I need to make a rational response to the circumstances and our resources. And not panic, or induce panic. The plan is to win by tries, by retaining possession and applying huge pressure. We've done it once with Rodney's try, we can do it again. That's the plan we came in with, that's the plan I'm sticking to.

Elissalde converts. 20–18 to France. We're behind for the first time in the game. The French are going off. They think they've got it. *This isn't supposed to happen!*

I try for a better picture, to change the channel: 2001, my first year with Canterbury, we're playing for the Ranfurly Shield against Wellington. We're down 29–12 with 15 to go, and our captain Todd Blackadder gets us around him and says, 'Don't for a minute believe that we're not going to win this.' And I don't believe him, I'm standing there thinking, *Bugger, my first decent shield defence and we're going to lose it.* When we got over Wellington and won it, that was a big lesson. *You've got to believe that it's not over.*

So that's what I tell them, gathered around me. What Toddy told me. And I try to put the bad pictures out of my head and believe it myself. *It's only two points and there's 10 minutes.*

But it doesn't begin well. From the restart, the French bomb and Siti takes it into the tackle too high, gets held up and France gets the put-in on our 10-metre line. Worse, Nick Evans is crocked in that maul and hobbles off. *What else?*

Luke comes into first-five, Ice — Isaia Toeava — goes to second.

The rejuvenated French scrum splinters us, but we pile into the loose fracas and turn the ball over, then break right. Ice makes an outside break, then throws the ball away. Clerc hoofs it downfield and we're back 10 metres out from our own line. *Fuck!*

Nine minutes to go. Ali's unbeatable in the air, Brendon kicks beautifully from the base, and Christophe Dominici is forced out five metres short of halfway.

Eight minutes to go. We overthrow to a short lineout, and I'm crash-tackled by Dusautoir, but manage to retain possession and we go right, where Luke grubbers in behind them. Ice is taken out by Jauzion's shoulder, a carbon copy of the move that got Luke a yellow card what seems an age ago. *Ref!* Barnes is right there, flaps his arms wide and says, 'Play on!'

Clerc takes the ball under no pressure, hoofs it into our in-goal and, again, we regroup for the 22, at the wrong end of the field.

Seven minutes to go. Harinordoquy collects our restart, thunders forward into contact, but we attack him like men possessed and turn it over. We pile drive through 14 brutal phases of pick-and-gos to get to 35 metres out from the French line.

Five minutes to go. Stick to the game plan. Attack narrow again, pick and go, get another try doing what has already worked. Failing that, a penalty. We haven't had a penalty in the second half. Law of averages, if we keep possession, keep the French under the hammer, they have to infringe. *Have to.*

Seventeenth phase. I burst down the blind to set it up 10 metres out from their line. Chris Masoe takes it another couple of metres, and after 19 phases we're right in front of the posts. Leon's at halfback and the rest of the backs are flat. Woody rumbles it up another metre. Horey takes it forward again. Luke calls for it, he can see numbers on the right, but we crunch it forward again, doing what we did to get Rodney's try. It's worked once, it will work again. We've got the French where we want them. If we don't get the try, we'll get a penalty. Either way, I believe we'll score. *It will happen.*

Three and a half minutes to go, we're on the twenty-sixth phase, two metres out from their line, when Harinordoquy plays the ball at the bottom of a ruck with his hands, sweeping it back to Elissalde. Barnes doesn't see it, or if he does, decides that he hasn't. Michalak clears, badly, from the dead-ball line, straight to Jacko, on his own, way out wide.

We get to him in time, recycle wide out on the 22, and go again. Mils gets in behind them, and we take it on through Luke and Woody and Rodney, until I get caught at the back of the ruck and the French get it back. Elissalde kicks it straight out.

Two minutes to go. Our lineout. Last throw of the dice.

What's happening? I've never known this sort of extended sequence play not to yield up something: a try or more likely a penalty for one side or the other, usually the attacking side. But as the game tightens up, Barnes seems to have gone from a ruck and maul martinet to Mister Anything Goes. I finally click to the fact that he's as fearful as we are of making a mistake. I realise, too late, he's not going to make a big call, that he's not making *any* penalty calls, no matter how blatant. This is Barnes' first big game and he's frozen. The pressure of a quarter-final at the RWC has got to him just like it's got to us. But I haven't seen that early enough. I should have realised sooner: *We're completely and utterly on our own out here.*

While we're assembling for the lineout, Carl reads my mind and asks about a drop-kick. I still don't want to make that call. But this is it. We're down to the last play. I compromise, tell Luke to have a crack at the drop if it's on. That's all I can do.

Ninety seconds to go. The ball is thrown in, Ali secures it. Siti steps through to their 22, and Rodney bulldozes it on and I pile in. We're right in front of the posts, 20 metres out, but when the ball is recycled the only one standing in the pocket is a prop. Woody. The backs are all lined out flat. Woody trudges across after the backs as they take it right and are smashed backwards by the French defence.

At the breakdown, France knock on, Barnes calls an advantage as we regurgitate the ball on our 10-metre mark, having lost 20 metres. We should take the scrum, but Luke is in the pocket finally and takes the drop-kick. The trouble is he's standing on the halfway mark, and the ball bounces twice before it gets to the goal-line. Advantage over. Traille runs it back and forth along the dead-ball line, using up time.

Thirty seconds to go. We're gone. Joe takes the restart on halfway, I power it up to the 10-metre mark. *Maybe not.* We go wide right, come back left, but we're going sideways, getting skittled. Time is up when Luke makes a half-break and Horey takes it on with a good drive, but the ball gets ripped away from him.

I finally stop, exhausted, disbelieving, and watch Elissalde grab the ball and dance triumphantly backwards and sideways almost to the sideline, waving one hand in the air, before booting the ball into the roaring French fans in the stands.

We've lost. It's over. That's the truth.

Ali and I try to find the words.

All choked up

The losers' dressing room turns out to be the right dressing room after all. Before I can get there, I'm stopped by a microphone and camera. An English voice points out the obvious, that the French just seem to have this ability to come back at us.

'Tell me about it. It's one of those days you just want to forget.' Knowing as I say it that I never will forget. He asks more questions. I shake my head, still shell-shocked, and tell him I'm lost for words.

I do have words to describe myself, but none that I can use. Angry. Devastated. Pissed off. Frustrated. Despondent. Angry. Remorseful. Did I say angry? Angry at myself, angry at the stupid passes we threw, the mistakes we made, the chances we blew. Angry at the ref for abdicating his responsibilities. Angry at not getting what I think — for all our mistakes — we deserved.

I forge on and see Andrew Mehrtens in front of me, comments man for TV3. Mehrts has his own bad pictures from '95 and '99. He doesn't know what to say to me. *Mehrts lost for words? Things must be bad.* He gives me a consolatory pat on the shoulder.

Someone offers me a chair to sit in while I wait my turn for the next interview. In front of me, Ibanez is doing his bit for French TV. I don't speak much French but the language of ecstasy is universal. *That should be me. What happened?*

I stumble through that one, and head to the false sanctuary of the dressing room. There is no sanctuary, but there are my mates, who are going through what I'm going through. Caveman Chabal is blocking my passage, excited about something. I realise he's upset about not being able to swap jerseys. He mentions Chris Jack. I don't know enough French to tell him Jacko might have a few other things on his mind right now, so I brush past.

I get to the dressing room. Anton, conjuring up an image from his extensive reading on the First World War, later describes it as being like 'no-man's-land in our hearts and minds. It feels desolate, decay, the putrid smell of, I don't know, death.' That's Anton. Never use a short word when several long ones will do almost as well.

Though, to be fair, he did also say at the time that no one actually died. And at least he's able to articulate something.

No one else knows what to say. Except the coaches, who move about, making consoling noises. The players seem lost in their separate worlds. There's no need for ice baths or recovery strategies. *It's over. We're out.* Most are sitting unchanged in their little cubicles, heads in hands.

We all thought — in so far as we'd considered losing at all — that Ted would take it the worst. But he's calm and collected, which is staggering. I know even then that this loss is more likely to be a career-defining event for him than it will be for me. I might get to go again: his chances of doing so are pretty slim, based on the response to past All Black coaches who have lost badly at RWC. The '99 coach, John Hart, was spat on at a horse race. After 2003, John Mitchell was cast into the wilderness. Ted is already 61, has had a long and distinguished career, but it seems now that he'll be remembered for two huge failures: the 2001 Lions Tour to Australia and the 2007 All Blacks RWC.

In the midst of my own despair, my admiration for Ted soars as he takes me aside and tells me that just he and I are going to do the big one with the assembled world media, that we're going to front up, play it straight down the line, pay the French respect, and as much as we might feel that we have gripes, there'll be no whingeing. He confirms what I already know in my gut: that if we complain, no matter what we say, no matter how justified we think it is, we'll look like sore losers. We have to front up and cop it on the chin.

That's what we try to do. I don't remember the details, except for one thing. I'm still in my rugby kit, covered in sweat and grime, and at one stage I rub my face and eyes with both hands. It's just one of those reflexive, unthinking actions. But as I do, I can feel the heat and light as the flash-bulbs pop. *Bugger, I've given them their front-page photo.*

Some time later, I get a message that my father and sister are at the players' entrance. I find them there with an old school friend and his father, in their black and silver supporters' kit, looking bewildered. Not my old man or my sister, Joanna. They're more concerned about how I am. I apologise for ruining their trip, and Dad tells me not to worry, that they'll have a good time anyway and they always knew there was a risk that the All Blacks wouldn't make it. He and Mum have never been part of the hype, and they're not now: he tells me that today was just one of those days. That's sport.

It's a perspective I desperately need. Sport is about winning and losing. There's no fudging, no smudging, no saying, well, that's not really what I meant. In RWC knockout, it's binary: two columns, win or loss; the classic zero sum equation: for every winner, there has to be a loser. If winning was pro forma, victory wouldn't be worth striving for. Victory is only sweet because you always risk losing. If you step into that combat zone, you accept everything that goes with it. You don't decide whether you want to stand under a bomb in front of the French forward pack

Bugger, I've given them their front-page photo.

when you're waiting for the ball to arrive. You don't decide once you're out there whether you want to be battered and bruised and humiliated. You have to make those decisions long before. The time to decide that losing is too painful is before you walk out on to the field.

I take some comfort from that, and also from what our psychologist Gilbert Enoka tells us when we gather in the team room back at our hotel, the Vale Glamorgan. 'Playing rugby is what you do,' says Bert. 'It's not who you are.'

But shortly after that, I'm called out to do one more interview, with Tony Johnson for Sky TV's *Reunion* programme. Tony's eyes are glistening with emotion as he talks about the end of the dream, and that's when it really hits me: what this loss will mean to so many people in our rugby community, our rugby nation. *Try telling them that supporting the All Blacks is what they do, it's not who they are.* I feel tears welling and struggle to get a grip.

We don't make it to Paris, of course. We don't see the big ball the NZRU has set up by the Champs-Elysées to promote the 2011 RWC, and we can't be part of the promotion. Thousands of New Zealand supporters do make it, many of them flying out from New Zealand on non-refundable package tours to see us play in the semis and finals. We probably pass them in the air somewhere over the Pacific as we fly home.

Twenty-four of the squad fly out of Heathrow on Japan Airlines. We'd agreed before we left New Zealand that win or lose we'd come home together, but there aren't enough seats for everyone, so we work out priorities for media duties and families and leave six behind.

There's an understandable trepidation on that plane as to what our reception will be. In 2003, when we'd also been favourites, we lost in the semi-final to Australia, but I was young and didn't have much profile, so was able to stay over there for a while, then slip back quietly into the country. This time, I'm coming back as the captain of the worst-performing All Black team in the history of the RWC.

Our fears aren't helped when we transit at Japan and get news of Doug Howlett's Heathrow high-jinks.

Doug had been one of the team who'd got stuck in at the bar of the Vale Glamorgan after the game. I'd gone to bed early, exhausted, played out. I didn't sleep well, but when I did, it was bliss. Escape. On Sunday morning, there was that moment between sleeping and waking, when the world was new, before the memory kicked in and hit me like a scrape on a raw nerve. *It happened.*

When I went down for breakfast, there were several who'd clearly put in an all-nighter and were a bit second hand. Some of them hadn't been selected to play and were, perhaps justifiably, pissed off. Maybe if we'd had the experience and composure of Doug and Aaron Mauger in that last 20, the result might have been different, but for me it was either way too late or way too early to be thinking about all that. I felt sorrier for guys like Ali and Rodney, who had played so well they deserved to be on the winning side.

I got out of there. Vale Glamorgan had its own sports complex and golf course, so I played nine holes of golf with a couple of the guys. Not well. Golf's one of those games that bites you if you're preoccupied with something else.

Later, Mum and Dad and Joanna called in. It was all pretty desultory. They did their best to cheer me up, and I did my best to make out I was okay. I must have already been looking ahead, though. Jo remembers me saying that I'd only be 30 by the time the next RWC rolled round.

Later, we were told the first flight out of London was not until the next day, so a few of us shot into town Sunday night and ended up at the Walkabout bar. The All Black tour parties had moved on, so we were spared the embarrassment of encountering any of the fans who'd been wandering stunned and bewildered around the streets of Cardiff after the game.

Letting go a bit seemed like a really good idea at the time, so we had a big night, and I was predictably as sick as a dog next morning. But I was still looking forward to the flight home as we bussed up to London. Through the hangover fog, I was thinking, *I don't want to be here, I just want to get home.*

But on the last leg home from Japan on Air New Zealand, the trepidation mounts. What's waiting for us? We know it's going to be very different from the send-off we got in August. Going on recent history, we can anticipate a harsh reception. It's reported that we're due in at midday and 'no homecoming welcome has been arranged at Auckland Airport'.

They're obviously gutted, but . . .

That might be because the only direct flight we can get out of Japan is to Christchurch, where to our huge surprise over a thousand people turn out to welcome us. They're obviously gutted, but so good about it, so sympathetic, that I'm not sure whether I feel better for their unflagging support, or worse, for letting such great fans down so badly.

When I get back to the townhouse, I realise that there's no family and non-rugby friends around, they're all in Europe. I only stay a couple of hours, repack my bag and head back to the airport.

Flying north, I can't help but see my face all over the front page of the *New Zealand Herald*. It's the money shot I was worried about during the Cardiff press conference, under a headline 'Déjà vu all over again . . . And again . . . And again . . . And again'. Underneath my photo, it says: 'So much promise, only tears to show for it'. Well, I was just rubbing my face, but why spoil a good story. 'The best team, the best players, the best coach, the most expensive and extensive preparation . . . A $50 million campaign . . . How did it come to this?'

What I find in the rest of the paper is nothing less than I expect, maybe more moderate.

There are opinion pieces from former All Blacks like John Drake and Richard Loe and coaches like Laurie Mains. They're understandably disappointed but urge the public to go easy on us. There are psychologists waxing lyrical about the grieving process we and the nation are going through, and even the editorial is headed 'No excuses, but keep a perspective'. Our GDP might have suffered from our loss, speculates James Ihaka '. . . judging by web traffic and office time and motion studies, the national product would have dipped substantially in the wake of the Cardiff calamity'.

In the best tradition of national disasters, All Black jokes are quoted. Have you heard about the new All Black bra? All support and no cups. What's the difference between the All Blacks and a tea bag? The tea bag stays in the cup longer.

The real brickbats come, mostly, from overseas. Under a column headed 'You've got to be choking', Peter O'Reilly reports that the result confirms the All Blacks' status as 'world class chokers'. Dave James asks what the All Blacks have got in common with tennis player Jana Novotna, NFL's Buffalo Bills and hosts of red-faced English soccer players. 'When the pressure's on, they all choked, and the meltdown has been public, painful and impossible to forget. Just ask New Zealand's rugby players. They trample all before them, but when the RWC comes round every four years, the All Blacks are all a tremble.'

And there's at least one of our own who's in that camp. Talkback host Murray Deaker says the result is a disaster. 'Sadly,' he says, 'we are a dumb rugby nation. We don't play the big matches well. We were a bunch of boof-heads. On the big occasions, we choke.'

Deaker has a book ready to sell on the back of the RWC. Rumour has it he's had to change the triumphant cover as a result of our loss. Perhaps to punish us for the inconvenience, he's written a new last chapter. It finishes with the words, 'The All Blacks choked.'

I know it's just tomorrow's fish-and-chip paper, but the constant 'choking' thing really chokes me up. It gives little credit to the French who, on the back of the right tactics, kicked brilliantly and put up a colossal defence, making 197 tackles to our 47. They played out of their skins and left everything they had on the field at Cardiff, which they were to prove the following weekend in the semi-final at Paris by losing abjectly to a very average England team.

There's a lot in the reports about France's ability to win when it counts. And yet in a few days' time, in that semi-final I won't be able to bring myself to watch, France will have lost two RWC semi-finals and the only two RWC finals they've played in. Is anyone talking about *Les ultimate chokeurs*? *Mais non!* France is wonderfully, excitingly, unpredictable due to their Gallic flair and *je ne sais quoi*. Jesus wept. Would that we were so *enigmatique*!

There's a lot of criticism of Barnes too. We lost so narrowly. Either Barnes or Kaplan could have picked up Traille's forward pass; we could have been awarded the penalties we'd earned. *Could have, would have, should have.*

I don't blame Barnes, but I do blame the people who appointed the most inexperienced referee on the roster to a RWC quarter-final between the hosts and the favourites. I thought both teams deserved a referee with experience. My beef isn't with Barnes so much as with his inexperience. This was Barnes' biggest game by far. On the big stage, an inexperienced referee is likely to become so afraid of making a mistake that he stops making any decisions at all. By the end of it, I thought Barnes was frozen with fear and wouldn't make any big calls.

That it's all in the mind at this level is borne out by another columnist in that Monday's *Herald* who is of particular interest to me: Crusaders coach Robbie Deans.

Robbie makes the point that the RWC is a unique challenge, unlike anything else the players will encounter. 'So how do you best prepare for a type of rugby that, as a team, you've never experienced?' He offers two solutions, both of which could be seen as implicit criticisms of Ted's selections. Pick players who have been there before and field established combinations.

I have a feeling this might be the first salvo in a battle which I, as captain of both the Crusaders and the All Blacks, am going to be caught in the middle of. Anton's no-man's-land metaphor might yet be apposite.

That looming conflict is borne out by the *Herald* headline in its sport section: 'Now it's off with their heads', meaning Henry, Hansen and Smith. Right under the headline is a photo of Robbie.

But when the flight arrives in Auckland, I put the newspaper down and decide to put all that out of my mind. The serious post-mortem will begin soon enough, and we've got tons of time — four more years. So has George Gregan, ironically — Australia got edged by England in one of the other quarter-finals.

I realise that the question *What went wrong?* will consume me and everyone around me for the next several months at least, but right now I want to dump that and think about something else.

It helps if you can swap one consuming passion for another. There's a beautiful bird sitting in Auckland waiting for me. She was going to be a reward for RWC success, but will serve just as well as consolation. She's been the stuff of fantasy for me, and I can't wait to get my hands on her.

The Discus 2C glider was brought down to Australia and New Zealand as a demo, and was about to be packed back to Germany when Gavin Wills, my mentor at the commercial gliding operation GlideOmarama, told me that the German manufacturer, Schempp-Hirth, might be persuaded to leave it here if they got the right price. He warned me that the Germans wouldn't negotiate; they had their price and that was it. I thought, *Oh, yeah*, and while I was in Auckland for the final Tri Nations test, I went out to the airfield at Drury.

As soon as I saw this stark white bird with its huge wings, snug cockpit and slick, streamlined body, I knew I was in trouble. The guy out there let me sit in it, and as soon as I slipped in there behind the controls, I knew. *Oh shit, you've got me buggered.*

Gavin tried to negotiate on my behalf, told the Germans it would be a great advertisement for Schempp-Hirth to have the first model of its type in the country being flown on a regular basis out of Omarama. He did well, got them to knock a couple of thousand euro off it, which meant I had to make a big decision. I made a phone call to the old man, and he agreed to put a bit in, so I did the deal.

I saw this stark white bird with huge wings . . .

It's only when I get to Auckland that I realise getting a rental with a tow-bar might be a problem, so I ring All Black sponsor Ford and ask them if they have anything with a tow-bar they want delivered to Wellington. Getting an XR8 is a bit of a bonus!

I pick up Hayley and we head out to Drury. The Discus is de-rigged and packed into its trailer, and a couple of hours later, I'm back to being a 26 year old with a girlfriend and a new toy, cruising south through heartland New Zealand in an XR8 in early summer.

Hayley isn't interested in talking about the RWC and neither am I.

On the plane home, the boys had joked about false beards and sunglasses, but the reception we got in Christchurch seems to be indicative of the mood out there. The rugby community is hurting, but wherever and whenever I'm recognised on the trip south, they tend to say 'Hard luck' rather than 'You suck', and I get the feeling they've developed a fairly mature and phlegmatic attitude to it all. Perhaps it's just the practice they've had at living with RWC disappointment. I learn not to duck my head at the prospect of recognition.

We stay overnight with an old mate at Palmerston North and next day get to the Wellington wharves and put the Discus on the interisland freight to Lyttelton.

I know there are black clouds on the horizon. The NZRU has already called for an official review of RWC 2007, and have announced that applications will be called for All Black coach, and a decision will be made before Christmas. I can see there's a shit-fight of epic proportions coming.

But every time I look at the Discus, I see clouds of a different kind, sweeping eastwards, rolling like waves across the Main Divide, crashing down on to the basin country.

Big sky

The clues are in the clouds. The wee puffy ones tell you there's thermal lift underneath, from the sun heating the earth and the earth heating the air, which rises. If the sun is on an angle to the side of the hill, it'll heat the ground more quickly. The air will keep heating as it rises up the hill and then shoot right off the top. That lift might take you up on to the mountain ridges that run along the western edge of the Mackenzie Country and from the foothills to the Main Divide, the Southern Alps. You get ridge lift if there's 10 knots or more blowing straight up, or convergences where different air masses meet, creating lift, and once you get up there, you can fly along the ridges, getting higher and higher . . .

When there's a nor'wester, you might see a big layered lenticular, a clue that the perfect wave might be on its way. The nor'wester hits the Southern Alps, drops its rain as it rises up and over, then creates a foehn effect as it crashes down the other side on to the hot basin country, which shoots it up into the air again. Underneath, you can use unstable rotary air to climb up through the stable inversion layer, where it's as smooth as silk, and then you can glide along the leading edge of this giant, invisible wave, like a surfer . . .

Flying along the wave, you can climb to 20,000 feet, zooming along at 160 kilometres an hour. You have to pick your path, because if you fall off the wave you descend at huge speeds too, and then you've got to get out. But if you do it right, you might take off at sunrise and not land till sunset.

I've heard the stories about the gun glider pilots who've been all the way over to the Landsborough and Mount Aspiring, right on the Main Divide. You can work on the converging east and west air masses if you're game enough, but if you fall into the cold sea air coming off the west coast, you won't get enough height to get home.

Getting home, that's always the challenge.

The Mackenzie Country is great for gliding because it's sheltered from the west and from the cold easterly coming off the other coast. The land heats up in the morning, allowing you to get up on top of the ridges before that easterly arrives. By the end of the day, the mountains are still hot, but the easterly has cooled Omarama and you're battling to get back. That's the intrigue of it, to be able to plot and pick your way around.

Before you go out, you know what the weather's likely to bring and you can look at terrain, sun and wind, and how those three will interact to enable you to plot a probable flight path. But it seldom works out exactly the way you planned it, so you have to know where you can bail out and land if you get low and can't find any lift along the way. Your mind has always got to be way out in front of the glider. If I don't get lift here, and I can't get to that airstrip, is there another strip I can get to?

It's easy enough to learn how to fly the glider, particularly if you've already got a power licence. A power pilot's training is heavily focused on managing the engine, so once you take the engine away and all you have is a stick and set of rudders and a few basic instruments, it's relatively easy to fly, to learn to take off and land, how to get the tow right.

Learning how to go places and to keep the glider in the air is the critical skill. That's where you have to understand the weather and topography; you have to learn how the atmosphere works, where and how to position the glider, often close to terrain, to take advantage of the atmospheric energy. I've been lucky at Omarama to have people like Gavin Wills to tutor me.

Gavin's my father's generation and has been part of the gliding scene at Omarama as long if not longer than my father and uncles. He's a former Chief Alpine Guide at Mount Cook and still has that tall, fit, rangy, bearded look about him. I went to Gavin because I knew he was into cross-country gliding. That's not true of all the instructors. Some glider pilots just want to get up and float around the local airfield and don't want the stress and challenge of cutting the umbilical cord and going cross-country. Once you leave the home airfield far behind, you're forced to rely on the decisions you make, based on the models you have in your head about how the atmosphere works. Some instructors put the fear of god into pilots who want to do that. Not Gavin.

I'd done some gliding at the Canterbury club, but wanted more intense tuition so that I could make more rapid progress. In gliding there's a clear gradation. Once you can take off and land, you go for your first solo and obtain your A Certificate, which is followed by the B Certificate. That means you stay up for short periods, soar around the airfield basically. Then you do some written tests, and finally you get your QGP, Qualified Glider Pilot licence. That gives you your passenger and cross-country ratings.

Gavin had me soloing after three or four days, and took me through advanced training, doing all my early cross-country training in two-seaters, then in single-seater lead-and-follows. He's a rigorous appraiser, so when he tells me he reckons I've got a real aptitude for it, I'm stoked, but I began with a big advantage: my family.

Soaring over Lake Pukaki on the edge of the Mackenzie Country.

Dad flies, his two brothers fly, a couple of my cousins fly, my aunty flies. We've got flying in common. When I go home to the old man, we sit and talk way more about flying than rugby. It's something he knows a lot more about than I do. That seems always to have been the case.

My father's two uncles, John and Robert Trotter, my grandmother's brothers, were foundation members of the North Otago Gliding Club. They got frustrated with the cold easterlies down at Oamaru, so they decided to base the club on my late grandfather's farm, run in partnership with my uncles, John and Ian McCaw. They built a strip in the late 70s, early 80s.

I was close to my grandfather before he died in 1996, so I grew up around it all. It might have been Grandad who inspired my father to get his power licence as soon as he left school. I never saw Grandad fly airplanes, only gliders, and then only very occasionally — I think my grandmother Cathie wouldn't let him, which was understandable once I was old enough for Grandad to start telling me what he did in the war.

Jim McCaw was a pilot with the Royal New Zealand Air Force 486 Squadron, based in England. The squadron's motto was Hiwa hau maka — Beware the wild winds. He flew the Hawker Typhoon and its improved version, the Hawker Tempest, a single-seat fighter-bomber and low-altitude interceptor, and was credited with shooting down 19.5 V-1 flying bombs. He told me lots of stories about the war, and I wish I'd recorded them for posterity. I remember him telling me that many pilots

Jim McCaw, DFC.

died in training, trying to land the things. I haven't seen a Tempest, but I've seen a Spitfire, which was slower than the Tempest, and I'm amazed at those guys. They were basically strapped on to the back of a huge engine with wings. Some of them were only aged 21, 22 and had less training than I got to fly a Cessna.

On one evening alone in July 1944, Grandad destroyed four V1s heading towards London, and scraped into Biggin Hill well past midnight with his fuel tanks showing empty. A couple of days after that he was awarded the Distinguished Flying Cross.

The really scary stories he made light of or probably just didn't mention at all. You had to talk to his mates in the bar to find out the truth about those. There's a famous piece of footage shot from the gun turret of a Tempest. The pilot has possibly misjudged his approach to a V1. He's very close when he finally manages to fire his cannon and blow it up. The pilot has to fly through the explosion and all the shrapnel and debris. It's pretty terrifying. Carnage. That pilot is the old fella. He came out the other side.

A lot didn't. Ten of his immediate colleagues and friends in 486 were killed that summer by V1 explosions as they attacked the bombs.

He was proud of his Scottish roots — his grandfather was born in the Borders — and safely sitting out hostilities from 10,000 miles' distance wasn't an option for him.

I'd love to tog up and fly for real in a Tempest. Just to get a feel of what it was like and experience in a very small way what he went through. I'm told they were incredible, very fast and untouchable in a dive but I'm not even sure there is one left in the air, although there are a couple in museums.

At Christmas, the whole tribe would grab the gliders and gear and decamp from my grandparents' farm and head across the river, up the Waitaki Valley and over the hill to Omarama, where we'd set up camp at Wardells, just round the corner from the town and airfield. The South Canterbury and Canterbury clubs would come down as well, and the gliders would stay there until the winter. That's the way it was for a decade or more, until we shifted the club permanently to Omarama, when numbers to keep the club operating weren't sufficient.

We sold our own farm in 2002, so Omarama has become more important as a continuing tie to the area, particularly since I went halves with my parents in a holiday home there last year.

On oxygen at 20,000 feet.

These days, I get to see the Haka Valley from the air mainly. We tend to go west in the gliders, but I often hire a plane from Christchurch and fly down to Omarama, and go over the Haka to check it out.

When I get down to Omarama with the Discus in tow, the gliding community is great. 'Sorry about the rugby,' they say, then we get on to flying. Omarama is a long way from most places, and the airfield environment is a separate, almost self-contained world within that, with hangars and accommodation units and its own laid-back little café. I love it, and Gavin reckons he can predict my arrival there to within about 48 hours of the finish of a tour or series.

Gavin helps me rig the Discus. That's all I want to talk about — I'm the newbie down here, all ears, trying to learn as much as I can. I'm a bit embarrassed about being such a novice and having a state-of-the-art machine like this, but Gavin is encouraging, tells me it'll be great to have a glider I can grow into.

When I finally get the Discus assembled and rigged, I lower myself into that snug cockpit and think, *Shit, it's too small* — in my excitement up north I didn't check that I'd actually fit the bloody thing. But once I'm in, it seems to mould itself around me, the perfect fit. I follow Gavin around to familiarise myself. The Discus is a gorgeous machine, and it's amazing to be up there at last in my own glider, and I feel like the luckiest guy in the world . . . If it wasn't for the Cardiff calamity playing out in my head, despite my best intentions to leave it behind.

We circle close to home, and at one stage we catch a thermal on the western ridge of the Kirklistons, and I can see directly down into the Haka Valley, our old farm, and the little school just down the road from the farm.

The Hakataramea Primary School closed in 2003, but it had two teachers and about 25 kids when I became a pupil at the age of five. The two little schoolrooms are still there, with a field out front, surrounded by a shelter belt of macrocarpas to keep out the raw southerlies and sou'westers. There was one set of farm-made goalposts hewn from hardwood and braced with iron footings. It was there that I started playing rugby, in pick-up games at intervals and lunchtimes, mixing it with kids of eight and nine. The bumps and bruises didn't put me off. Mum says that's all I wanted to do. Get to school so I could play rugby.

When I was seven, Dad took me across the river to Kurow on Saturday mornings, where I began playing in age-group teams for the Kurow Rugby Club, full of good North Otago names, like McCone, Stringer, Gard, McIlraith, Perriam and McGill. That first year, Barney McCone was our coach, because he had a son, Ross, in the team.

Barney farmed Domett Downs on the foothills of Mount Domett on the southern side of the Waitaki Valley, and was an ex-halfback and a great mate of Phil Gard, Kurow's All Black, who played outside Barney at first-five. Barney was also assistant coach of the Kurow seniors, so rugby was part of every day of his week and he was a real thinker about the game. We were very lucky to come under his tutelage so early in our playing careers.

He wouldn't let us play in competition that first year, for instance. We had to spend the first season learning skills. So every Saturday morning, Barney would teach us all how to catch and pass and tackle, and at the end we'd play a game among ourselves. We didn't know it at the time, but that was a huge advantage Barney gave us. He quickly picked up that I liked contact and was pretty fearless, and he knew that it was really important to teach me to tackle properly, so that I didn't damage myself. As a result he spent a lot of time with us on correct body position, straight back, eyes open, all that basic but essential stuff.

When we entered the North Otago Under 9s competition the following year, straight into full tackle, playing against the Oamaru teams, Athies, Old Boys, Excelsior, and the surrounding hamlets, Maheno from down near Kakanui, and Valley from the Wairareka, we won it. Every week we used to get on the bus and go down and play rugby in Oamaru. That was a big day out. For half the kids the highlight was the pie and the Coke afterwards at the dairy on the way back. A few other parents would help Barney, and I think pretty much every week, bar one or two, in the five years I played for Kurow, Dad would've been on the bus to come down with me.

The best thing about Barney's coaching was that he made us all part of the team. His mantra was that everyone loves playing good footie, and good teams produce

Carrying the ball for Kurow Under 9s against Union.

good players. He rotated the captaincy every week, rotated the kicking duties, both for touch and for goal, and kept meticulous records of who did what in his exercise books. He wanted everyone to share in the team responsibilities. He had a cup that he used to award to the player of the day, which never went to the kid who scored the most tries, it always went to the kid who had lifted his game the most from the week before.

The one thing he did stick to was the positions he chose to play us in. He'd had a year to look at us by then, assess our skills, size, speed and agility, and he must have had a pretty good eye, because most of us played out our careers in the position that Barney chose for us. That said, I mostly played No. 8, and occasionally lock, because of my size.

Barney remembers me as being 'ball hungry', but there was no individual starring stuff. You couldn't be selfish with the ball — you got a metaphorical boot up the arse if you didn't pass the ball — and it was all about using the backs. That taught me a hell of a lot. I watch kids play sometimes, and quite often some guy will get the ball and that's it, particularly if he's one of the bigger kids.

I was one of those bigger kids. I was born on 31 December, so I could have almost played in the year below, I was right on the edge, but I still used to get questioned about my age every week. Mums would come up and ask, 'How old are you?' Thankfully, it was only age that counted in North Otago. I was a bit chubby — 'solid, very solid,' according to Barney — until Dad got me running when I was 12, and weight-wise, I certainly had a bit of an advantage. In the cities there used

1989

#	Name	Maheno 15/4/89	Athletic 22/4/89	Union 29/4/89	Athletic 6/5/89	Maheno 24/?/89	Union 3/6/89	Old Boys 30/6/89	Excelsior 24/6/89	Valley 1/7/89	Union 22/7/89	Maheno 29/7/89	Valley 5/8/89	Excelsior 19/8/89
1	Justin Tipa	Prop (CPT)	Prop	Prop		Prop	½	Prop	Prop	Prop	Prop	Prop	Prop	Prop
2	John Pearson	Hook	HK	HK		HK	HK	½	—		HK	HK	U10	U10
3	Chris Linwood	Prop	Prop	Prop		Prop	½	Prop	½	Prop	Prop	Prop	Prop	Prop
4	Rick McCaw	Lock	Prop	Lock	CPT	½	Prop	Lock	Prop	Lock	Lock	NO8	Lock	Lock
5	Andrew Hayes	Lock	Wing	—		½	Wing	—	Wing	FB	Lock	Lock	U10	Lock
6	Alec Stringer	Centre	—	—		—								
7	Mark Reid	NO8	Lock	—		½	Lock	½	HK	HK		—	Lock	
8	Guy McCone	NO8	Lock	Lock		½	Lock	Lock	Lock	Lock	·	Lock	Lock	U10
9	Ross McCone	Half	Half	Half		½	Half	Half	Half	Half	Half	Half	Half	Half
10	Ben Whitworth	1st 5/8	1st 5/8	1st 5/8		1st 5/8	½	1st 5/8	½	1st 5/8	1st 5/8	1st 5/8	1st 5/8	1st 5/8
12	Andrew Gard	Centre/2nd 5/8	2nd 5/8	2nd 5/8		½	2nd	½	½	2nd 5/8	2nd 5/8	Half	2nd 5/8	2nd 5/8
13	Rob McIlraith	2nd	—	Centre		2nd	½	Cent	2nd	Cent	Cent	Cnt	Cnt	Cnt
11	Scott Willson	Wing	Centre	Wing		Wing	Wing	Wing/Cnt	Wing	Wing	Wing	Wing	Wing	Wing
14	Hayden McGill	Wing	Wing	Wing		½	Wing	½	Wing	Wing	Wing	Wing	Wing	Wing
15	Glen Turnbull	Wing/NO8	NO8	NO8		½	NO8	NO8	½	N8	N8	-·	HK	HC

Barney McCone's exercise book, full of good North Otago names.

to be Under 45 kg then Under 58 kg for the bigger kids in Form Two, but I would have been struggling to even make that.

I finished at Haka School in Standard Four at age 10, and travelled to Kurow Area School each day for Forms One and Two, an hour each way in the bus because I was first on, and we had to go right round the loop road. I think that was when Dad and I made the goalposts on the farm, so that I could have a kick around after I got off the bus. Between that and my running, I'd be totally busy until Mum called me for tea.

That Kurow team stayed together for five years, through Under 9s, Under 10s, Under 11s, Under 12s and Under 13s, until I went away to boarding school, and I think we lost only three or four games in that time. We quite often used to win by 70 or 80 points, even though we seldom had 15 players. I was selected for North Otago rep teams from Under 9s through to Under 13s, and twice for the Hanan Shield Under 11s and 12s, encompassing the North Otago, South Canterbury and Mid Canterbury rugby unions but, ironically, I didn't get selected for the Under 13s the year I did all that running. I did get second in the school cross-country that year, though, an event I'd never featured in before. That was a wow moment.

Barney remembers one recurring problem with me. He was strict about having our jerseys tucked in and our socks pulled up, but I'd forget to bring the tape and within 10 minutes my socks would be around my ankles and my jersey around my knees.

When we'd played our last game together at 12, and we were about to scatter to the four winds, Barney made a speech and told us 'a couple of you have got the ability to go all the way'. He never singled out who. He wanted us all to harbour

First day at Kurow Area School, with sister Jo.

With Mum and Dad, about to head off to Otago Boys'.

our dreams; that was Barney's way. And we knew it was possible, because we had our own heroes from the Waitaki Valley.

Barney's best friend, Phil Gard, who also farmed just south of Kurow, made it all the way to the All Blacks from one of the tiniest clubs in one of the tiniest unions. Phil once played for two years, club footy for Kurow and rep for North Otago, without winning a game, until he was selected for the South Island in 1969 and they beat the North Island. In Barney's estimation, Phil was one of the most complete footballers he ever saw and played mightily for the Hanan Shield Combined side against the 1971 Lions. He was selected for the All Blacks for the fourth test that year at second-five. That was his only cap, but he played on until 1977 for North Otago, was on the committee at Kurow, then President, and I remember him being around at practice. Phil died far too young, of cancer, at the age of 42 in 1990.

Shortly after Phil, Ian 'Archie' Hurst also made the All Blacks, for the 1972–73 tour of the UK, also as a second-five/centre. Ian had played for North Otago when he was still at Waitaki Boys' High School, but made the All Blacks from the fierce Canterbury team of the early seventies, when he became a student at Lincoln University. We'd pass Ian and Gloria's farm at Papakaio on the way down to Oamaru every weekend on the bus. That's about as close as I got to him then, but more recently I've had a lot more to do with him, through playing with his son Ben at the Crusaders and flatting with his daughter Sarah in Christchurch.

The important thing was that all us kids knew we had All Blacks from our neck of the woods, who were farmers and locals just like us, and who we saw in the flesh from time to time, so we had it in the backs of our minds that to rise so high wasn't completely impossible.

And, at school, we found out that Kurow had played its part in New Zealand's political and economic history too, by providing two of the biggest building blocks for the development of the modern nation.

We learnt that Kurow's Presbyterian manse had been the birthplace of New Zealand's modern welfare state back in the early 1930s, when the local Presbyterian minister, Arnold Nordmeyer, Kurow school's headmaster, Andrew Davidson, and the local doctor, Gervan McMillan, prepared the blueprint for the Social Security Act introduced by the first Labour Government.

It should have been no surprise that such a compassionate approach emanated from our area: for all the spectral beauty of the place, it was harsh terrain to wrest a living from in those days, with snow most winters, very hot in summer, little water and a lot of drought. Before irrigation, the crops that grew most naturally were stones and rabbits. The road up the Waitaki was white shingle, and some of the tributaries had to be forded when the little wooden one-way bridges were taken out by floods.

There'd been a hydro dam built just north of the town in 1928, but the real changes came in 1956, when Kurow became the staging post for the Benmore

Driving the old Model M crawler tractor, aged 13.

dam, further up the river. At the time, Benmore was the biggest earth dam in the southern hemisphere. The third big dam on the Waitaki, Aviemore, completed in 1968, came with a painful family history. It resulted in my grandmother Cathie's family losing their land. The Trotters' station, Garguston, was compulsorily acquired by the government, and the drowning of their beautiful farm remained a sore point with their family for many years, and probably still is today. A lake-edge residential development ensures that the name Garguston lives on, above where the road used to run down to the homestead.

When I look down at the Haka Valley on that first flight in the Discus, it's with mixed feelings. I know I couldn't have accomplished what I've done and have the life I have if I'd stayed there, but what a start in life it gave me.

I was seldom inside. I'd just take off. If I wasn't kicking the ball or running, I'd go and play in the creek, go rabbit shooting, or I'd be out helping the old man on the farm. We did a lot of cropping, so I'd get out there and row paddocks with grubbers and stuff, driving the tractor. Shift an irrigator. At 10 years old, I'd be flying round the paddocks on a motorbike. I got to do all that outside stuff. Occasionally, I'd hear a yell 'Where are ya?', but they weren't really worried. It was nothing out of the ordinary. You made your own fun. It wasn't until I got out of the Haka that I thought, 'What an upbringing! How lucky was that?'

As I swoop off the Kirklistons in the Discus, I remember something else.

When we sold the farm in 2002 and I went back to clear out my room, I found pinned up behind the wardrobe the table napkin that Uncle Bigsy had helped me put together while we were waiting for our burgers in Timaru. When I looked at the target dates for all the teams, I realised that I'd beaten them all, making the All Blacks in 2001, three years before the 2004 team I'd targeted.

The only goal I hadn't fulfilled was the last one, the *G.A.B.*

And I realise, five years later, as I start the glide back to Omarama, that I'm not much closer to achieving that particular goal than I was back in 2002.

Superficially, there aren't a lot of similarities between gliding and rugby. Gliding teaches you that you've got to be as prepared as you possibly can be for whatever contingencies of terrain and weather might eventuate once you're up there. At the same time, you have to acknowledge that no matter how much you prepare, no matter how thorough you are, you can't anticipate everything that Nature or Fate might throw at you. Sometimes Fate throws you a curve ball. You have to deal with it the best way you can, survive it, then learn what you can from it.

As I set myself for landing at the airfield in Omarama, I think *G.A.B.* might be a handy frame of reference when it comes to consider what I do next, how I respond to the Cardiff calamity. What would a *G.A.B.* do?

The first thing would be to admit that I didn't play to my best in that game. One bad game doesn't suddenly make you a bad player. I remember a quote I've heard: 'Every great All Black has been dropped at some point.' I've got to face the possibility that I might be dropped after Cardiff. But even if I'm not, what happened there, getting beaten when we shouldn't have, is almost like being dropped.

But there's no real question in my mind about walking away. I don't want to play overseas, and I signed a contract with the NZRU just days before that quarter-final. It might have been silly to be doing it in the middle of the RWC, but it had to be signed then, otherwise I wouldn't have been eligible for Super Rugby in 2008. It wasn't really that much of a distraction because I was always going to stay. There was never any doubt about that. Now I'm thinking I might have been lucky — they might not have offered me a contract on those terms after the game!

There's another issue. My captaincy is being called into question, constantly I'm told, in the sports pages I'm not reading and on the talk-back radio I'm not listening to. It's a legitimate question: Am I the right man for the job?

There's an option in front of me which would make everyone feel good: take a neutral position, say that if I'm not the right man for the job, I'm happy to step aside. Give everyone, myself included, an out.

But at bedrock, I think: no, bugger it. I still believe I can do it. It's scary, but if I'm going to become the captain I want to be, I've got to put myself up for it, I've got to survive Cardiff and come out the other side stronger for the experience.

I think about Uncle Bigsy and the *G.A.B.* What do I want to be remembered as? The guy who gave up when it got hard?

Robbie & Ted
& Smithy & Shag

In late November, Graham Henry makes it public that he's going to reapply for All Black coach, and Wayne Smith and Steve Hansen recommit as well. It doesn't take me by surprise — I reckon that if I deserve a second chance, so do the coaches — but it seems to surprise many in the media. From the time the NZRU announced there'd be a review and that applications would be invited for the All Black coaching position, a lot of people simply assumed that that amounted to the chop for Ted and Smithy and Shag.

That's probably the way Ted & Co. viewed it too when I saw them in Wellington earlier that month. I was up there for other business, and banged into them at NZRU just after they'd been told the news that if they wanted their jobs back they'd have to reapply, and they were debating whether it was worthwhile even putting themselves up for it.

I told them they should. I told them that I wanted another crack and so should they. I accepted that after Cardiff there were no guarantees for anyone involved, that I was expecting to have to fight to retain the captaincy, and perhaps even my place in the All Blacks, and that was only right because I was one of the ones out on the field who had stuffed up. We'd made mistakes collectively, and it'd be nice to think that we all got a chance to profit from them. I was trying to reassure Ted that he hadn't lost the changing room, and other senior players were telling him the same thing. Ted seemed down, but I could see that he was open to the idea at least.

All Black coaches are very accountable. Every year, they undergo 360ies, an anonymous on-line review system. Players, co-coaches, management, NZRU staff, some media and sponsors complete a series of questions about each coach. They even do some public focus groups. Ted and Smithy and Shag must have been reassured by what the 360ies were telling them as they came in, because at the end of November, Ted says they're going to reapply. I'm pleased.

Robbie Deans has also thrown his hat in the ring, though when he tells me he's done that, he also says that he's not sure that the position is genuinely up for grabs. I tell him that's news to me.

The fact that I'm hearing the same doubts from both the major applicants indicates how conflicted I feel: up to my ears. I owe both Robbie and Ted huge debts for my development as a player.

Robbie has been my mentor at Super 14 level since 2001, and was also there as John Mitchell's assistant when I first made the All Blacks. When we were dumped out of the 2003 tournament in the semi by the Aussies, both were sacked, but their subsequent career paths have been very different. John Mitchell has had to struggle to rehabilitate his reputation, but Robbie returned to the Crusaders and won back-to-back Super titles in 2005 and 2006, and got us to the semis in 2007, when we were battling to get our top team on the park. By December 2007, when the interviews are being conducted, Robbie Deans is the only credible alternative to Ted & Co.

The problem is that some in the media have already anointed Robbie Deans and they're affronted that Ted has had the gall to put his name forward again. It's pretty brutal: if he'd won the RWC, he'd have been up for an Order of Merit at the very least, whereas now they're clamouring for the Order of the Boot.

Publicly, I have to maintain a strict neutrality, but privately, when I start working through my own evaluations of them, I develop a strong preference as to which choice would better serve the All Blacks and our chances in the 2011 RWC.

The first step in that evaluation is to be rigorously honest about what went wrong in Cardiff.

As the who-will-coach-the-All Blacks saga develops, with formal applications to the NZRU and interviews, Hayley and I rent a bach at Raglan, the west coast surf spot near Hamilton, a great place to lie low and think. We're joined there by Ali Williams and his girlfriend, Casey.

Ali has remained loyal to Ted, and down at Raglan, in so far as we discuss developments at NZRU HQ in Wellington, Ali speaks as highly of Ted as ever. He's got no regrets about the last four years with Ted, and has gone public with his view that his involvement in the All Black set-up with Ted and Shag and Smithy has not only made him a better player but a better person.

That motto, 'Better people make better All Blacks', has been a guiding philosophy for the All Blacks since Ted & Co. were appointed in 2004.

By that time Ted was already in his late fifties, a former headmaster from southern stock, and could have been excused for sticking to methods which were tried and true across a long career. But what you see of Ted — a slightly curmudgeonly, at times grumpy-looking and conservative late-middle-aged man — is not what you get. In the last four years he's proven himself to be an innovative, enlightened thinker, with the energy and openness to new ideas of a man half his age.

Instead of harking back to what worked so brilliantly with the likes of Fitzy and Zinny and the great Blues team of the mid to late nineties, Ted recognised when he took over the All Blacks that the make-up of the modern team had inevitably changed along with the demographics of the country. The modern All Blacks are culturally and ethnically more diverse, and Ted and the people around him made a point of embracing all that, not fighting it.

One of the first signs of Ted's approach was appointing Tana Umaga to be his captain. I've spoken to players of Ted's vintage who tell me that not only would someone with dreadlocks never have been in the running for All Black captain in their time, he would have been lucky to have worn the silver fern in any capacity.

Ted's said that being principal of Kelston Boys' High School, a decile 4 school, helped immensely. There was a high percentage of Polynesians in the school and he got to know a wider cross-section of New Zealand society than he might have done down south, or if he'd stayed at Auckland Grammar. He learnt that what was important to the European kid might be quite different from what was important to the Samoan, or to the Tongan or Fijian, and he learnt to respect the differences.

He's carried that over to the All Black environment, where he's worked hard to make sure that everyone in the team knows and respects everyone else's culture.

But if there's one single outstanding and innovative element to what he's done with us since he took over in 2004, it's the ownership he's encouraged each player to have over what we're doing as a group. The coaching team put a lot of effort into growing us as people, and developing our leadership and decision-making skills. The only way of doing that is by giving us players real power over our own systems and protocols, and by integrating them into all the major decisions.

The perfect illustration of this is the controversial rotation and reconditioning system, which was endorsed by the players. The pity of it is that we didn't get far enough through the RWC tournament to show its true value. If we'd had to play a semi-final the week after Cardiff, we'd have been without a number of front-line players, and the game time that some of the other guys had had during the year and in the earlier RWC matches against the likes of Italy and Portugal and Scotland would have been of critical importance.

Okay, we got stuffed in the quarter-final, but you have to plan as if you're going all the way.

There'd also been a lot of criticism about the NZRU taking the All Blacks out of the early Super 14 games, and the way we rotated through the Tri Nations etc, but from my own point of view, I was absolutely knackered at the end of 2006, and I needed that extra window of recuperation and conditioning at the beginning of 2007.

In retrospect, it's a hard one to call.

It's true that in 2007, we never quite had the physical edge we had in 2006. Maybe the critics are right and it was due to the fact that the core of the team didn't play together enough. The other possibility is that our opponents stepped up a gear. The timing of the RWC means that the northern hemisphere teams get a six-week window to prepare solely for the tournament with no other distractions, and that can turn them into a different proposition from the teams we play at other times, when the demands of their long club season wear them down.

That's the thing: Ted & Co. have given us huge success at every level, except the RWC.

Me and Ted — 2006 was a very good year.

We were the Laureus Sports Academy team of 2006, along with the Italian soccer team and the European Ryder Cup team, and in their time at the helm Ted & Co. have cemented the All Blacks as one of the premier global sporting brands.

That's terribly important: the All Blacks don't have the critical mass of fan base and revenue that an England or a South Africa has. New Zealand rugby simply can't afford for the All Blacks to stuff around and get it wrong for three years in the hope that they'll pull everything together for the RWC. We'd be down the drain. The number-one ranking is almost as important as the RWC.

However, for virtually every success attributed to Ted, you could say the same about Robbie Deans.

The All Blacks have won 42 out of 48 games under Ted, and won 22 out of 27 under John Mitchell and Robbie. Before the 2003 RWC semi, the All Blacks under John Mitchell and Robbie played stunning rugby, running up record scores against the Aussies and Springboks. And Robbie's record at Super rugby level with the Crusaders is phenomenal — three Super titles in his seven seasons as head coach, so far, and only missing the play-offs in one season. Robbie's also enhanced a culture where a diverse group of players could thrive — guys like Ron Cribb, Rico Gear, Mose Tuiali'i, Ross Filipo, Norm Berryman and Rua Tipoki have all come to the Crusaders with question marks against them, but have produced the goods in the Crusaders environment.

No one can afford to stand still, and, like Ted, Robbie's had to keep developing his skills. In 2004, the Crusaders were not all happy campers. There were a lot of disgruntled players and discontented rumblings, mostly about Robbie's man-management around who was playing and not playing. While there's a view that the only thing a player hears when he's dropped are those words — 'You're out' — the reality in the professional environment is that every player needs to be told why he's not playing and what he needs to work on. The truth may not be what he wants to hear, but it's what he needs to hear: every player wants to improve, it's a basic light-at-the-end-of-the-tunnel aspiration. If he's not being given the right information, or any information, it's difficult for him to move forward. Players were being told they were playing okay, but being rested, or were being told that the minor niggle they'd reported was the reason they weren't playing this week. Robbie may have been trying to keep everyone happy, but fudging the truth had the opposite effect.

So, before I took on the captaincy in 2005, Reuben Thorne and I asked for a sit-down with Robbie. We discussed the situation, told him that some players were unhappy and why. It turned into a very human moment, when Robbie opened up and said that telling players they weren't selected was the part of the job he found most difficult. Once the problem was identified, he addressed it in a professional way and improved that aspect of his communication with the players.

I feel I owe it to Robbie to give what happened in Cardiff more than a quick once-over. There are questions arising out of that game that need honest answers, now that I've got the time to do it.

Reuben and I frame Robbie.

Where was the vaunted leadership group in that last 20 minutes?

Quite a few of them weren't on the field. Anton, Byron, Dan and Jerry had either been injured or subbed. Guys like Aaron Mauger and Dougie Howlett were sitting in the stand.

For all the work Ted & Co. have done on our leadership and decision-making skills, I'd be struggling to give myself or anyone else in our leadership group a pass mark when it came to the crunch in Cardiff.

Down there in the cauldron of noise, it was bit like the silence of the lambs. Carl Hayman and others in the pack were still voluble, but where we most needed direction, there was a lack of decisiveness. Luke was inexperienced and had inherited first-five by default after Dan and Nick went off. Perhaps I should have seen that he needed more help and direction from me, particularly when he had Ice, equally inexperienced, outside him.

We did a lot of good things in that last 20 minutes, got ourselves into positions where we should have won the game. The fact that we didn't wasn't for lack of effort — if anything, individuals began trying to win it on their own. But we needed a little more coolness under fire in critical positions.

I keep replaying one sequence in my head. With 90 seconds to go, Ali had secured the pill from the lineout, Siti had stepped through to their 22, and Rodney bulldozed it on and then I piled in to secure the recycle. We were right in front of the posts, 20 metres out, but the only one standing in the pocket was Woody, a prop.

If Dan or Nick or even Aaron had been on the field, I like to think they would have been in the pocket, making the call, taking the responsibility for winning or losing the game.

The guts of it is that in that moment, our leadership group failed under pressure. That includes me. Rather than saying, 'Have a pot if it's on,' I should have been more directive — and so should the senior players in the backline. But it also includes the coaches: we didn't have a drop-kick in our play-book.

We hadn't as a group run through the scenario of what happens if it gets tight and we need one or two things to happen to win the game. We believed that we were good enough to go out and play well. We never imagined ourselves to be in a sticky situation like that, despite history showing that all RWC-winning teams have been in those situations. In that sense it was a failure of imagination as much as anything.

If there's a next time, we need to expect to be in that situation, rather than hope we won't be.

Were the tactics right?

We went out there to play our game, high pace, high intensity, believing we could win by scoring tries.

We had variations on that plan of course, but we never considered for a moment that we'd be in the kind of hole that required a kick, whether a penalty or drop-goal, to win the game. That wasn't an option, and when it came to the crunch and we needed a drop-kick, we didn't have a play we could go to in order to execute that. We had to fall back on the improvisational abilities of our play-makers, and when you're down to your third first-five in the game, that's something you can't rely on.

The All Blacks have routinely been labelled arrogant by some of the northern hemisphere media. I've always thought the New Zealand media have brought that down on us by not respecting the opposition in their pre-game analyses. Some of the predictions about how much the All Blacks are going to win by are both ludicrous and disrespectful. But while I think the All Blacks are generally pretty grounded and humble as individuals, maybe the arrogant tag is true of the way we try to play in world cups.

France knew what we were going to do; we had no idea what they were going to do, really. When we'd whacked them in Lyon and Paris in 2006, they'd tried to play rugby against us, what we might call traditional French rugby, keeping the ball in hand and running at us. We lapped that up. We turned the ball over and punished them. It should really have been no surprise that they tried something different in Cardiff.

Instead of employing that running game, known in France apparently as the 'Toulouse style', they decided to implement the 'Biarritz style', which is shorthand for spoiling rugby, keeping it tight and kicking. They kicked very well and defended brilliantly, stopping our go-forward and our offloads. We got frustrated and made mistakes. They did a Biarritz on us and it worked — as, I'm told, that style usually works against Toulouse.

I don't think we played dumb on the day. We adjusted hugely in fact, narrowed our game drastically in the last quarter, and played for a mistake that never came — or if it did, was missed by the referee.

Nevertheless, tactically we were arrogant and naive. We thought we would roll them with Plan A, and when we didn't, our Plan B lacked options and execution because we hadn't anticipated having to use it.

Were the selections right?

Robbie Deans in his *New Zealand Herald* column made two important points: that because the RWC knockout is like nothing else the players have ever experienced, you need to select players who have been there before, and you need to select established combinations to operate under that pressure.

Robbie's wisdom was hard-earned: he was instrumental in not selecting a fit Tana Umaga for the semi-final in 2003. Instead, he and John Mitchell pushed Leon into an unfamiliar role at centre. The Australian centre Stirling Mortlock was a dominant figure, just as he was when we lost to Australia in Melbourne in June, this time against Luke, who was playing out of position at centre. After that game Stirling was reported as saying that the All Blacks hadn't solved the problem of how to replace Tana.

We hadn't solved it by Cardiff either. Conrad Smith had been injured earlier in the tournament and there were doubts about his match fitness, so, once again, we improvised at centre for a crucial RWC knockout match. So much so that when Mils got the nod at Tuesday practice that he was playing at centre against France, not fullback, he was surprised.

One lesson from history that we ought to always keep in mind is that the best All Black teams have very experienced specialists at centre. Crusties like Joe Stanley and Frank Bunce and Tana Umaga had hard-headed attitudes and considerable age in common: all of them played great rugby into their early thirties.

But who played centre wasn't the only pertinent question.

Doug Howlett would have been a stronger defensive option on the right wing, and might have been a critical element when France scored their second try. And while Luke McAlister played very well, particularly in the first half, there's no doubt in my mind that we lacked Aaron Mauger's experience and decisiveness in that last 20 minutes, and that he should have at least been on the bench. But who would have guessed that neither of the starting first-fives, Dan and Nick, would be there for the end-game?

On the positive side, you'd have to say that Ted & Co. got the forward pack right. The scrums, lineouts and restarts were excellent. Ali and Rodney had fine games, and the front-rowers bested their opponents. Keith Robinson did well enough and Jacko lifted us when he came on. I wasn't the presence at second phase that I usually was, and Jerry wasn't his usual self either, though he had an excuse after he got crippled by Dusautoir.

But the game was won and lost in that last 20, and you'd have to say we didn't have the right people in the right places for that critical time. Some were absent through injury, but a couple were sitting in the stand.

Continuity or a new broom?

I remember a quote I use a bit: 'If you learn from your own mistakes you pick up experience, if you learn from someone else's mistakes you pick up wisdom.'

Choosing between Ted and Robbie on the basis of RWC experience is inconclusive. They've both been there, made mistakes, come home with their tails between their legs.

Given their formidable rugby intelligence and dedication to their craft, they were both going to learn from their experience and from others', and be better and wiser coaches in that environment next time round.

The question is whether it's better to stay with the incumbent or get a new broom in there and start again. Because that's what a choice in favour of Robbie would mean.

As a player and captain, I already know I'm going to be asking for another chance at RWC glory. Talking with Ali and Mils and others, there's a feeling that surely we can be better for this, surely we can build on the good things that we've done, if we're given the chance. Should Ted expect the same opportunity?

However, I'm beginning to realise that *Ted or Robbie?* is the wrong question.

The applications in front of the NZRU are telling. Robbie hasn't named his assistants, though Pat Lam's name has been mentioned in some reports. But Pat hasn't coached at Super 14 level yet. So the question actually is: *Graham Henry, Wayne Smith and Steve Hansen or Robbie Deans and Unknown Assistant Coaches?*

That's a critical difference right there.

While Ted's the man in charge, maintains a bit of distance, and is tough to get to know, he works well as part of a team. He's great at the big picture, always looking ahead, getting a handle on who we're coming up against. He watches an awful lot of rugby and looks at trends, where we need to be, what we need to do to get there, while we're busy just looking at our own stuff. He'll say, 'This is what I've seen from the northern hemisphere, this is what I see from Super rugby.'

Before we went on the Grand Slam tour in 2005, for instance, he knew that the biggest game was going to be England, the third one. He was planning around how to get to that. I didn't think England had been playing that well, but he was dead right and that was the toughest by far.

Again, in 2005, after we'd dealt to the Lions, he knew that South Africa were going to be the toughest in the Tri Nations. He'd have in mind how we were going to play against South Africa and what we needed to do to be right for that. He'd have regular meetings with the senior players and plan what we needed to do to win the campaign, rather than get lost in what's ahead of us this week or next week. It's pretty easy to get caught up in that.

Ted had all the percentages. He'd be looking at stuff like tries from turnovers and where they come from, what the northern hemisphere were doing to create tries. How the game had changed. 'Okay, what's our strength,' he'd say, 'and how are we going to make that work for us?' For all that, he was never a one-man band in this or in anything else.

Smithy's similar to Ted in that he does a shit-load of research about what other teams are doing and how to exploit what they're doing — and most importantly, he has an understanding of what might actually work in the heat of battle.

While he's big on stats, it's because he can interpret them in a useful way. He's not blinded by them, uses them as a good indicator, but isn't bluffed by quantitative measurements — he's looking for the quality. Twenty tackles against a player's name is meaningless, unless you further analyse how many of them were weak and how many were dominant or turnover tackles. Smithy's got a great eye for detail and how to translate that detail to individual skill-sets. He's big on systems but also sharp on detail.

At the same time — and this is probably the paradox with Smithy — as much as he likes a good stat, he's also big on emotive drivers. What gives a team that mental edge?

Steve Hansen has a different but very complementary approach. He has a great feel for how things are now, and he's able to get in front of the team without doing as much homework but work his way in and get the best out of the players. He's bloody good at handling stuff on the fly. He'll be your good mate, but has a way of being able to have a straight conversation with a player. Instead of saying, 'This is what I think,' he'll ask, 'What do you see?' You end up picking your game over. He won't blow wind up your bum, but you'll go away thinking that you really got something out of the session.

Steve was apparently quite tough on the Welsh team when he went there in 2001, but he turned them around, and some of the Welsh boys who worked under him have told me they'd die for him.

The three of them make such a strong unit, that's the thing. Smithy and Steve have been international head coaches in their own right and they're happy to defer to one another, and all of them are prepared to try stuff and then put up their hands and say, 'I got that wrong.' Notwithstanding all that, there's never any doubt that Ted makes the final decision if one is needed.

For me, the fact that Smithy and Steve have committed again to Ted speaks volumes. That must have been a difficult decision for both of them. Smithy won't have done that without a lot of thought, and Steve probably considered putting his own hand up.

Then there's the support staff those guys have put around us: Sir Brian Lochore, and the specialist coaches — Mike Cron with the scrum, Mick Byrne with the kicking

Is it a bird, is it a ball? Or am I boring them?

and catching, Graham Lowe, the trainer, Gilbert Enoka, the sports psychologist. It's such a powerful coaching nexus.

Robbie is different.

Robbie doesn't appear to want to be challenged by his assistants and won't allow the kind of full-on debate that Ted encourages with Smithy and Steve. Robbie's approach is to say, 'This is what we're doing,' then convince people that that's the way it's got to be. He's very good at that.

But when you look at the record of Robbie's assistant coaches, there's quite a lot of turnover and fallout. Robbie's intransigence and reluctance to delegate might have been a factor.

It was certainly a factor with Steve Hansen, who was Robbie's assistant at Canterbury and the Crusaders from 1997 through to 2001, before Steve departed for Wales. I was involved off and on in the 2001 Crusaders campaign and it was pretty average: we finished tenth, and there was a lot of tension between Robbie and Steve. It was then decided that you couldn't coach at NPC and Super rugby level, so Robbie got the Crusaders and Steve got hold of the NPC team. Steve brought some good ideas to that NPC team, got buy-in from the guys, and we had a really successful year — and a lot of fun.

But Steve is just one case in point, if you look at the names of some of Robbie's assistants. Colin Cooper, Vern Cotter, Don Hayes, Todd Blackadder. It's tempting to draw the conclusion that if Robbie gets a strong assistant coach, the assistant won't last, and if he gets one that lasts, he's not that strong.

Despite that history, Robbie's stature is such that he could have pulled some excellent coaching assistance in with him for the application to the NZRU — after all, a year as Robbie's assistant is probably going to teach you more than most other positions in world rugby.

So when I see that Robbie hasn't really nailed anyone down to back him up, I wonder whether Robbie's gone into the process believing that he hasn't really got a fair shot and is just going through the motions.

There'd be some history in support of that attitude.

Some in the media see a Crusaders monopoly in the NZRU, with Steve Tew and Darren Shand and Shag and Smithy — not to mention me — all with strong Canterbury and Crusaders connections (even Ted was born and raised in Christchurch), and imagine there's a Canterbury power bloc running New Zealand rugby, but nothing could be further from the truth.

When Robbie was sacked as All Black coach after the 2003 RWC, his nemesis Steve Hansen came back from Wales and stepped into the All Black coaching team, and Steve wasn't alone in making that move from the Crusaders to the All Blacks. Steve Tew, the CEO, left the Crusaders for the same job at the NZRU, Darren Shand left as manager of the Crusaders to become manager of the All Blacks, even Errol Collins, the Crusaders baggage man who'd been around a long time and had been part of the glue of the team, left for the same position with the All Blacks.

These changes could all be explained in terms of career opportunities, but I'm not sure if Robbie and Hamish Riach, the Crusaders CEO who replaced Steve Tew, shared that sort of equanimity about the movement of Crusaders personnel to the NZRU. Both Robbie and Hamish are paid to work their own corner, and I could be wrong, but my feeling is that the ones who left were seen as defectors from the cause.

That's been borne out by the All Blacks not really being made welcome when it comes to using Canterbury facilities. Every other franchise around the country gets the NPC team to move out for the week the All Blacks are in town. Canterbury just said no, which was a bit embarrassing when so many of us, management included, were from Canterbury.

On the positive side, if Robbie was appointed All Black coach, it would bring an end to all that, you'd hope. But that's not a good enough reason to change the All Black coaching set-up, to throw everything out and start again.

The conclusion I come to has an inevitability about it.

While *Ted versus Robbie* might have been a fair fight, *Ted and Smithy and Shag versus Robbie and Persons Unknown* never could be.

So when Steve Tew phones me for an informal catch-up on this and that, I tell him I'm happy to work with either, but I do have a view on which option might be better for the All Blacks.

Whatever decision the NZRU make, I'm about to spend the next six months with Robbie and the Crusaders. I hope expressing my views won't come back and bite me on the bum.

Canterbury tales

etting back to the Crusaders set-up for a new season at Rugby Park, St Albans is a bit like sinking into a warm bath. Familiar settings and people, a ritual I've been part of since 2002, and before that with Canterbury.

This time, it's not quite so comfortable. There's an anxiety hanging over everything, born out of uncertainty. We know that Robbie's up for the All Black coaching job, and there's been a lot of media speculation about the Aussies courting him too. If either eventuates, where does that leave the Crusaders?

I can imagine the NZRU allowing Robbie to see out the Crusaders season as incoming All Black coach, but if he misses out on that and gets the Aussie job, he's suddenly in the enemy camp, and how will that sit with being coach of a New Zealand franchise?

My own state of mind isn't helped by my conflict over the Robbie vs Ted contest still being played out, and the bath really loses its heat when Robbie tells me that he and I need to have a sit-down.

We adjourn to the little café just across the road from Rugby Park. Robbie has a great shock of hair and the face of eternal youth, but when he's serious, you know it. His first question confirms it.

'Captain of the Crusaders,' he says. 'Do you want to do it?'

I'm a bit startled at the question. I tell him I don't see why not.

'I want you to tell me why you want to do it,' he insists.

By now I'm getting a bit defensive. I'm wondering if he's heard a whisper. 'There's no one else really, is there?'

'That's not a good enough reason,' he says. 'I want you to give me a good reason why you want to do this.'

I'm thinking, *Oh shit, what's going on here?* But once I get over that, I realise it's a fair question and gives me a chance to think whether I really do want to do it and, if so, why. It's wonderful how quickly this threat to my captaincy of the Crusaders crystallises things for me.

Happiness is . . . leading Canterbury to the 2004 NPC Division One title.

I tell Robbie I know I can be a better captain for the experiences that I've been through — and I'm not just referring to Cardiff or to the All Blacks. I've been on a huge learning curve since I was appointed captain of the Canterbury NPC team in 2004. That year, I tried to be one of the boys too much and went over the top instead of just being myself. I tell Robbie I still feel like I've only just started, and while I've still got so much to learn, I know I can contribute a hell of a lot more than before.

That's what he wants to hear. There's no ulterior motive, it's just Robbie being the great coach he is, making me recommit to the captaincy, instead of just rolling up and expecting things to be the same this year because that's the way it was last year.

On the way home, I take a leaf out of Barney McCone's book, 94 leaves actually, when I buy a Warwick 2B4 ruled page exercise book and start putting my thoughts together on the page. I write down a heading — *Why I Want to be Captain*. It helps to write it down: that I enjoy having an influence on how the team operates and performs; that I like the pressure and responsibility that comes with the captaincy; that I believe I can improve with experience; that I care about how the team goes and want to help set high standards; and that, selfishly, it helps me stay engaged and become a better player.

That prompt from Robbie is an example of the much talked-about Canterbury/

Crusaders culture in action, which Robbie has played a huge part in building. There are different elements to it, but one of the biggest mantras is that no player is bigger than the team: the team always comes first. All the guys know that, we respect each other for that: pricks don't last. And although we're all well looked after from the word go, we're not feather-bedded.

In that first year as captain of the Canterbury NPC team, I missed the start of the season because I got badly concussed playing for the All Blacks against England and was out for three months. When I came back to the NPC team, I lacked confidence and suggested to coach Aussie McLean that I forgo the captaincy for the first game at least, until I got rid of the doubts and found my feet. He said he'd discussed the situation with Steve Hansen, and they wouldn't have a bar of it. Aussie told me that I'd agreed at the start of the season to be captain, and that if I played at all, I was playing as captain. I was initially taken aback, but it was the best thing he could have done: the captaincy forced me to put aside my self-doubts, stop thinking about my problems and commit myself to the team.

That sort of psychological savvy is the Canterbury/Crusaders way. It's why I came here straight out of school, though putting it like that makes it sound a lot more straightforward than it was.

I was an age-group player for Otago when I first became aware of the Canterbury phenomenon.

I was selected for the Otago Under 16s and we travelled to Ashburton for the South Island inter-provincial tournament. We were still mucking around, getting ourselves and our gear organised, when the Canterbury team arrived in a flash bus, immaculate gear, organised, ready to go. We were billeted; they stayed in a motel. None of that would have mattered particularly. What mattered was they thrashed everyone.

I went back to Otago Boys' and kept developing my game, with the help of some great rugby mentors. As in Kurow, I was able to move through the grades with the same group of guys, with the same coach, David Cook. That made for enduring friendships and a real feeling for each other, on and off the field.

In the fifth form, the First XV coach, Brian Ashwin, gave me a couple of games for the First XV. They were club games, not inter-schools, but we played in the Under 21 grade in the local club competition in Dunedin, against the likes of Otago University students who were up to five years older. I was used to battling for survival against older boys — as a five year old at Haka Primary, I was in boots and all for the pick-up games at intervals and lunchtimes. That served me well as a 15 year old when I went up against 20 and 21 year olds in my first game for OBHS First XV against Taieri at Peter Johnstone Park. By halftime I was a bit battered and bruised, and it didn't help to overhear the Taieri coach urging his players to climb into 'these effing schoolboys, get some boots and hair flying so they don't want to be here'. That certainly hardened me up for the following year, when I became a regular in the First XV.

The last time I appeared in the blue and gold: Otago Under 18s; I'm fourth from left.

That year, when I was a sixth former, Brian Ashwin made an inspired decision to enlist the aid of David Cook, because David had already been with us for a couple of years and knew us so well.

Brian became another of my important rugby mentors. He was utterly dedicated to the school and to rugby, and also taught me Accounting. He was always available in class for a chat about rugby, but it couldn't have been too much of a distraction from the academic side, because in the seventh form, I won Scholarship in Accounting under his tutelage. I remember myself as being a bit shy and reticent, but Brian remembers me sitting up the front of class asking questions.

That Canterbury encounter, and others in the Otago Under 18s, must have simmered away as I completed my sixth and seventh form years, because halfway through my last year I heard that Lincoln University had a rugby scholarship that paid all your fees. My family had always assumed I'd go to Lincoln University and do a Bachelor of Agricultural Science degree, so when Lincoln got back to me and offered me the scholarship, it all seemed to fit; the die seemed cast.

This was 1998, so rugby was in its third year of being professional, but I had no real thought of becoming a professional rugby player. The steps on Uncle Bigsy's stairway to rugby heaven didn't have dollar signs on them: it was about playing for the All Blacks; it wasn't about making a living from rugby. Perhaps I was naive, but that was the way I thought.

But a couple of things happened in the latter part of my last year at Otago Boys' that made me think — and also put my commitment to going to Lincoln University and Canterbury back in the balance.

When Mum and Dad dropped me off at Otago Boys', they'd told me to make sure I made the most of the opportunity, to get stuck in, don't waste this chance. I took their advice to heart to an almost ridiculous degree and had a crack at everything. Orienteering. Drums. Rowing. Tennis. I got a bit carried away, but some things stuck.

I was a waste of everyone's time on the drums, but at the end of my first year, we had a hostel Christmas dinner and another third former got up and played the bagpipes and I thought, *Oh Jeez that's cool. Right, I'm going to do that*. I quizzed him and ended up learning the bagpipes with him twice a week at lunchtime. We would stay at school instead of going back to the hostel for lunch. I'd either get a cut lunch or I'd just go without lunch pretty much. In the end, there were four or five of us, and an old fella called Airdrie Stewart, a really good piper, used to come in and teach us. We had a couple of drummers and we played in a wee band at some concerts at school, but my aspirations were fairly modest — I didn't want to be in a pipe band, I just wanted to be able to pull them out on special occasions and bust out three or four tunes.

I'd never played cricket because they didn't have cricket in Kurow — I'd played tennis on Saturdays during summer. The only cricket I'd played was on the back lawn with Dad and/or Jo. When the cricket trials came up at Otago Boys', they told us to turn up only if you'd made rep teams or played a lot of cricket before, but I thought bugger that and turned up anyway. I told them I wanted to be a 'batter' — batsman — but I was about as useful at that as I was at playing the drums, so they gave me the ball and told me to hurl a few down in the nets. Turns out I was a natural left-arm seamer. One of my mates was there in the nets. He'd been in the North Otago underage cricket team, and he kept missing, and complaining that I was making him look bad.

A couple of days later, one of the teachers came up and said they'd put me in the third form second team. 'We were going to put you in the top team,

Winning lineout ball for Otago Boys' against the visiting Rugby School of England.

At 'boot camp' for the Lincoln Rugby Scholarship, Burnham Military Camp, 1999.

but there's another left-armer, so we've put you in the second team for now.' I thought that was pretty cool.

By taking a punt and getting a bit of encouragement to keep developing, I finally made the First XI in the seventh form.

My academic development paralleled my cricket career.

When I started in the third form, I wasn't in the top class, but I got there in the fourth form.

In the seventh form, I made Head Boy and did Chemistry, Physics, Stats, Calculus and Accounting, and was runner-up to the dux. I did better than the dux in the end-of-year externals, but the dux had beaten me in the internal exams, which I put down to the extracurricular demands of inter-schools rugby and cricket. Even then, I was very competitive and didn't like getting second! Maybe it was because I had to work hard for everything I got. So hard that I copped a bit of stick for being a geek — though not from my mates, and I was saved from the worst of it by my sporting prowess.

But the geek calls didn't put me off — just the opposite. It probably brought out my competitive nature. I wanted to be top. I wanted to be first in the class. In retrospect, I think I probably overdid it, and wonder whether it was really that important, but when it came to leaving school and moving on, those academic achievements opened up a few doors, and suddenly, instead of a degree at Lincoln being a lay-down misere, I had other options thrust in front of me.

When I went up to Christchurch for a look around Lincoln, it was suggested that I also have a scout around Canterbury University, with a view to doing an engineering degree. So I looked at the campus and the college house where I might board, but it didn't really grab me.

By that time, my rugby was really blossoming too. My rugby path at Otago Boys' had been easier than cricket because I'd made North Otago and Hanan Shield rep teams and had some pedigree. I played for the top Otago Boys' teams in third and fourth form, and was selected for Otago age-group representation in Under 16s and Under 18s, but missed out on the New Zealand Schools side to my nemesis from Christ's College, Sam Harding.

But in my last year, Christ's College didn't make the National First XV Championship, so I had a stage that, for once, wasn't shared by Sam. The top three North Island First XVs and the top South Island First XV played in a tournament in Christchurch. Otago Boys' just scraped past a very good Southland Boys' side, with the likes of Clarke Dermody, Corey Flynn and Jeff Wright at No. 7, to finish top South Island First XV.

We thought we had a pretty good team, with Captain Ryan Martin at halfback, a bit of Polynesian muscle in the pack, headed by Filipo Levi, and pace and power in the backs with Jason Kawau at centre, but Kelston were something else. They had guys like Mils Muliaina, Sam Tuitupou, Steve Bates and Boris Stankovich, who ended up playing hooker for Bath in the UK. They looked very big and very dark,

One of us looks the part! Hostel 'formal' at Otago Boys' with mate William Lowe.

compared to us. They did their haka first and it was so powerful and impressive that we just knew that the little white boys from down south weren't going to cut it, so we flagged ours. We hadn't really recovered by the time the whistle blew. In one movement, they scored under the posts: 7–0. I remember thinking, *Jeez, I hope this is less than 50 points.*

We were shell-shocked, but knuckled down and tackled our hearts out. As the game wore on, we tackled and tackled, and they couldn't score again, and it seemed to surprise them that we hadn't just capitulated. We won narrowly with a kick from near halfway that was aimed at the corner posts and was blown in by the wind. Then we drew the final against Rotorua Boys', and ended up joint winners of the tournament.

Those two games, particularly the game against Kelston, got me into the trials for the New Zealand Under 19s, and it also brought me to the notice of a certain Steve Hansen, who was running the Canterbury Academy. Steve reportedly told Canterbury, 'Get him up here', and was presumably told to relax, that I was coming to Lincoln, and everything was sweet.

Meanwhile, word about my intentions filtered back to Otago. The headmaster at Otago Boys' collared me and asked me why I was going to Lincoln. He told me I had the ability to do medicine at Otago. When I said that didn't appeal, he said that it was a waste my going 'up there' and I should stay 'down here'.

It didn't end there. I was at a leavers' dinner with businessman Eion Edgar's son, Adam, who was in my year at Otago Boys'. Eion had — and still has — huge official and unofficial heft in the Otago Rugby Union. When Eion found out I was off to

Lincoln, he repeated the question — 'What the hell are you going up there for?'

The very next day, I got the same question from Des Smith, who'd been one of my masters at Otago Boys' but was now working for the Otago Rugby Union. 'What the hell are you going up there for?' He told me if I wanted to stay, he'd organise some accommodation and I could do a degree at Otago. He even arranged for Tony Gilbert, the Otago coach at the time, to show me around Otago Uni and the Unicol residential towers. Wow.

'Have a think,' said Tony, 'and get back to us.'

Steve Hansen must have heard a rumour that I was in danger of changing my mind about coming to Lincoln, and next minute I had him on the phone. At least there was a slight variation in the question: 'What the hell are you staying down there for?'

I'd heard that Canterbury and Otago had an informal pact not to poach each other's players, but I'd also heard a whisper that Otago had lured the New Zealand Schools No. 7, Sam Harding, down from Christ's College with blandishments of fees and accommodation. So perhaps Canterbury were trying to get their own back by coming after me. Sam 'The Dominator' was a bloody good player, had basically beaten me for every team we'd been up for, so that was playing in the back of my mind too — Otago had preferred Sam; I was a bit of an afterthought.

Still, I had a girlfriend I was keen on in Dunedin.

I left it and left it and didn't know what to do. I felt a bit overwhelmed with all the attention. It got to Christmas and I still hadn't made a decision. After Christmas, I got a call from Steve Tew. I had no idea who he was until he identified himself as CEO of the Crusaders, who had won the 1998 Super title.

'I'm just ringing to see if there are any problems or if you're still coming up?'

I still didn't know what to do, but I felt I couldn't justify changing my original decision.

'Oh,' I said, 'I think, um, yeah, I'm still coming.'

And that was it. Later I heard that Steve Hansen put him up to it.

It might have taken me a while to make, but it was the right decision. I'm sure I wouldn't have made the All Blacks as quickly with Otago. If it had been the other way round, and Sam and I had both stayed where we were, Sam might have made the All Blacks before me because of the superior way Canterbury was organised.

An example of that was the Rugby Academy, the first in the country I think, run by Steve Hansen, with a trainer to help him. They really kept tabs on you.

In my second week of uni, I played in a final trial for the Under 19s, and was selected for the team — the first time I'd beaten Sam Harding for any team! All of a sudden, it seemed, I was on a plane for Wales — my first real trip overseas, apart from Australia — to play in a world tournament, New Zealand's first at Under 19 level.

Two weeks in Newport may not seem like everyone's idea of a great trip away, but for me it was magic. We stayed in a hotel, not a billet, which I thought was extremely cool, and played four games, beating Ireland in the semi and Wales in the final. Graham Henry was coaching Wales and at that stage was going pretty well, being the Great Redeemer and all that, so it was a great place to play with the silver fern on your chest. Many of those players kicked on — Clarke Dermody, Campbell Johnstone, Brad Mika, Steven Bates, Jerry Collins, Aaron Mauger, Mils Muliaina and Tony Woodcock all went on to play for the All Blacks.

When I got back to start the academic year at Lincoln, Steve Tew rang me up again and said, 'We're paying Aaron $5000 on an academy contract, so we'll give you that as well.'

Wow. First year at uni, and I'm getting my fees paid and $5k on top of that, for playing rugby, effectively.

That might have been the first inkling I had that there might be more to playing rugby than sheer pleasure.

Being part of the Academy introduced me to the facilities at Rugby Park in St Albans.

In those days, there was just a weights room in the bowels of the grandstand, where the trainer ran sessions and taught us how to train with weights. There'd be Mehrts and Blackadder and the like floating around. I never had the front to talk to them, but I thought it was pretty cool just being that close.

We were given guidance on nutrition, and encouraged to share any problems we had at uni. I was set a programme to follow, which was a hell of a lot more sophisticated than flogging myself up and down the road, though I still did that as well. We did Mondays and Wednesdays with the Academy, on top of club practice on Tuesdays and Thursdays, and every so often we'd be taken away for camps.

In hindsight, it was all valuable preparation for becoming a professional, and it was reinforced by sometimes seeing the Crusaders and NPC stars at close quarters.

I made the Canterbury Under 19s that year, as scheduled by Uncle Bigsy, and we had a similar playing schedule to the Canterbury As. So when they were playing in town, we were also playing in town. That had its advantages: there were always big line-ups at the entrance to the pub, and whenever we tried to bluff our way in, we'd stuff up and get told to bugger off for being under age, but we discovered that if we turned up in our suits, they thought we were part of the NPC team and we were in, no questions asked. Sweet.

Of course, being in the Academy also meant they could keep an eye on you, and you couldn't just bugger off, but I couldn't see a downside in any of that.

A couple of years later, Rugby Park at St Albans was developed into a state-of-the art facility, and over the years it's become a second home to me. What seemed so state-of-the-art back at the turn of the century now seems a bit rumpled and old-fashioned in comparison to the facilities of some of the other Super franchises I've seen, but there's comfort and security that comes from familiarity and past success all round me here, happy memories of people and events that have been a huge part of my adult life.

When I swipe my card at the door that leads straight into the weights room under the old wooden grandstand, I'm hit by that welcome home aroma of sweat and liniment. The room is just a big old torture chamber with steel racks and frames and a big single-hand clock on the front wall to measure the minutes of your pain. Not my favourite place, and I tried to avoid it as much as I could and go running, but back in about 2003 I could feel the guys I was tackling and wrestling with at the breakdown getting stronger and stronger and knew that I had to get stuck in, right here in this room. There's no escaping it.

It had another benefit too. I had a chronic back problem and was told that if I strengthened my core, it'd help my back. I didn't really believe it, but it worked. Even now, if I forget to do the core stuff, my back starts reminding me.

The trainer's room is at the far end, and leads through to a couple of prefabs, a team room where we order in lunch a couple of times a week and eat as a team, and beyond that the physio room.

Turn back to the old grandstand and stairs lead you up to a series of rooms built into the roof, which look out over the field. There's management and administration offices, then the Canterbury NPC coaches' office, then the Crusaders coaches' office, with video rooms behind.

Down in the depths of the grandstand, our changing room, plunge pool and showers are at the end closest to the field, with pretty ordinary unpainted chipboard 'cubicles', just shallow recesses with a seat and shelves and hangers. Mine is #17 down the end closest to the players' tunnel.

Back through a short corridor is a big room with no windows, the strategy room. This is the hub of Crusaders rugby; for me, it's the heart of the beast.

The floor is taped out as an accurate-to-scale rugby field, with little plastic cones in various colours that can be manoeuvred around, and pins with numbers on, which can, say, indicate spaces we want to kick to or attack. Up front there are whiteboards and a big roll-down screen for video projection, but what always strikes me when I walk through the door is the façade of what looks like a Greek temple or one of those grand old limestone buildings in Oamaru, which fills the far wall.

It looks like grey granite but it's polystyrene — foundation stones across the bottom, Corinthian columns soaring up to plinths and gables, topped off by the Crusaders shield, with the arm wielding a sword. Underneath that, *Our House* is across the top of the gable. Beneath that, across the central plinth, is *Excellence*, then the six Corinthian columns are headed *Nutrition*, *Physical*, *Technical*, *Practical*, *Teamness* and *Mental*, with the body of each column full of pinned-on typewritten aphorisms about each of those aspects of the game. The content of the columns changes from season to season, from week to week, but the truth of some of the sayings never changes — *Failing to prepare is preparing to fail. Go hard or go home. Excellence is a habit, not a skill.*

The foundation stones at the bottom hold up the whole structure — *Loyalty*, *Enjoyment* and *Integrity* supported by *Respect*, *Team-First* (the centre-stone) and *Work Ethic*.

Coaches announced: the result is the perfect quinella for me and, it seems, for Ted and Robbie.

It's funny how often, if the team's not going well, you look at those foundation stones and find the reason in there somewhere.

Once I'm back here, and past Robbie's interrogation of my reasons for wanting to be captain again, I find, like the other returning All Blacks, that I desperately want to get back to playing rugby, to get stuck in for the Crusaders, move on from Cardiff, leave all the political fallout behind . . .

But that's not so easy with all the publicity around what's happening at NZRU HQ in Wellington.

On 6 December, Robbie's shown leaving with a big smile on his face after his interview. There's a photo of Ted too, looking, well, just like Ted.

There's speculation that the Board's deliberations could drag on until Christmas, but, as it turns out, the decision comes quickly.

On 7 December, the NZRU confirms Graham Henry's reappointment as coach of the All Blacks for the next two years, with assistants Steve Hansen and Wayne Smith. Not everyone is pleased.

'The spirit of New Zealand rugby died yesterday,' writes Tony Smith in Saturday's *Press*. 'We are witnessing a once-proud sport in the delirium tremens of denial as it bounces around its padded cell.'

Chris Rattue, as usual, is equally moderate and considered in the *New Zealand Herald*. Under the headline 'Ship of fools welcomes the skipper back', he writes 'What a black moment for rugby union in this land, and a mighty victory for dunderhead thinking.'

Things get rapidly worse for the Robbie Deans Fourth Estate Fan Club. Within the week, Robbie is confirmed as the new coach of the Wallabies. Australian Greg Growden tries not to crow: 'Those in the know in the Shaky Isles are deeply concerned by the Deans appointment. They realise the All Blacks head into 2008 with the wrong coach and their best export will now be conspiring against them.'

Ten minutes before John O'Neill makes the Deans announcement in Sydney, Robbie gathers the Crusaders around him on the field at St Albans. We stand in a circle with our arms linked over shoulders and prepare ourselves for the worst. Robbie tells us that, yes, he's accepted the position as coach of the Wallabies, and, yes, he'll be seeing out the 2008 Super 14 season as coach of the Crusaders.

For dunderheads like me who aren't in the know and are suffering from the delirium tremens of denial, the result is the perfect quinella: there's coaching continuity for both the All Blacks and the Crusaders.

We're so relieved that there's laughter, and we give Robbie a cheer and try to prepare him for the future with the green and gold chant — 'Aussie Aussie Aussie, Oi Oi Oi!'

It's sorted, finally. Time to move on. We've got other challenges ahead of us. Last year's Super 14 was an unsatisfying mess, spoilt by players being rested and an inevitable focus on the RWC. I want to put that right before even thinking about the larger challenge of the All Blacks.

Survival of the fittest

The 2008 Crusaders have some of the usual challenges in front of them, but also some that are unique.

Changes in personnel happen every season, but this year we've lost four of our best: Chris Jack and Aaron Mauger have gone to club rugby in England, and Rico Gear and Kevin Senio have gone too. Countering those losses, we've got some promising youngsters who seem ready to step up — the likes of Tim Bateman, Kahn Fotuali'i, Sean Maitland and Kade Poki.

We've also gained some grunt in the pack. Ali Williams has come down from the Blues, and on the strength of his showing at Cardiff has to be rated one of the best locks in the world. He's staying with me in the townhouse, so at the very least I'm in for an interesting and entertaining year off the paddock.

Ali's an interesting case, a hard case, one out of the box, as they say. He has all the attributes of a top international lock: genuine size at two metres tall and 115 kilograms, allied to real athleticism and power and great ball skills. In 2005 against the Lions, he was up there with Victor Matfield as one of the best couple of locks in the world, and he was probably our best player at Cardiff. But Ali's personality, most charitably described as mercurial and irrepressibly irreverent, is different from your average Kiwi rugby player's, and he can rub some people up the wrong way.

Some of those people happen to be coaches.

Most recently, during the 2007 Super 14, he's had a very public falling out with Auckland Blues coach David Nucifora. I've only heard Ali's side of the story, true, but one test for these things is whether the disciplinary response causes more negative repercussions than the original offence. In this case, it seems to me that Nucifora overreacted to Ali's birthday celebration drink by banishing him from the team. To my way of thinking, Nucifora compounded that decision by hiding behind the senior Blues players, telling the media that it was them, not him, who sent Ali home from the Blues Super 14 campaign in South Africa.

Justin Marshall takes exception to Ali's attempt to rearrange the part in my hair, 2005.

For me, that took the concept of the leadership group to a new high, or low.

Whatever the details, the upshot was that Ali didn't want another year with Nucifora and is coming to the Crusaders for the 2008 Super 14. The Blues' loss is the Crusaders' gain, and Robbie Deans, who coached Ali at All Black level as John Mitchell's assistant, has no doubts about Ali's value to the Crusaders.

Neither have I, though I've had my own issues with Ali in the past.

In a Blues/Crusaders Super 14 game in 2005, he and another couple of Blues players got stuck into me on the ground with their boots. I was pissed off at the time because it felt like they were attacking my head, and Ali and the other two players copped suspensions. But it's hard to stay mad at Ali for long, and I've accepted his explanation that while he wanted to give me a bit of a rark-up with his sprigs in the old-fashioned (and outlawed) tradition, he wasn't going for my head. I just put it down to Ali's boots being a lot further from his brain than most people's and that much harder to control.

Graham Henry may also have had his problems with Ali, but the difference between Ted and the likes of Nucifora is that Ted has never wavered in his belief that Ali, if handled correctly, would be a committed and endearingly positive bugger to have around in the team environment. As a result of Ted's faith, Ali has almost always delivered for the All Blacks and Robbie shares that faith in terms of what Ali can bring to the Crusaders.

The other recruit in the locking department is more of an unknown quantity.

Brad Thorn is back, after turning down the All Blacks in 2001 and going back to league with the Broncos in 2005. When he first came to the Crusaders, he was tried as blindside flanker and No. 8, but found the calls and the different lines too complicated to master after a lifetime in league, and reverted to the second row.

This time, he's back to bolster our locking stocks, though my understanding is that he's with us on a temporary basis, helping us out and getting in a bit of rugby before taking up a contract in Europe later in the year. I think Robbie had to convince the rugby union to contract him — he'd been thinking about going to Dunedin, but he really wanted to come to the Crusaders and Robbie made it happen.

I reckon it's great he's back, and he proves his value at the first scrummaging practice. Ali is a bloody good tighthead lock, but when the two big boys get down to the serious pushing, Big Bad Brad simply can't be beat. As one of the tighthead props says: 'It's like having a V8 up your arse.'

Brad pushes so hard in the scrums that even *his* strainer posts turn to jelly and he sees stars. He likes that, revels in it. He's immensely strong, trains like a Trojan, and has developed a very simple approach on his return to rugby: shift bodies in rucks, push like a bloody bulldozer in the scrums and catch the ball at the front of the lineout. If he gets the ball in hand, he's going to take a very direct route forward, and if he sees anyone in front of him with the ball in hand, he's going to snot him. He's absolutely single-minded in pursuit of those goals, so much so that he's sometimes a difficult guy to talk to on the field. His mind is on his core jobs, what he's got to do next — he never misses a lineout call, for instance — and he's not that interested in the finer points of team strategy.

The finer points of team strategy have been getting more than passing attention this year, because the ELVs are coming, whether we're ready or not.

The stated aim of the Experimental Law Variations to be trialled during the Super 14 is to keep the ball in play longer, promote fewer stoppages, more running rugby and a more free-flowing and exciting style of play.

To that end, the IRB has ruled that there'll be free kicks for most infringements other than offside and foul play, each backline has to stay five metres behind the hindmost foot in the scrum, and you can't kick it out on the full if you take it back inside your own 22.

All of that suits the Crusaders' cause, and, even if it doesn't, that's what Robbie tells us. We're going to embrace this new style of rugby and make it our own. That's the right message.

The new laws were trialled in the provincial second division in 2007, and reports from those involved confirm that there's a hell of a lot more running and therefore a requirement for a higher degree of aerobic fitness.

All of that looks like it might suit me.

My biggest attribute is fitness. I've always worked bloody hard at it. If you're fast and strong but you can't get there, then your speed and strength are no use to anyone. And oxygen debt doesn't help your decision making.

Some guys don't like running and they go to the gym, but if I had the choice, I'd always pick going for a run. At the end of the '99 season I broke my wrist and had quite a long time in plaster after an operation. All I could do was run, so that's what I did. That base, with what I did when I was younger, really helps, particularly when I've been sidelined with injury. I can be out for six weeks or longer, like when I was concussed, but I can get back into it quickly and not be too far off.

I've always had the goal that I want to be among the top one or two forwards in the country fitness-wise. In the All Blacks I always make sure I'm at the top.

Having said that, weight training plays a huge part, too. When I first played for the All Blacks in 2001, I was under 100 kg, and I thought that bigger would be better. When I got home that summer, I was 21 and my body was mature enough to handle it, so I did really specific weight training for the first time, focused on gaining weight, and came out the other end at 107 kg. That was too big and I lost some edge, so I trimmed back to 105.

That's turned out to be about the right playing weight for me: it made me a little bigger than most out-and-out fetchers, which was an advantage, but also gave me more strings to my bow when I had to adapt my game. I wasn't a natural ball carrier, for instance, but I put a lot of work into that, and the extra weight helped.

I got a heap of turnovers in the first couple of years. When I was playing for Canterbury, that's what we were scoring all our tries off. I'd get two or three turnovers a game and sometimes that would be two tries. The more I got, the more I wanted, so I was in there every time. Then people started to work me out as I went up the levels, from NPC to Super to tests. I began to get very frustrated, because the turnovers were harder to get. Finally, Robbie took me aside and told me I didn't need to be a hero every time. 'Just do your job. If you do your job, good things will happen.'

I took Robbie's advice on board, and instead of counting the turnovers, began breaking my game down into four key roles: tackling, clearing rucks, flogging the opposition ball or pressuring it, and carrying the ball. I found that if I went out there and made sure I did those four things as well as I possibly could, the opportunity for a big play would come along, whereas if I went searching for it, I'd end up being inaccurate. Some days there were no big plays, nothing spectacular, but I found that was okay if I could come off the field knowing that I did those four things well.

I've developed that further, and now measure my impact on influence, not numbers of turnovers. It's much more nebulous, but I know when I've had a decisive impact or influenced a key moment in the game. Increasingly, my own assessment of a game is about what I've done with the influence I have, not how much I've done.

I'm also used to adapting as I go along, because every year, it seems, someone else comes up with a bright idea to 'modify' or 'reinterpret' the much-maligned tackled ball rule.

Part of my role as a representative of the Rugby Players' Association — the players' union — is to give feedback on the rules of the game. I enjoy that — I've been on the Board since 2005 and we work closely with the NZRU on a wide range of issues that influence the playing environment here. We don't always agree, but we're lucky to have a good working relationship and most of the time we're able to get to the right place to ensure the game here thrives. A lot of that is down to Rob Nicol, Executive Director of the RPA, who's been outstanding in organising the players and making sure the right areas are addressed. But dealing with the IRB over rule changes and interpretations is something else. The RPA and the NZRU try to present a united front, but there's no guarantee that our advocacy will make much of a difference there and, as an active player, at a certain point, I've got to just accept whatever the IRB decides: you make 'em, I'll play 'em.

The ELVs are no exception. There's an offside line drawn as soon as the tackle occurs, we've got to enter the breakdown area through an imaginary gate behind the hindmost foot, and the halfback can't be touched unless he has his hands on the ball.

I make sure I know the new rules inside out, that I've got a full understanding of exactly what they are, not just because I'm captain and might need to make representations to the referee from time to time, but also for the requirements of my own position.

You have to accept too that the finer interpretations will change from week to week, from referee to referee. You're always asking yourself, 'What am I allowed to get away with?' That's not cheating; it's a legitimate question you have to ask if you want to do the job.

In 2007, it paid to be an assist tackler. I could ride the ball carrier to the ground, stay on my feet and stay right on the ball. I didn't have to back off or let the ball carrier go, so I got a lot of reward through being the assist tackler.

That looks like being the same this year, but I'll monitor it week by week. From week to week, I'm consciously thinking about ways to have an impact. I want to make it as difficult as I can for them, whether it's our ball or theirs. I either do that through how I tackle, if I can wrap the ball up, or where I end up, and a lot of that is mental, thinking through scenarios, visualising what might happen.

I often do this visualising kind of work on my own, going through the motions out on the training ground, repeating the exact moves I'll have to make. It must look weird to anyone watching, but it actually saves me from having to practise the moves quite so much in contact. I'm not sure where this comes from — maybe it springs from being on my own a lot as a kid and having to get things sorted without anyone to train with.

Most of the techniques don't change, so I practise the same things: how I enter the breakdown from different angles to make sure I look after our ball, how to get rid of someone, or, if someone's locked on to the ball, what I'm going to do.

If they've got possession, it's about how I tackle to slow the ball up rather than

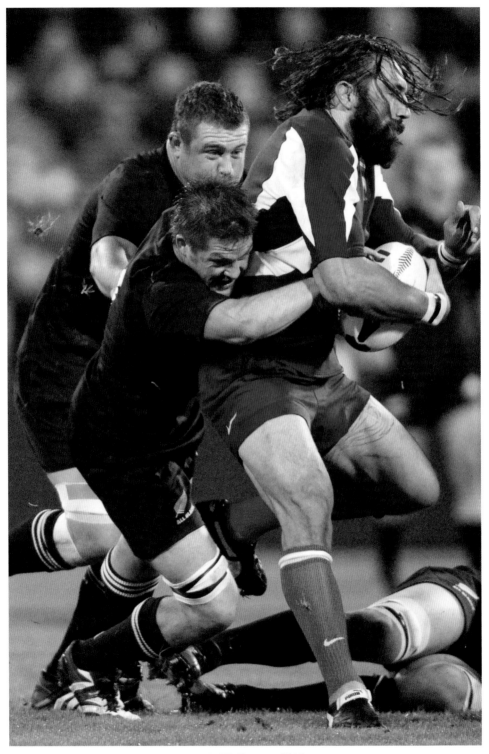

Caveman Chabal about to return to earth, Wellington, 2007.

actually trying to win it. How to get them in a bad position so that their ball is compromised. Or when I arrive, make sure that they have to clean me out to end up on top, so it slows their delivery. That's what I want. A full turnover is great, but if the ball's been compromised or they've at least hesitated, that's enough.

I'll go right back to walking it through, then work it up to full pace. That'll happen at least once a week, when I and the other loosies will get together at the end of training just to make sure we get that right.

When it comes to different rules, like the ELVs, you have to ask: How does this change what I do? Often, any change is quite subtle. So much is about feel and being able to sum up the situation.

To help me do that, I look at the video of breakdowns and ask really specific questions: about the decision to be at that breakdown; whether my technique and timing were right; whether my positioning was good.

The process of finding answers to those questions helps me make an impact next game. Maybe I have to pull back and pick my time better. If it's a technique problem, then I just try and work on it.

With the ELVs, the gate behind the breakdown isn't new, but the change of sanction to the short-arm penalty or free kick is going to be interesting.

That's putting the devil of temptation in front of loose forwards like me. Risk versus reward. There are people who will find this hard to believe, but I never actually deliberately infringe. However, I might be more prepared to risk a 50/50 to stop the opposition scoring if the penalty is a bent arm, because they don't get a kick at goal out of it. The refs can only award a straight-arm penalty if they believe the offence was deliberate. That puts a huge onus on the refs to make a decision about intent in the heat of the moment.

For my money, the best ELV in terms of attacking rugby is the five-metre gap behind the hindmost foot in the scrum. It's going to make it quite tough to defend, and I do a lot of work with Dan, trying to work out how best to manage it. I'm used to him being right beside me in defence, so we can cut the space down very quickly. But under the new ELV, if the opposing No. 8 takes it off the back of the scrum, for instance, and our halfback is on the other side, there's a lot more space to shut down.

When we loosies talk it through then walk it through, it becomes clear that it's going to be very difficult to defend off a good scrum. With Ali and V8 Brad, we know we're going to have a good scrum. Everyone's talking about tap-and-gos for the free kicks, and the demise of the scrum, but they're maybe forgetting that the captain has another option for the bent-arm penalty: the scrum.

I keep that in mind, and we prepare as best we can for the new scenarios created by the ELVs. We know the real test is going to be when the whistle blows for the first game, and who's blowing it.

We *think* we're ready, and as the 2008 Super season descends on us in what seems like high summer, another unintended consequence of the 2007 conditioning programme becomes clearer.

I'm used to Dan being right beside me . . .

To be fair, what I and the other All Blacks in the Crusaders are feeling as the season approaches, the lightness of tread, the gleam in the eye, is not just a consequence of Ted's conditioning group holiday, but it certainly helped.

In 2006, I'd played a total of 25 games (13 for the Crusaders and 12 tests for the All Blacks), whereas in 2007, I played only eight games of Super rugby, and, due to a shortened Tri Nations, started in only six tests before Cardiff. There was no end-of-year northern tour, so my load for 2007 was a total of 15 games. That's 40 per cent less, year on year: 10 games of high-pressure rugby my body didn't need to get through.

Given that, it's no surprise that come February 2008, I feel refreshed, rejuvenated and straining at the leash to get back into rugby.

The other All Blacks at the Crusaders are feeling much the same.

You could say that Ted's conditioning programme worked. The cruel irony is that it seems to have kicked in about three months too late for the RWC.

Whatever, that's gone. I'm determined to make it work now for the Crusaders' benefit.

Crusade

The English Premiership has been described as a marathon, compared with Super rugby's sprint. That might have been true of the Super 6 or even 12, but with 14 rounds, semis and finals, the Super 14 is more like a lung-busting middle-distance race, where you have to get out of the blocks quickly, sustain close to maximum pace through the middle stages, work to make sure you're in the right position at the top of the final straight, and try to finish over the top of them. Last year we got the staggers at the tape: in 2008 we think we're ready.

By the luck of the draw, we get an early opportunity to find out how ready. Rounds 2 and 3 are in South Africa.

A drought-breaking late summer deluge at Jade makes it difficult to judge the true effect of the ELVs in the first game played under the new laws. We beat the Brumbies comfortably enough, 34–3, and there are some promising signs in the way Leon MacDonald counter-attacks to set up the first try for Mose Tuiali'i. Mose runs powerfully for his second after halftime, then Brad and Dan score — right on fulltime — to get the bonus point.

However, the biggest thing we take out of that game is that our thoughts about the power of a dominant scrum prove well-founded. Our scrum is so dominant that I take that option every time we get a free kick, and it keeps the Brumbies under the hammer.

As we board the plane next day for the now familiar trek to Africa, we're aware that neither the Brumbies nor the weather conditions at Jade is much of an indication of what we're about to strike next. Last year's champions, the Bulls, are waiting for us at Loftus Versfeld, scene of our ignominious semi-final exit last year, and we have no idea how the Bulls will adapt to the new rules.

The answer becomes apparent quite early in the game. They haven't.

For the first half hour, they do much as they did the year before, take it forward with the panzer division, one pass off the ruck looking for the collision, two passes if they're really chancing their arm, then hoof it high. And for the first half hour it works — Derick Hougaard kicks four penalties. Bulls 12, Crusaders nil.

We're struggling to find our rhythm, and it's shaping up as a replay of last year, but the new rules — even if you don't embrace them — keep the ball in play longer and have a cumulative effect which the Bulls clearly haven't trained for. We're certainly feeling jaded, but as time goes on we can sense they're feeling it more than us. The pace quickens if anything, and there are suddenly a lot of wide open spaces on the high veldt to attack. The scoreline for the second half hour is Crusaders 35, Bulls nil.

At fulltime, it's Crusaders 54, Bulls 19.

Journalist Paul Lewis sums it up: 'New Age Crusaders, Stone Age Bulls'.

Okay, no Bryan Habana, no Matfield, no Bakkies Botha for the Bulls, but we're still able to take some big pointers from the game. Robbie's strategy to get us fit enough to take advantage of the space the ELVs create seems to work.

And we appear to have the personnel to execute that strategy. We have a powerful pack which is also very mobile. Mose is a so-far unsung hero — big ball carries and powerful defence. Ali is bringing aerial command and pace and power to the middle row, and Brad is a unique mix of power and mobility and stamina. Stephen Brett at second-five is loving the space Dan's giving him, and guys like little Kade Poki are really dangerous one on one, particularly with the direction they're getting from Leon at the back. Leon seems custom-made for the new rules.

South Africa is so vast, and the differences between Pretoria and Cape Town so pronounced, that it's entirely possible that the Stormers will have a very different approach to that of the Bulls. Richard Knowler of *The Press*, who's travelling with us, describes Pretoria as Margaret Thatcher, compared to Cape Town's Catherine Zeta-Jones. I'm glad *he* said that!

Certainly, Cape Town seems to have more than its fair share of beautiful women, and the hotel we stay in is an easy stroll from the waterfront bars and bistros and has a dramatic outlook to the Atlantic Ocean. The Crusaders seem to have a lot of local support in Cape Town and there are a lot of people floating around the hotel getting photos and autographs, but for all that, Newlands is a damn hard place to win at. It's too early in the season to have much intelligence about how the Stormers are playing, but there's no reason to suppose that they'll be as conservative and anachronistic as the Bulls, particularly with a new coach, Rassie Erasmus, in charge.

At Newlands on Saturday, Kade Poki pulls a hamstring in the warm-up, and Sean Maitland gets his first start. When Kade pulls up lame and Sean is promoted off the bench, it causes a bit of consternation up in the lounge. Hamish Gard has just knocked off his first beer when he's told to get down to the changing room and get his gear on, he's replacing Sean on the bench. I think that was the beginning of a new protocol — no beers until after the whistle for kick-off has sounded!

It's a game of two halves, as they say, but this time they're perfectly balanced: a try and a penalty in the first half for an 11-point lead, exactly replicated in the second half, when Sean gets the critical try.

The most pleasing thing about the 22–nil scoreline is the 'nil'. If defence is about

Man of the Match against the Stormers.

attitude, then keeping the Stormers scoreless — not even a penalty goal — for 80 minutes of rugby under the new rules says a lot about the determination and spirit of the 2008 Crusaders.

I'm happy with my form too. I get Man of the Match for both games in Africa, and as much as that's a bit of a pluck out of the hat, it's an indication that I'm back in the groove and putting last year behind me.

It's our first clean sweep of South Africa since 2002, and we fly out to Perth with a real sense of mission accomplished, leaving a lot of questions behind for the new world champions. Already Fourie du Preez and Bryan Habana, two players who might have profited most from the ELVs, have instead publicly lamented the damage the ELVs are doing to their structured game. Their protests don't bode well for the ELVs' review at the end of the competition.

That sense of mission accomplished almost turns out to be a banana skin in Perth. Part of the problem might be the time we have to kill — eight days. As beautiful as Perth is, and as much as we try to take advantage of the beaches and golf courses, hanging round for eight days waiting for the game is too long, particularly given it's our third week on the road. Robbie's right when he says that you tend to lose track of the days, from game day to game day, and the days of the week don't mean much.

Then, five hours after the end of the game, we have to get on the midnighter to Sydney. That means you pack up at the hotel and leave from the stadium directly after the game. There's always a risk that you've got one foot on the plane before the game starts.

None of this can be used as an excuse if we fall over, and we damn near do. Two years previously, we escaped with a draw in Perth when Marius Jonker ruled out what looked like a legit try, and it almost happens again.

The Force are 17–12 up at halftime and could have had another five points on us but for a forward pass by Cameron Shepherd. They quickly remedy that in the second half, going up 24–12. But we level up with tries from Ali and Andy Ellis, then when Matt Giteau misses touch, we counter-attack and Casey Laulala scores what proves to be the winner.

We've crabbed ahead 29–24 by the last quarter, but it's squeaky bum time — Nathan Sharpe throws a loose pass into touch with the line open. That would have tied it; a conversion would have won it for them. It's a warmish night and we're buggered by the time the ref blows the whistle for fulltime.

The Brumbies, Bulls and Stormers got one try against us. The Force score four and could have had, should have had, two more. You've got to hand it to coach John Mitchell. He got them to go wide against us and put runners into space: in other words, his approach to the new rules is the same as Robbie's, and it almost pays dividends.

Mitchell is a good coach, and his partnership with Robbie might have worked for the All Blacks if it had been the other way round — Robbie head coach and John Mitchell his assistant. That might have saved us all from some of his cryptic answers at the media conferences. I used to sit there thinking *'F'christsakes man, just bloody say how it is. Just answer the bloody question!'*

Back at Jade, we pull up our socks and hoe into the Cheetahs, to the tune of 55–7, despite benching Ali, Greg Somerville, Mose and Corey Flynn, and losing Stephen Brett to injury in the first half. This game shows the value — again — of trusting the whole squad.

At the following Thursday training, we have some interested spectators — Ted and Smithy and Kieran Crowley, who's just been appointed to coach Canada. They're going round the franchises, talking with the Super 14 coaches about what they're looking for in the All Blacks. Clearly, they're not going to do that with the new Wallaby coach, and they maintain a respectful distance. It's all a bit tense and difficult, but it's been like that between the Crusaders and the All Blacks for a few years, so nothing much has changed.

The atmosphere might still be a bit unsettling, though, because we're really off our game in the first half against the Waratahs, dropping passes, not looking after the ball at breakdowns, and find ourselves down 6–7 early in the second half. But, again, the fitness factor tells in the last quarter — we start hearing the sweet music of their forwards gasping for breath. We hold on to the ball and grind them down. It takes 17 phases to get Mose over the chalk, but that kills them off, and we get another two tries, the last one for a bonus point right on the hooter. The final score of

34–7 was never in prospect at halftime, but it shows again that the most critical change precipitated by the new rules is time: ball in play time.

It seems extraordinary to be six rounds down without having faced one New Zealand side. The Hurricanes in Wellington remedy that. As the Force under Mitchell proved, New Zealand coaches seem to have a more positive attitude towards the changes, and we know we can't count on the Canes running out of breath in the last quarter.

There's a bit on the line for this game, all sorts of individual match-ups for a start. Kieran Read, Mose and me up against Chris Masoe, Jerry Collins and Rodney So'oialo, Ali and Brad versus Craig Clarke and Jason Eaton, Corey Flynn versus Andrew Hore, Andy Ellis versus Piri Weepu, and Casey versus Conrad Smith. Some were left out of the All Blacks in '07, some were injured, and those that did play mostly didn't play well and are looking for redemption. It's a virtual All Black trial, mate against mate. That gives extra motivation and these derbies can often be pretty brutal and intense — you go hell for leather but within limits, and what happens on the field stays there.

Tough grind: Waratahs, 2008.

We're heading into the bye, so we know we can give it everything and we do, in front of 31,500 fans at Westpac Stadium. It's the toughest game of the season so far, and, sure enough, Jerry fells Kieran with a coat-hanger early in the second half. Six months after being brothers in arms at Cardiff, I'm in referee Steve Walsh's ear, trying to convince him that Jerry's a nasty recidivist who has to be sent off. Doesn't work. Instead, Walsh yellow cards Mose with 15 to go for tackled ball infringements. Horey scores a couple of minutes later and it's all on, with our defence getting us home 20–13.

The week off is timely: we're knackered, but satisfied — top of the table, stage one completed, time for reflection.

The ELVs have certainly made a difference, but the biggest difference is not really in the individual rule changes, but rather the cumulative effect they have in increasing the time the ball is in play. That's the critical factor and it comes back to fitness. Maybe that has had some effect on some of the big boys if they lack mobility, players like Jone Tawake and Sione Lauaki, maybe even our own Campbell Johnstone. But it's too early to be definitive about that.

Certainly, the five-metre scrum gap gives a dominant scrum a real advantage, both as an attacking weapon and a means to manipulate the defensive alignment, but other than that, there's not a hell of a lot of difference to the basic game, and I'm a bit bemused by the bleats of protest coming mainly from South African teams who are using the ELVs as an excuse for playing poorly. What we work on each week is what we've always worked on.

We come back from the bye and crush the Lions 31–6 at Jade.

All in all, I'm in a happy place, with the weekly routine of play, recover, recondition, prepare, play. The team is going well, and I'm back on top of my game to a degree I never quite managed in 2007.

Throwing myself into the Crusaders campaign has worked — with every week that passes, the pain of Cardiff recedes a little. I'm putting it behind me and feel that, finally, I'm able to move on . . .

A feeling that turns out to be more than slightly premature.

Back when the NZRU called for applications for the All Black coaching position, the Board had an opportunity to quiz the applicants and thoroughly canvass whatever opinions they needed from their stakeholders and the players — all of which I know they did — before making their choice. Surely that was the de facto review that mattered. We all know what happened. Done and dusted.

But no. I'd forgotten all about the other review, the official one, the one the NZRU instituted as a knee-jerk reaction in the immediate aftermath of Cardiff. Until I get a phone call from Steve Tew mid-April.

Steve tells me there's a bit of criticism of my captaincy in the official review. 'About what?'

'The drop-kick.'

Again? Jeez, I'd like to drop-kick that bloody drop-kick . . .

Steve Tew says the coaches were asked 'Did you send a message down?' and that they had to say, 'Yes, we did.' That it then looked like I just ignored the message.

Steve intimates to me that if I feel that is too tough, he'll try to get it cut from the public version of the report.

The easy option would be to ask Steve to cut it. Everyone in the loop already knows about it, so is it essential that the public know too?

I'm dreading the looming publicity, the public relitigation of the whole shemozzle that it's going to bring with it. A drop-kick was never in the play-book, we'd never used it in the past, we'd always got home in the last quarter by sticking to our guns, et cetera, et bloody cetera. But even given all that, and as much as I want to avoid being dragged into it, I can't bring myself to ask Steve to cut it.

Would people then have a right to ask: 'Why isn't the captain mentioned?' It would seem like a glaring omission. I *was* the captain. I was in charge, the buck stopped with me on the field.

And besides, there's a question of basic morality and propriety. If the NZRU thinks it should be cut, they should make that decision, not ask me to collude in it. If I'm the person in the gun, I shouldn't have the right to decide what does and

Ted tries to defend me at the 2007 RWC Campaign Review press conference.

doesn't go public. That just doesn't smell right, that's not how it should work.

So I duck my head and try to lose myself again in the Crusaders campaign as I wait for the media heat.

Sure enough within the week, the shit hits the media fan and away we go again.

The NZRU gets a lot of flak, not so much for the report's conclusions — Tony Smith writes in *The Press* that Blind Pew, an under sevens midget coach and the corner grocer could have reached the same conclusions — but for the timing and cost. It's seen as a waste of time and money, despite Mike Heron and Don Tricker's diligent approach to the job — 41 people or organisations were interviewed.

Of course, the element of the report that attracts most attention is the bloody drop-kick. 'In the dying minutes of that critical game, the leadership model failed to deliver what was its most important objective — decisions which give the best chance of winning the game . . .'

At the press conference to release the report on Thursday, 17 April, Ted mounts a passionate defence of my captaincy, which is much appreciated but kind of begs a question which seems not to have been asked by Messrs Heron and Tricker. Yes, the message was delivered, but was a drop-kick ever in the play-book? Was it ever practised?

If flying to the moon had been the right option, but we didn't have an astronaut and hadn't practised take-off, can you still call it a viable option?

Heron and Tricker seemed to assume that ordering it was enough, that it would just happen — and maybe if Dan or Nick or Aaron had been on the field it might have happened, without any intervention or direction from me. But they weren't there at the critical time, and I had to make a decision as to whether to call an option that we'd never practised as a unit. We'd never practised setting up the play, manoeuvring the scrum or ruck to protect the pocket, and putting a player in the pocket to execute that option.

That lack of preparation was a contributing factor to my not having the confidence to call that option out on the field in the heat of the moment, where one mistake would lose us the game. If I had been able to call a move that everyone understood and had practised, that would have made it a hell of a lot more attractive.

The bulk of the report is unstinting in its praise of the team's organisation:

'The overwhelming impression from our review of the documents, reports, our interviews and the 360-degree feedback is that the quality of the planning and preparation was of the highest calibre. It was universally described to us both at interview and in the documents as "meticulous", "excellent", "superb", and "incredibly efficient".' An adidas representative apparently described the All Blacks as the 'most professionally organised team I have ever seen'. And Ross Young, the general manager of Rugby World Cup Ltd, 'gave the impression that the All Blacks were the most demanding and exacting team in terms of their planning and attention to detail'.

All of which is great, but none of that helps me in the great drop-kick debate.

As much as I try desperately hard not to be affected by all this, and not let it show, I am affected. I can't speak for the other guys in the team, but I hope the other All Blacks aren't feeling the vibe. That big black cloud. Here we go again.

The night of Ted's impassioned defence of my captaincy, I play my worst game of the season so far and we're deservedly bludgeoned 5–18 by the Chiefs in front of a capacity crowd at Waikato Stadium. Our winning run is over.

Somewhere in the midst of all this, I'm summoned to Auckland for a seminar on leadership. It turns out to be quite positive, but in a way the organisers probably hadn't anticipated.

Ted, Shag and Smithy are there, along with Steve Tew, Jock Hobbs, Paul Quinn, Mike Eagle, Darren Shand, Gilbert Enoka, Mils, Dan and me. The day was organised by the NZRU and a number of speakers are lined up, who've all been briefed to give us their views on how they see team environments and how they get the leadership right and how they get the teams to be successful. We have Kerry Spackman, who wrote *The Winner's Bible*, we have former Aussie cricket coach John Buchanan, we have an academic, we have Mainfreight CEO Don Braid, and we have Pat Lam, who gives us a Polynesian perspective.

It's all terribly interesting, and we're sitting there thinking that this or that might be useful in the future, when Wayne Bennett, coach of the Broncos, walks on to the podium, looks straight at Ted, Shag and Smithy and says, 'I don't know why the fuck you're sitting there and still got your jobs.'

After Ted's impassioned defence, I play my worst game of the '08 season, against the Chiefs.

Whoa!

Then he looks at all of us and says, 'I wouldn't be giving any of you your fucken jobs back.'

It'd be fair to say that we're all sinking a bit lower in our seats as he turns his attention to Steve and Jock. 'But you bastards have got balls. At least you've fucken done something different.'

'Why were you playing guys out of position?' he asks the coaches.

While they're pondering that one, Bennett walks over to Mils, who's kind of scrunched down in his seat. 'Did you want to play 13?'

'Ah . . .'

'Where do you want to fucken play, son?'

'Ah, fullback,' says Mils, almost apologetically.

'Well, what the fuck were you doing playing centre?'

Mils understands that the question is rhetorical, or at least directed at Ted, not him, and says nothing.

I can't remember much else of what's said at that seminar, but some of Wayne Bennett's words stay with me when I get back to Christchurch.

'I tell my guys that if I stop chipping them, you better make a real quick decision,' said Bennett. 'You're either perfect or you're gone.'

That's a positive I can take out of the criticism of my captaincy at Cardiff: at least everyone's still interested!

I come away from all that determined to get my focus back. There're four rounds left to secure a home semi.

First up is the Blues, an emotional tester for Ali, who might feel he has a point to prove, not so much to his old mates from up north, but to David Nucifora, the coach who humiliated him by putting him on the plane back from Africa before the Blues' semi-final. That history hypes the media interest, and I can see that Ali's feeling the heat a bit. He jokes about making an appearance as Spiderman — he and Dan have got lots of party costumes, all the superheroes etc — and I think, *Yeah, good joke Ali*, and forget it, until bugger me he turns up to the interview wearing his Spiderman suit, and talks about himself in the third person!

The media don't seem to be terribly impressed, think he's taking the piss out of them, whereas it's just Ali's way of trying to take the heat out of the *situation* — his looming confrontation with his old mates in the Blues. It does actually defuse things.

Ali's spent a lot of his downtime back in Auckland, but he's been a great flatmate for me, even if he doesn't know how to cook toast. That's been okay, as I like to cook if I'm home — nothing cordon bleu, pretty much meat and three veges, maybe a stir-fry — and Ali does the dishes. That week, I can see that he's got a bit of an edge, and I remind him to just go out and play well and try not to get personal.

The usual Super Rugby attrition is making the playing XV a week-by-week exercise in manipulation of resources — we've not been able to field the same backline for consecutive rounds at any stage. This week Casey's out, not recovered from being KO'd by the Chiefs, Dan's ankle is still not right from a bad sprain, but Stephen Brett is back from a shoulder injury and Leon's back too.

Nucifora pulls a switch before the game, pushing Nick Evans to fullback and Isa Nacewa to first-five. The Blues scrum goes well and it's a tight game, but Spiderman rules the air with a commanding display in the lineouts, and in the end we get there 26–22 and secure a home semi. Corey Flynn scores two tries and gets Man of the Match, despite being sin-binned for a shoulder charge, but the award could easily have gone to Leon, who sets me up for a try. The loss more or less pushes the Blues out of contention, which might be some satisfaction for Ali, though I doubt it.

The Sharks are next up, contenders for a home semi position after an unbeaten home run, but now on the slide and desperate after being beaten by the Brumbies and the Waratahs in a five-game slog through Australasia. We get there 18–10,

Sure you've got the right person, ref? Off to the bin against the Sharks.

which sounds a hell of a lot more comfortable than it is. Their athletic No. 8, Ryan Kankowski, scores a great individual try, and the game's in the balance until five minutes to go, when we feed off a handling mistake and Wyatt Crockett scores. It's a reminder how physical the South Africans are — they steamroller us a couple of times with mauls and are fierce in the collisions. Our situation's not helped by the 10 minutes I spend in the sin-bin for a professional foul.

We go to Brisbane needing just one point to finish top of the table and get hosting rights for the play-offs. The Reds started the early rounds badly, but are playing good attacking rugby in the latter stages of the competition, and Suncorp is always a tough place to play. Robbie decides to rest Ali, Corey, Andy Ellis and others, but the biggest point of interest for us is Dan's presence on the bench, ready to get back into it after a long absence with that ankle sprain.

The danger is that we've already got our minds on the play-offs, and as much as we think we've factored that in, we're still sloppy on attack, lazy on defence and 21–8 down well into the second half. Pride is on the line, particularly after Quade Cooper dummies Leon and me to score.

Robbie has had enough after 55 minutes and gets Dan and Ali and Andy Ellis into the game. That improves things a little — we get to 15–21 with 13 minutes to go. We get a break — well-earned, we've got them on the ropes — when their

We play poorly against the Highlanders and get done. Johnny Leota drags Dan and me.

halfback Ben Lucas resorts to a professional foul and gets a yellow card. They've already got Digby Ioane in the bin for a spear tackle on Casey, so they're briefly down to 13 men. Ali scores, Dan converts, then scores in the corner, and we fly home and try to take some comfort from the last 20 minutes, when we woke up and pulled the game out of the fire.

The strain is definitely showing, and although we talk the talk before the last round against the Highlanders, say all the right words, we get done. There's no miracle finish this time. We play poorly and get dicked.

Afterwards, Robbie is pretty restrained in his comments to the media, dismissing what happened against the Highlanders as irrelevant, but he knows and we know that that's not true.

At practice it feels like we've come to a rocky patch. We've lost something and we're not even training well. Robbie doesn't flog us, just watches us for a couple of sessions, then reveals how much finishing with a title means to him.

He has a great knack of picking out the times where you expect him to get angry and doing something different, being reassuring, and then when things are ticking along nicely, bang, he'll give it to you between the eyes about staying on the job. He's always picked his moments really well, giving confidence that he — and we — have it sorted. He's usually really measured under pressure. That's bloody

Kieran Read scores against the Canes in our Super 14 semi-final. Reado's rise has been one of the features of the season.

important. Same with the captaincy — if you're shitting yourself, don't ever let that show because the team will pick up on it real quick.

This time, although we're going badly, there's no hiding from Robbie's wrath. He gets us on the line and really fires up. 'Are we going to come this far and let it slip? Like hell we are! Harden up!'

That one. Stay on the job.

We're up against the Canes in the first semi, while the Waratahs play the Sharks in Sydney.

During the build-up, it becomes apparent that they have a belief that we're there for the taking. The Canes' loose forward trio, Jerry and Rodney and Chris Masoe, have been labelled The Bouncers by their fans, and Kieran will certainly remember being bounced by a stiff-armer from Jerry in Round 7, but as it happens, Rodney is sidelined by a rib injury, and Kieran proves he's the coming man by outplaying Jerry in the van of a dominant pack.

The game illustrates the difference that attitude makes. We're on edge and bring that edge to the match-ups, dominating the breakdowns, making the advantage line with pick-and-gos, then taking the legs away from them by sweeping wide on attack. They're only five points down at the break, but in the second half they run out of juice. Conrad later admits that bringing the line forward on defence was difficult because he was so knackered.

We take the semi 33–22, with their score inflated a little by a Neemia Tialata try after the fulltime hooter.

I watch Jerry toe-kick the conversion and realise that the great warrior's All Black career is over.

So are Corey Flynn's immediate prospects — another broken arm, sidelining him for three months. He's been in top form, one of our best: sheer bad luck, not just for the final, but for his All Black aspirations.

Over in Sydney, the Waratahs roll the Sharks, so it's an Australasian final, a re-run of the 2005 final, which we won 35–25, only getting away in the last few minutes. The Tahs destroyed the Sharks' lineout, and with Dan Vickerman, Dean Mumm and Rocky Elsom as targets, they'll doubtless try to again.

Which makes it a huge game for Ti'i Paulo, starting in Corey's place. Robbie makes some changes to what has been the playing XV, though that's been in such a state of flux through injuries, it's been hard to say what the top XV is. Tim Bateman's preferred at second-five over Stephen Brett, who has struggled since his shoulder injury. And Kieran's retained his starting spot on the blindside, ahead of Reuben Thorne for what we know will be his last match for us, after having a hand in every title won by the Crusaders.

Kieran's rise has been one of the features of the season. He's a big man, quick, good with ball in hand and he works hard — you can rely on him to turn up where he needs to be. In that respect he's like Reuben, but a more explosive ball carrier and, if anything, even better than Reuben in the lineout. For a young guy, he's got a calmness about him and thinks well, to go with really good instincts around the game.

Reuben's the ultimate team man and has handled the demotion with good grace, giving Kieran a great deal of help. Caleb Ralph is also finishing. These two guys have been benchmark players and team men for the Crusaders team.

The strange twist is that it's also a farewell match for both coaches — Robbie's off on Monday to start coaching some of the players we're trying to bash on Saturday, and Ewen McKenzie was sacked by the Waratahs Board mid-season and has no job to go to. We don't want to give him a chance to shove it up the Tahs' Board by brandishing the trophy.

During the build-up, there's pressure on Robbie to vent a bit of emotion in public, but he's focused on the game and won't talk about what lies ahead after the weekend; if anything, he's more curt than usual.

The game, like Cardiff, could have turned on a sin-binning. Sixteen minutes into the second half, we think Wyatt's scored, only to find one of the touchies has his flag up 60 metres back downfield. He reports that Brad's thrown a punch and the ref has no choice but to haul out the yellow card.

I'm surprised, because Brad just doesn't do that, but it's hard to miss or deny, when the replays show him chasing some Tah across the field and punching him,

Dan's dropped goal against the Waratahs in the final proves what a loss he was at Cardiff.

after being blindsided with a cheap shot. Brad sinks into the chair, holds his head in his hands, wondering what the hell he's done, as the bloody Tahs flanker Phil Waugh yells at him that he's just cost his team the Super title. Phil knows that Brad's desperate to win a Super title after two losing finals, yet he's blown it by succumbing to the red mist.

Almost. With Crocky's try, we could have been 19–12 up going into the last quarter, but instead we've only got a two-point lead and are one man down.

The character and defensive fortitude the guys show in the next 10 minutes wins us the game. Plus Dan's kicking. He emphasises what a loss he was in the last quarter at Cardiff by drop-kicking a goal to get us out to 17–12 and then kicks his fourth penalty, for a final score of 20–12.

Good, tough game, worthy of a Super final, and the perfect send-off for Robbie — his fifth title as head coach, plus two as manager.

The moment that matters. The 2008 Super 14 trophy.

We have a lunch together on Sunday, nursing our hangovers, but there are no memorable last moments between me and Robbie — apart from when we held up the trophy after the game, which, in the end, is the moment that matters.

The irony is that if you win the final, you don't get time to celebrate it properly. Robbie is due in Sydney on Monday to begin his duties as Wallaby coach, and I and the other All Blacks are due in camp to prepare for the Irish. The next time we see Robbie, he'll be in the green and gold coaches' box plotting our downfall.

That's all in the future. What matters right now is that we've won the Super 14.

It's not redemption for Cardiff, but it's a step towards it. The real thing can only happen in a black jersey.

Locked and loaded

Jerry Collins gets an early release from his NZRU contract and is gone, with some not very gracious words from Ted ringing in his ears — which doesn't help Ted's battle to win back the hearts and minds of Kiwi rugby fans. Jerry's only 27, same age as me, and what surprises me is the rapidity of his decline. One moment he's the warrior with an unquenchable thirst for battle, and the next he's had enough, all appetite gone. When the desire goes, the body and form aren't far behind.

I know that Cardiff eroded his spirit, but is Jerry's fall a marker for the toll taken by the modern professional game? If so, how many years can any of us count on? Deb Robinson, the All Black doctor, who's seen it all in terms of battered bodies and bones, is quoted as saying that without a significant change to the rugby calendar, there is a real chance that careers will get shorter. In the meantime, the game gets more physical every year.

It reinforces one of the little pre-game mantras I always write down in my Warwick 2B4: *Enjoy*. Enjoy today. A rugby career is as fragile as your knee joint.

Jerry isn't the only one going or gone. The traditional post RWC clean-out includes not just Jerry, Aaron Mauger, Anton Oliver, Chris Jack, Carl Hayman, Byron Kelleher, Reuben Thorne and Doug Howlett, but also Nick Evans and Chris Masoe, along with a whole swag of players who give the New Zealand game depth, like Jimmy Gopperth, Shannon Paku, Craig Newby, Troy Flavell, Hoani MacDonald and Tom Willis. Most of these were anticipated or expected.

The name that isn't expected and the one that has alarm bells ringing is Dan Carter. For months, during the Super 14, there's been speculation that Dan is going, and he's been linked with every club from Toulon to Timbuktu. This is a huge worry for me, because I know he's serious about leaving.

Dan takes a while to get to know, but he and I have a lot of things in common. Born and raised in tiny South Island rural settlements, pin-pricks on most maps, we shared that country-boy reserve and an almost instinctive understanding of each other, even though we're very different people and we don't live in each other's pockets. I know that Dan needs to get away from rugby more than I do, and at times I'm sure he gets annoyed at my being in his ear, but he's become bloody good at telling me what he thinks and we're quite tight. So when it becomes clear that he's seriously considering going overseas, it worries the hell out of me, because I know the All Blacks can't be the same team without him.

When he first came into the Canterbury NPC team in 2002, he was seen more as a second-five, and he was big enough and defensively secure enough to play well there and made the All Blacks in 2003. In 2004, he moved into first-five for the All Blacks and became the man in charge. In 2005 he played sublimely against the Lions and was acknowledged as not just the best first-five in world rugby, but arguably the best ever in that position.

And the pundits were right. The thing about Dan is that he can do everything and, like most great athletes, seems to have all the time in the world to do it. You get first-fives who can kick or run, but can't do both, or are great at directing the team around the field, but can't tackle to save themselves, can't defend their channel or cover defend. Dan's got real pace, accelerates from languid to full in a split second, uses his low centre of gravity to good effect with hip-bump, body swerve or step. His only weakness initially was a reluctance to call the shots, impose himself, direct the show, but he's grown into that.

Given that the captain and the play-maker have to be on the same page, having him on the field makes it so much easier for me. Dan and I share a similar outlook on how to play the game and he and I have had some good debates with Ted.

It'd be fair to say that Dan and I are more conservative than Ted, who wants to push things more, play more expansively. That creative tension works, I think — most times we've managed to get the balance right.

The prospect of getting through the next four years to 2011 and winning the RWC without Dan is almost unimaginable. And yet I've got to be really careful because I know what he's going through. He's pretty much unflappable on the field, but the whole RWC experience really tested that. He played the quarter-final with a bad calf that, even before it forced him off, prevented him from playing at full capacity and showing his stuff on the biggest stage there is.

Then there's the public recognition factor.

The thing about fame is that you can't switch it off when you've had enough. I've seen Dan go from reserved country boy to a superstar in his underpants on billboards in what seems, in retrospect, the blink of an eye. I know there's a part of him that's had a gutsful, that wants at the very least a change of scenery, a change of lifestyle in a place where he'd be less recognisable, can go and have a beer with his mates, or sit at an outdoor table at a café with his girl without posing for photos and signing autographs. I know all this, and I know he's got a right to make his own decisions, but, back in April in the middle of the Super 14 campaign, I feel I have to at least let him know what I'm thinking.

I'm also aware that there's a core group of All Blacks we'll need in 2011 who

Me and Warren Alcock, of Essentially Group. He's been there for me since 2000.

haven't re-signed, and that if Dan goes, quite a few others might decide to go too. If I'm honest, it would knock me too, and make me think that maybe I should have a look at my options. In Cardiff I signed a contract for a further two years, and if Dan and other key men go, I'd have to think again about extending, because his absence would make it so much tougher.

When I go round to see him at his place, I try to be careful, tell him that I understand it's his decision and his alone to make, and that I don't want to put any pressure on him, but, in the end, I get to it . . . 'I want you to know that I really want you here to help me. I need you.'

To my great relief, Dan tells me that he's looking at a sabbatical, and that he's sorting through the options, but he's still pretty keen to be around.

Dan staying is a huge fillip for me. Back in Cardiff, when I'd signed on for another two years, I'd wanted a longer term, but in the end we'd run out of negotiating time and I'd signed something I wasn't entirely happy with, so that I made the deadline for Super 14 eligibility.

But now, with Dan committing through to 2011, that's what I want to do too. Since Cardiff, it was always going to be about that next RWC here in New Zealand, so I go back to Warren Alcock, one of my agents at Essentially Group, and ask him to talk to the NZRU about having another look at my contract.

Warren's been there for me since about 2000, when I was given an academy contract with the NZRU, and I looked at it and thought, *What do I do with this!* This was early days on the professional rugby scene, and there weren't that many agents around. I waved the contract in front of the guy who looked after us at the Academy, the trainer, and asked him, 'Who do I see about this?' and he mentioned this solicitor in Dunedin. My parents were in Dunedin, so they went to see Warren. At that stage he was still working as a lawyer in partnership with Iain Gallaway, the esteemed cricket and rugby commentator, and he told Mum and Dad he'd be happy to look at the contract for me.

I liked Warren immediately. It helped that he was a real rugby fan, ex-coach of the Dunedin Club, loved New Zealand rugby — had an encyclopaedic knowledge of the game in fact. So while he's always absolutely in my corner, he's also aware of the big picture and is realistic.

Dan found his own way to Warren a few years later, and he now acts for both of us. I guess that helps when it comes to renegotiating my contract with the NZRU, because Warren knows exactly where Dan is at, and the upshot is that, sort of on Dan's coat-tails, I re-sign with the NZRU through to 2011.

Steve Tew later says that signing Dan and me is almost as significant as Jock Hobbs securing the signatures of Josh Kronfeld and Jeff Wilson back in 1995. Jock's actions saved All Black rugby, so I wouldn't put our signings up there with that, but it did mean that the core group of players we think we'll need for 2011 start getting aboard for the trip: Ali Williams, Andrew Hore, Rodney So'oialo, Tony Woodcock, Sitiveni Sivivatu and Keven Mealamu all sign shortly after, followed by younger guys like Ma'a Nonu, Liam Messam and Richard Kahui. Once Mils Muliaina is finally signed, I know we're locked and loaded for 2011.

When the All Black team goes into camp for the 2008 June tests, a one-off against Ireland and two against England, there's a different feeling as we go about putting the nuts and bolts of team protocols together. Part of it is all the new faces. There seem to be a lot more than usual.

There's also been a change of approach. 'Because of time,' Darren Shand tells the media, 'we have had to be quite dictatorial . . . Say this is what we are going to do and just get on with it.'

It isn't quite as dictatorial as it seems. We've already made some critical decisions before we go into camp. That the leadership group, for instance, formerly 10 of us, is going to be downsized and split into two — an on-field group of me, Rodney, Dan, Horey and Mils, and an off-field group of Greg Somerville, Kevvy Mealamu and Conrad Smith.

But the biggest change is going to be in how we approach the challenge set out by the NZRU review: making the right decisions under pressure. We'd believed that if we gave players more responsibility peripherally, that would translate to them being able to take more responsibility on the field. Cardiff indicated that something was being lost in the jump from off-field theory to on-field execution, so we've decided to go back to our core task. Performing on the field, winning games, is what the All Blacks are about. We'll start from there. To that end, we'll try to re-create game pressure in training.

Early in the week, you're going over calls and moves repetitively, but as we get closer to the game, it changes to bang — you need to get this right now, what are you going to do? You need to win the ball at this lineout and you haven't been — what are you going to do? Decide right now. You get one crack at it.

There's also a feeling that we're on probation. In one sense that's just the norm: All Black coaches and players will always be under the most intense scrutiny, that's just the way it is. You've got to regard that attention as a privilege, earned by the guys who wore the jersey before you. But there's also Cardiff. During the Super 14, there was some respite from it, but now that we're All Blacks again, it hangs over everything still, even for the new guys who weren't there, like Brad and Ma'a Nonu and Jerome Kaino.

'When the All Blacks turn out tomorrow against Ireland,' Wynne Gray writes in the *New Zealand Herald*, 'it will snap a 245-day hiatus in which controversy and uncertainty have cloaked the national sport. Financial pressures, player exits, faltering competition structures, erratic crowd and television viewer-ships, a sceptical fourth estate, coaches and administrative blotches, new playing laws — there's not been a dull moment since the All Blacks went belly up in Cardiff . . . Victory will not be balm for all the discontent . . . it will not reduce the forgiveness levels by much but it should create some diversion from the rancour and ill-feeling.'

Bugger that — I'm not buying into any of it. We have five days before our first test against Ireland and all of a sudden I feel different. Rather than please everyone, fuck it, *I'm* going to do it, I'm going to make sure I get others to help, sure, but I want to set things down my way and not tiptoe around and make sure everyone's happy.

So, if you're a reserve and you're a bit disappointed that you're not playing, well tough. You're in the All Blacks and someone has to do that job and it's you, and you better do it bloody well.

That certainty around what I want to do comes from a feeling that this is my team in a way that previous teams weren't.

When I was appointed captain in 2006, I was very aware that there were guys in the team with a lot more experience than me, guys who had even captained the All Blacks before, like Reuben and Anton. They were always supportive, but the thought would sometimes come to me when I was fronting the team: *What are they really thinking? Do they really think I'm doing a good job?* This time, when we get together, there are no longer any whispers of doubt in my mind. I'm the captain, and they're my team.

That extra security means I'm happy to ask the senior guys, what do you reckon? Tell them I'm not sure and then be happy to go with what they think. I don't feel any more that because I'm the captain I need to know everything. When you're not comfortable in the role, you don't want to show any weakness.

Whatever happens, I'm in charge, and I'll accept everything that flows from that.

The Irish have been responsible for a couple of highs and lows in my career.

In 2001 I played my first test against Ireland as a 20 year old at Lansdowne Road, and won Man of the Match. It was a terrible game, and the Irish had the winning of it early in the second half when they were 24–12 up. We managed to let Jonah loose on the left and eventually got home 40–29. David Humphreys, who was the Irish No. 10 that day, said that game is his biggest regret, that they finally had us there for the taking after never having beaten us, and they blew it.

In retrospect, I think they had too much time left in the game to think about it. It felt similar to my first game as captain against Wales in 2004. With 10 to go Wales had got to within four points and had us pinned on our line. We were just holding on and the winning try seemed inevitable. But when they were awarded a penalty, they took the shot, even though three points wouldn't win it for them. All it did was let us off the hook. What a relief — that might have been the only way we were going to get back to halfway! We held on and won by that point.

The Man of the Match award in Dublin in 2001 was the best riposte to Josh Kronfeld, who'd cast doubt on the wisdom of picking me after just 17 first-class games. 'You might as well just give All Black jerseys to everybody,' said Josh. 'The fact they picked guys off one NPC season is bloody incredible.'

Maybe that was why John Mitchell took me aside in the build-up to the game and reassured me that I was the best in the country, that was why I'd been chosen, and to just go out there and play.

After the game, at a formal dinner attended by both teams and several hundred UK rugby luminaries, I was awarded my first test cap, along with Aaron Mauger and Dave Hewett. When my name was called to come forward, former Lion great Syd Millar, later Chairman of the IRB, rose to his feet and began clapping. Keith Wood, the Irish captain of the day, followed Syd to his feet, then the whole room rose in acknowledgement. That was an amazing introduction to test rugby.

Not so amazing was the next time we played them, at Carisbrook the following year. We won 15–6 but got booed off the field by our own crowd.

I was bewildered, didn't know how to handle it. It was a shit game in cold, wet conditions and we hadn't scored a try, and it was probably boring for the spectators, but even so . . . We sat there in the changing room afterwards thinking, *Man, we just won a test match. Do they know how tough that is?*

There was also the incident where Irish and Lions captain Brian O'Driscoll was injured and invalided out of the Lions tour in 2005. I thought Woodward and his PR man got that terribly wrong, and I was disappointed that O'Driscoll went along with it. I can understand his anguish at being knocked out of the tour a few minutes into the first test, but there was no way it was intentional. He got caught

Ireland, 2001, an amazing introduction to test rugby. Top: me, Aaron Mauger and Dave Hewett with our first test caps and, below, taking on the Irish defence.

Lote Tuqiri's spear tackle on me . . . 'Honestly, mate, there was no malice intended.'

in a clean-out where in the spur of the moment neither of the two cleaners, Tana and Kevvy, knew exactly what the other one was doing. It was because of that lack of coordination that Brian got flipped, and landed awkwardly.

I know from experience how unsettling it is if you think that the opposition is targeting you outside the law. The collisions within the laws are bad enough, but if you become aware during a game that someone has been told, or has decided, to take you out, then that's bloody unnerving, because if you're playing the game and doing your job, there's going to be any number of opportunities for someone with intent to seriously hurt you.

I got that feeling at Eden Park in 2006 against Australia. Lote Tuqiri spear-tackled me, then I got stiff-armed by Phil Waugh shortly after, which broke my nose. There are high tackles and high tackles. A reflexive high tackle from a defender who's been caught off balance is one thing. Coming in from the blindside and attacking a static guy's head with your arm is quite another.

Next day, I got a hand-written note.

To Richie. Hey mate, I walked past you last night in between our press conferences, instructed not to say anything until we knew what was going on with myself being charged or not regarding that tackle . . . I was going to call you this morning to see how you were, but you're not in town, so I'm writing this letter instead. Honestly mate, there was no malice intended, and I hope you're not feeling too bad today . . . Hope to catch up sometime soon. Cheers mate. Lote Tuqiri.

That's class, and made me feel far better disposed towards Lote afterwards than to Phil Waugh.

Something along the lines of Lote's note might have happened with Brian O'Driscoll if Woodward and Campbell hadn't decided to blow it up. Their reaction made any conciliatory gesture impossible — and really fired us up. When Tana made a statement to the media, the whole team lined up behind him. Before we ran out for the captain's run on the Friday, we haka'd Tana in the changing room. What followed was one of our best-ever performances.

In my hotel room before the test against Ireland, in that quiet time after game day lunch, I take out my Warwick 2B4 and start writing, same as I always do before a test, trying to reduce my role to some simple maxims that I can keep coming back to during the game. I find that writing them down embeds them in my psyche better:

Start again
Get involved early
DMJ — Do My Job —
    tackle, go thru, clean, low to high, past ball, aggressive, shoulders on
    steal — pick my time
    link — run hard
Work rate — just keep getting up
Clarity to boys
Trust me, back my instincts
Just play
Enjoy
G.A.B.

The list doesn't vary much game on game, or even year on year. Sometimes I'll refer to something more specific, like my right shoulder in tackles, because it's more natural to hit with my left and I have to consciously practise getting my feet and body in the correct position to hit with my right.

I feel good to go.

I reckon I played right up to my best in the 2008 Super 14 semi and final. A possible complication is that we're back to playing the old rules. The ELVs aren't being used because the Irish haven't played those rules. It seems a retrograde step, but we know that whatever happens at IRB level, the northern hemisphere teams cannot, must not, be disadvantaged, so it's out with the new and in with the old.

Ted's picked a team with one new cap, right wing Anthony Tuitavake and three others on the bench. But perhaps the most interesting experiment is swapping Rodney to No. 6 and putting Jerome in at No. 8. That reflects the need to find the right replacement for Jerry — Adam Thomson is lurking on the bench.

Irish loose forward Alan Quinlan makes all the right noises about the new-look team before the match, and says that while a few years ago, Ireland didn't believe it could win, now there's a confidence that 'if we play to our potential we certainly have a good chance'.

There's the difference between Ireland and New Zealand right there; if I said before a game that we had a good chance of winning, it would be regarded as defeatist.

All the heat is in the pre-game — the match itself is played in as cold conditions as I've ever struck. We're locked together at 11 all in the Westpac fridge before we lift the tempo in the final quarter, if only to avoid hypothermia. Dan isn't having a great game — he's had a kick charged and misdirected other kicks, one of which nearly gives them a try — but in the sixty-second minute he breaks on the outside of O'Gara, and puts Ma'a over the line. That's the game. 'It took one moment of genius to create the difference,' laments the Irish coach.

I'm stoked with the way the new-look pack finishes over the top of them and pretty happy with my own game in the dreadful conditions.

We all head to Auckland feeling that England will be a tougher test, particularly since this time they haven't sent their traditional D for Down Under team.

A novel element is the inclusion of Tom Palmer, who played with me in the Otago Boys' First XV in 1997 and went on to make that year's New Zealand Schools side. Interesting guy, Tom, brought up in Kenya and then Edinburgh, then came to Dunedin to further his rugby education. I brought him back to the farm with me one weekend and we did the Haka thing, motorbikes round the ploughed paddock, night-shoots and Dad took us for a ride in the plane.

Tom's part of your typical English pack — full of behemoths like Andrew Sheridan whose declared intention is to 'outmuscle' us. And, bugger me, the way they start almost blows us away. The first five or 10 minutes they throw big numbers into all the breakdowns and, after the Super 14 where there's seldom more than a couple of guys to clean out, we're shocked out of our stride. They knock us off our own ball a couple of times, and it's like, holy hell, back to test rugby!

But the longer the game goes on, the more we get our multi-phase rhythm going, and even without the ELVs, England can only compete fitfully with the pace of our game. We're soon beating them in the collisions and even in the scrums, and win 37–20. Dan is back in command, and one really great development is the combination outside him, between Ma'a and Conrad. Ma'a busts the line, then throws a sublime pass to put Mils over.

England get castigated in the New Zealand media — 'bulk and bluster', one scribe calls them, 'clueless and bumbling', says another — and far be it from me to

With Rodney So'oialo in the dressing room after the second test against England in 2008. Rodders had been one of our best for so many years, always combative, super-fit, tough.

describe UK rugby writer Stephen Jones as more rational, but at least he gives us some credit for 'pace, wit, efficiency and passion'.

Whatever, it's great to be back playing tests and winning. While I'm not sure we're playing like world beaters — particularly our lineout — I don't think Ireland and England are complete donkeys either, and I'm really happy with the way the 'new-look' team is coming together, on and off the field. I'm already looking forward to the much more torrid tests of the Tri Nations.

And I'm happy with my own form — I've been able to maintain a consistently high standard since the Super 14 semi, one of the benefits of having an injury-free run.

I should have known it couldn't last.

Twenty-eight minutes into the second test at Jade, I'm trying to support Ma'a and the guy who's tackling him cannons sideways into me, trapping my ankle underneath. I feel it go snap and I think I've broken my leg. When I try to get up — *Keep getting up* — I can't.

I sit on the sideline until halftime, then Steve Donald and Jimmy Cowan help me into the dressing shed. Ali's already there — his ankle's given way again — so after a shower, the two crocks sit there in comfort and watch England get torn to shreds, 44 to 12. Richard Kahui demonstrates that Conrad isn't the only option at centre. It looks to me like a much more complete All Black performance than last week, even though their loose forwards James Haskell and Tom Rees show real physicality at the breakdown, and some guts and desire.

But this week, as they head through to the departure gate, England have no friends, even among their own media.

I spend that night in hospital. When they put me under general to have a look, they warn me I might wake up with a bolt in there.

Perhaps it's an over-reaction to being crocked again just when I was feeling on top of everything, this sneaking suspicion that maybe the media assessment is pretty accurate and that beating these guys from the northern hemisphere is no indication of success in the Tri Nations, due to start without me in two weeks' time . . .

But even so, I have no idea that this fledgling team of mine will be thrown so immediately into crisis.

Numero uno

Six weeks later, just about the only thing that's gone well is rehab — no bolt, just a high ankle sprain — and I'm almost ready to play again. Almost is good enough. We're in the shit. If rugby is a religion in New Zealand, there's now a schism: Ted vs Robbie. There's a kind of madness out there. The taxi driver in from the airport tells me he's not supporting the All Blacks any more, he's supporting the Wallabies.

'Right. So you've always supported teams because of who the coach is?'

'No, no,' he says, 'but I'm pissed off with what's happened, so bugger you guys.'

He's not the only one pissed off. 'Mate,' I tell him, 'I don't want to talk about this.'

And we sit there in silence all the way into the Heritage, the beginning of a huge week. I'm fuming, thinking how much worse can it get? *An Auckland taxi driver supporting Robbie Deans! Clown.*

But he's not the only one who's pissed me off.

Last Saturday night I was in Sydney, watching the team get thumped in one of the worst performances I've seen from the All Blacks. We were really poor; we just got it all wrong. But what really pissed me off was the sight of their analyst and media guy in dinky-di green and gold uniforms dancing around on the sideline after the game like they'd just won Lotto. They were both Kiwis, ex Crusaders, Andrew Sullivan and Matt McIlraith. At least Robbie kept a bit of dignity as his new team smashed us.

But it's not just about the Aussies in Sydney. We got stuffed by the Springboks the game before that in Dunedin, after beating them in Wellington.

In that opening Tri Nations match, we were brutal and clinical, and Brad showed he was really going to add some steel to our pack. Unfortunately, he overdid it, dumped John Smit on his head and got a one-week suspension.

That made it a pretty green pack the following week at Carisbrook, particularly when Ali's ankle gave up the ghost after 20 minutes and Kevin O'Neill came on for his first test, to join Anthony Boric, playing his third test. We had guys with similar experience — or lack of it — at tighthead prop, blindside flanker and No. 8, and Rodney playing No. 7. Even so, it was pretty woeful, and when Ricky Januarie pulled off a brilliant kick-and-chase to win it, the Springboks had broken their 87-year hoodoo at Carisbrook and the media, quite correctly, began to speculate about whether the exodus of experienced players had come back to bite us.

But that had been lost in the frenzied build-up to the clash in Sydney. It wasn't New Zealand versus Australia, it was Robbie versus Ted. In the two weeks before that game, Kaingaroa Forest might have been felled to provide the newsprint for the big face-off. The continuing debate over whether Ted & Co. should have been reappointed inevitably reopened the festering sore of Cardiff.

There was also more constructive criticism: that Robbie's experience with the ELVs through Super 14 might have given him an advantage over Ted & Shag & Smithy. But that was no excuse for our players and what happened out on the field at Olympic Stadium. There was no tactical nous — we tried to run it from everywhere and got bowled. Daniel Braid was playing openside and wasn't match-fit after being out with injury, and when he was replaced by Sione Lauaki, that option was crossed off the list as he waved Rocky Elsom past on a 30-metre jog to the try-line.

Lauaki wasn't the only one who let himself down. Watching good players play badly was really frustrating. Being professional means working out how you get yourself ready to perform *every* week. It has to be a combination of self-reliance, self-knowledge and self-discipline — coaches and colleagues can't get you there. I'd rather have a guy who can give me an eight every week than someone who's a 10 one week and a six the next. You can't make a coherent plan around that.

The 34–19 scoreline wasn't a loss, it was a dicking, and the Dingo Deans lobby went into overdrive. Sitting in the stand with Hayley, I felt that the win wasn't really due to the Aussies being particularly smart or brilliant: we were so awful, they didn't have to be.

Afterwards, Smithy, as usual, was excoriatingly honest. 'I've been out-coached before,' he said, 'and I'll be out-coached again.'

But not this Saturday, surely.

Those two losses in a row have put our season on the skids. Robbie's new-look team beat the South Africans in Perth and now lead the Tri Nations points table with two wins. If we lose the return game at Eden Park, right before we hop on a plane to South Africa, that's the Tri Nations effectively gone and we're dog tucker.

There's open speculation that Ted & Smithy and Shag will be too. Sacking an All Black coach in the middle of his tenure is unprecedented, but feelings are running high, and what happened in Sydney must have been an embarrassment to the NZRU Board.

'The net result of the World Cup fallout is that I'll never cheer for a team coached by Henry,' writes a sports hack in our major metropolitan daily. 'No team in black will ever represent my sporting fervour while he is in charge. There will never be a time soon enough for Henry's departure.' I won't embarrass this guy by naming him: I hope his fervour is keeping him warm at night.

My first crack against the Aussies at Eden Park in 2008. Ali reckoned I'd win all the plaudits.

At least it's not getting to Ali. When I get out of that taxi and into the foyer of the Heritage, he's an unmissable totem pole. 'You know what's going to happen,' he says with his usual grin. 'We'll all front this Saturday because we have to, but you'll be the bloody hero because you came back and saved us.'

And that's more or less how it pans out.

Robbie picks two opensides, Phil Waugh and George Smith, even though we've been deliberately ambivalent about whether I'll play. Robbie knows I'm going to be there.

That's going to make it really tough on a dodgy ankle after six weeks on the sidelines and a couple of runs. Phil and George are both natural opensides, but have different styles, which might be complementary.

Phil's in there at the breakdown every time, having a sniff, and is easier to control because you always know where he's going to be. If we play him right, he'll become inaccurate.

George is much harder to play against because he picks his times. You lose track of him, don't know where he is, then — bang! — he's in there, usually when it matters. George is smart and his interventions usually make a difference. Like me, he's put the work into becoming more effective as a carrier, so potentially, the Wallabies shouldn't lose much by having him play No. 6.

Before I get to training, I've written in the Warwick at the top of the page *Need to be more desperate*. And that's the guts of what we need to put out there, along with work-rate and belief. At the bottom of the list, I write: *When we get behind, must build pressure and not give it away with soft shit*.

But we never are behind, as Dan kicks sublimely and we chase with purpose. We keep the ball behind them, play in their half and belt them. We belt them in the scrums, in the collisions, at the breakdown: even our lineout goes well. Woody scores two tries, the second from an attacking lineout move called Teabag. The move will only work if you're sure the defending lineout will contest the ball in the air close to their line. I know the Aussies will fancy their chances and have a go, and when we split the pods, it creates a hole for Woody to charge through to the goal-line. Perfection.

By the 60-minute mark, when Phil Waugh is subbed off, the game is ours. Ali's right: I get the plaudits, but in truth it's a huge lift from everyone. We play smarter tactics; we're focused and a lot better at the breakdown.

The relief in the coaches' box is evident as Ted & Smithy & Shag do the old man's version of high fives. It's good to see. They've been so under the hammer.

But I haven't forgotten what I saw in Sydney.

The following week, we're at the airport hotel for an early call to board the plane for South Africa. I call a team meeting for even earlier, 4.30 am, which is apt, because I want to talk to them about not relaxing, not getting comfortable.

There are no coaches or management, just me and the team. I tell them that last week's game is the perfect illustration of the difference between genuine preparation and faking it. I name a couple of names, to show the difference in their performances when they prepped genuinely and when they didn't. I tell them that last week doesn't mean shit if we can't do it again next week at Newlands. Preparing genuinely means being tough enough mentally to do what is required between now and next Saturday. Cape Town's got a lot of temptations, and I'm not talking about no fun, but we need to be tough bastards if we are to get what we're after.

'I'm asking you all to be fucking genuine this week,' I tell them. 'Before you leave here, just decide if you are willing to do that and, if you're not, I suggest you don't bother getting on the bus.'

There's utter silence, which I take as assent, then I tell them about the exercises that Gilbert Enoka and I want them to do on the flight, things to think about, visualisations about preparation and playing.

The week goes well. I've told the leaders that I need them to help set the attitudes for the week, both on- and off-field, and to be demanding, so that I don't always have to be the voice in their ears.

The game at Newlands is a benchmark performance for the team and for me. We beat the World Champions 19–nil, and the nil is as impressive as the 19. Our defence is massive. It's the first time South Africa has been kept scoreless in a home test. We could have had a lot more — Dan had one of his less accurate goal-kicking days.

Robbie's sitting in the stands at Newlands, and obviously picks up something useful. The Aussies beat South Africa the following week and it's all set up for Brisbane: winner take all — the Tri Nations and the Bledisloe, and, for the media, Robbie or Ted.

That contest is 1–1 too.

Suncorp is a hard place to win. Expat Kiwis in Queensland ensure we have great support, but the Aussies seem to grow an extra leg there, and they score either side of halftime and after 60 minutes we're 10 points down. The Wallabies are playing superbly and exerting huge pressure on us. We can't seem to get on the front foot and at times we're just holding on. We try Teabag again, splitting the pods in the lineout, and they're ready for it this time, so that's that one to put away for a rainy day.

In some strange way, it's where I want to be. Last quarter, everything on the line, almost a year after we blew it all in a similar situation at Cardiff. We've talked the talk, trained hard and thought hard about what we'd do in this situation. Can we execute?

In the huddle after they score, Mils tells us what he's seeing from the back — the kicking game we'd planned isn't working. So Dan and Piri start attacking the fringes with the ball in hand, Rodney has a huge last 30 minutes and gives us some go-forward, and the game gradually changes.

It helps that the ELVs are working their space magic as the game goes on. Under the new rules, it's as exhausting to attack as defend, and when Conrad wriggles free on the 10-metre line there's space in front of him, apart from a lone defender. He looks outside for Siti and sees instead all 120 kilos of Tony Woodcock. What the hell, Conrad draws and passes perfectly, and Woody thunders down the left-touch like a white rhino — it might have been 20 metres or 60, depending on who's telling the story — and scores in the corner. Dan slots the conversion from the sideline, closing to within three.

Now, we start turning the screws. There's composure and focus. We pin them on their line and work them over, patiently, relentlessly, until Siti dabs and Piri finds the hole.

It's a close-run thing right to the end, when the Aussies turn over our scrum on the hooter and almost score.

There's enormous satisfaction — and relief — in holding up the Bledisloe and Tri Nations Cups after the game. Neither is the cup we really wanted, but we had them in the cupboard at the beginning of the year, and if we'd lost them, that would have been the end-point for a few careers, inside and outside the coaches' box.

Instead, guys like Jimmy Cowan and Jerome Kaino and Brad and Conrad have really found their feet in test rugby, while the core of the team has kept developing.

Way back at the beginning of the year, when Robbie asked me to give him a reason why I should be captain of the Crusaders, I'd told him I believed the experiences I'd been through would make me a better captain than I had been. I reckon I've delivered on that — and I think Robbie, to his cost, might be the first one to agree that I have.

All the sweeter out of the Big Cup . . . Suncorp Stadium, Brisbane, 2008.

Playing well has definitely helped me captain well. There's a symbiotic relationship. People speak of the Suncorp test against Australia in 2006 as my best ever, but I reckon my form in the games against Australia at Eden Park and against South Africa at Newlands is up there with anything I've ever done in the All Black jersey.

We've all, coaches and players, come a long way in a long year of rugby, gone through a hell of a lot, emotionally and physically.

But it's not over.

Almost a year to the day after Cardiff, I spend a couple of hours with Gilbert Enoka, refining objectives for me and the team on the eve of our departure for London. We talk about the leadership challenges of a five-week tour, like how to keep everyone fresh and emotionally connected, how to avoid a culture of secrecy in a touring party of 35 where cliques could easily develop, and how to get bone-deep commitment out of players every week, instead of skin deep.

Ahead of us, we've got consecutive weekly tests against Scotland, Ireland, Wales and England, with an extra midweek game against Munster sandwiched in between Ireland and Wales. It's another opportunity to complete a Grand Slam. The last one was in 2005.

But when we look at what we want out of this tour, the Grand Slam is incidental to a larger goal that we want much more.

Job done: at the back of the bus with Rodders, Kevvy, Woody and Mils after our Grand Slam-clinching victory over England.

We've got to wait another three years before we get an opportunity to call ourselves World Champions, but we've worked out that if we can win those four tests we'll have won the number-one world ranking back from South Africa.

That's what we really want.

On the way to that assignment, we play Australia again in Hong Kong. The promoters of this experimental game, a revenue opportunity for the NZRU and ARU, would have preferred it to be the decider for the Bledisloe. It's not, but we want to be worthy holders, and know that 3–1 will feel a hell of a lot better than 2–2, but the fact that the Cup is already in the cabinet could be a potential motivational problem for us. Luckily, Matt Dunning steps up with a few choice comments about Woody being 'a myth'.

On the day, we're not that convincing and have to come from behind again to pull it out of the fire. I think I've nailed Giteau, but he throws a miracle no-look pass to Drew Mitchell who goes over. We get home narrowly 19–14, partly through sheer stamina and partly because Dan gets back into first-five in the second half, after playing outside Stephen Donald in the first, and pulls the right strings.

The rest of the tests are pretty comfortable, at least on the scoreboard: 32–6 against Scotland, after a brave first 10 minutes, a much tougher battle against Ireland at Croke Park than 22–3 would indicate, 29–9 against Wales and a smashing of England, 32–6 again. Apart from Scotland, we have to play at tempo for 60 minutes to reap the rewards in the last quarter. We take enormous satisfaction that in those four tests we don't concede one try.

The week after we beat Wales, they tip over Australia, which is an indication of our quality.

The toughest test turns out to be the one game that isn't a test.

At Limerick, we're taken to see a play about Munster's 1978 defeat of the All Blacks. Our visit is reported in the *Daily Telegraph*.

'The cast of *Alone It Stands* have performed their little masterpiece more than 1000 times on four continents but half an hour before "kick-off" at the Millennium Theatre at Limerick on Sunday night came a bombshell from playwright John Breen. On Monday the entire 50-strong All Black party would be in the audience.

'It is one thing doing your version of the haka, not to mention your approximation of a New Zealand accent, among those of a Munster or neutral disposition, but quite another poking fun — albeit gentle — at the All Blacks when the modern day warriors are seated 10 yards away in the small and intimate auditorium.'

We get a standing ovation before the play begins, and we reciprocate when it ends. In between, though, it's moving and a bit unnerving. As the actors do their best to mimic the All Blacks and Munster players of the time, I can't help thinking that there's no way I want some Irish actor playing Richie McCaw 30 years down the track to commemorate a victory!

Yet it damn near happens.

We're there to help Munster celebrate the opening of their new ground, Thomond Park, and the atmosphere is festive, given the weather. Munster don't have any of their internationals playing, apart from Dougie Howlett on the wing, so it should be one of those games you win easily. And that's the way it's shaping up when Stephen Donald scores an early try. I settle back and enjoy the atmosphere, and wait for us to really get going.

Trouble is, we don't, and at halftime it's still close. I'm sitting beside Jimmy Cowan up among some Munster Rugby Union guys and one of these guys says, 'Oh well, you never know, that's what dreams are made of.'

The game wears on and we can't kick clear, it's a complete bloody arm-wrestle and then Jimmy tells me he's got a bad feeling.

'No, no,' I tell him, 'we'll be right.'

'You don't play for Southland,' he says. 'When you play for a team that shouldn't win and you get this close, you grow another leg.'

Shit. At five minutes to go, the crowd is going crazy, willing them home, and I consider getting up and going down to the changing room so I don't have to watch it. But with seconds on the clock Joe Rokocoko scores in the corner to win the game. The defender who Joe Rocks runs through to score is Doug Howlett. Good old Dougie!

It's a great day in the end — beating them by 50 or 100 wouldn't have been nearly as special, but Christ, we're glad to sneak away to Cardiff with that one under our belt.

With roommate John Smit after the Baabaas game at the end of '08.

Some of the old All Blacks lament the lack of midweek games, but they're dreaming. It's just too tough now. The playing XV need a full week's preparation for a test match these days. We had a few guys from the test team against Wales on the bench against Munster, so they had to train with them and train with us. Doesn't sound like a major, but it is.

The test against England isn't my last for the year. Joe Rocks and I have been asked to play for the Barbarians. I've been asked a few times before and always said no, but this time I'm already in London and the game is at Wembley. How many chances does an All Black get to play at Wembley?

I'm carrying a bit of a hip spiker from the England game, but it frees up under the strict Barbarians training regime of beer and laughs, and I think I might be okay for 40 minutes, which is all they want. At halftime they ask if I can do another five minutes, then straight away in the second half a couple of their front-rowers get injured so they pull our props off also and go golden oldies, which means I have to play out the full 80. It seems like the game that never ends on top of the season that never ends. I'm out there thinking, *Is this finished yet?*

Eventually, it is over, the game and the season, and I'm glad I've done it, if only for the chance to mix with some of my fiercest competitors in a different context. I get to play with George Gregan and Schalk Burger and Jean de Villiers, and room with John Smit. There's always a bit of intrigue as to how your opponents do things, and it's great being able to sit and have a beer with them and be involved in a common endeavour, instead of being at each other's throats. They impress me as being pretty good men — I reckon you have to be to stay in top-level rugby for any length of time. We're not that different in outlook, and we play the game for much the same reasons. The Baabaas experience means that I might be able to start developing friendships with some of these guys that go beyond the standard post-game 'How's it going?'

It's a Wednesday game, and after little or no sleep, Joe Rocks and I have to get on a flight first thing on Thursday morning and fly to Milan where we join the rest of the All Blacks for a day set up by adidas. We have a day floating around Milan doing promotional stuff with AC Milan and then have another big night out before we hop on the plane home. That's one long, long day on top of a long, long season, but that's finally the end of it. I don't have to worry about the next game for a couple of months.

And I discover that number one in the world sounds even better in Italian — *numero uno del mondo.*

On the flight home, during the few hours I'm not asleep, I reflect on a hell of a year.

Both the Crusaders and the All Blacks have won pretty much everything they've been up for, despite hiccups in the middle of both campaigns: Super 14, Tri Nations, the Bledisloe Cup, the Grand Slam and the number-one ranking in the world.

Looking back, I'm happy with the way I played, and I can see that it's taken me three years to really find my feet as captain, which isn't a lot different from the experience of guys like Sean Fitzpatrick.

I'm knackered, but a hell of a lot better in body and in spirit than I was at this time last year. A year on from Cardiff, this is definitely a nicer place to be. Back on track.

After a season like we've just had, some guys talk of a summer with no stone under the beach towel. I prefer to think of no stone under my seat, the one in my carbon and Kevlar beauty, full harness locked, with the snow-tipped Southern Alps on one side and the wide brown Mackenzie Basin on the other.

Partners

Gavin Wills is right. Within 48 hours of touching down in Christchurch, I'm back at Omarama, unfolding the Discus from her winter hibernation, going through all the little rituals that culminate in the tow-rope release, then the big sky . . .

Gavin takes me on a lead-and-follow, which sounds easier than it is, because we see these veil clouds and a split cloud base, signs of a convergence of the two air masses, the moist cool sea air and the inland air which is being pushed to the western side of the Main Divide by light south-easterlies. These take us west of Mount Aspiring into wild rugged West Coast country and I hear Gavin's voice telling me, 'Don't lose me, because you have no idea where the alternative landings are, and there aren't many out here. It's just riverbeds and beaches unless we go all the way over to Haast.'

We find little whiskers of clouds from not particularly high levels — we're at ridge-top, a little bit above — and we get inside them or on the edge of them and climb up and then move on to the next one.

'Don't lose it,' Gavin tells me. 'Don't lose me.'

I don't. I'm loving it.

A couple of times, we cross a valley, misread it on the other side and end up down in the wrong air mass, falling. The only way out is to go deeper back towards the Main Divide and try to find the other air mass and climb up on this side of it. Gavin's making tough decisions. In some ways we're putting our heads deeper into the lion's jaws, and he's trying to teach me just how far we can push it before the lion gags and shuts his mouth. That's what we're grappling with.

Gavin tells me later that at one stage, coming north up the West Coast, looking for a lift back across the Southern Alps, with not a lot of landing options if we don't, he has this moment where he thinks, 'Jesus, I've got the captain of the All Blacks out here. I bet his coaches have no idea where their boy is today!'

He's able to put that out of his mind because, he tells me, I've earned his trust. He reckons I've got good 'situational awareness'. Part of that is knowing I'm the newbie,

Gliding mentor Gavin Wills
and newbie . . .

and I do what I'd expect any newbie to do in the All Blacks. If I don't understand something I'll ask. If he tells me I'd better stick to his tail, I bloody well do.

Gavin's right about something else too. He reckons he knows which girlfriends will last. He gives them the speech about my future as an ace glider pilot, and watches their eyes glaze over. He says that's what happened with Hayley. I wish it was that easy to tell!

Turns out he's right, though, and Hayley and I don't last much longer. That's just the way it goes, and it's no one's fault and no one else's business.

Being available to media and sponsors is part of my contractual obligations to the NZRU, so a public profile or persona is an inevitable result of doing my job. I kind of trust the media to respect that, to know where the boundaries are. When Hayley or anyone else has a relationship with me, there's no implied contract that the details have to be shared in the public forum. It's the same when I'm with my mates from school or Lincoln — they're not part of any deal I've made with the devil.

I've always been deliberately guarded in my public utterances, because whether I'm officially on duty or not, I'm talking as All Black captain and my words carry the weight and expectation of that position. I decided when I got the captaincy that I'd rather be seen as boring than say something that ends up as an embarrassing headline.

That pressure is not just on me. The All Blacks are given a wee book with all the protocols and expectations in it. One of the first things it says is that if you're an All Black, you're an All Black 24/7.

Whether you're in an All Black environment or you're at home, or out and about, you're still an All Black and you're representing the team and so you should act as if you are. That's a tough one for a lot of the players to get their heads around. You've got downtime at home, you're not in the All Black environment, you're out with your mates, relaxing, switching off, winding down, chilling out . . . You're still an All Black, because that's what the headline will say if you stuff up.

I have trouble with the 24/7 thing too sometimes, knowing where the line in the sand is for instance, when you're not with the All Blacks, not in that environment where you expect fans to want autographs and photos. If I'm by myself, okay, I try to manage it and still do what I need to do. As much as I appreciate that the attention and interest is a privilege that comes with being an All Black, some days it seems relentless and gets on top of me, and I either get a bit short with people

Being able to put a smile on some young kid's face is pretty cool.

or, worse, decide that going out is too much trouble. I wish it was written into my contract — 10 autographs and photos is okay on one outing, 50 is too many!

It can become really irritating if I'm with a friend or friends who are not All Blacks or anything to do with the public spotlight, and the attention starts inhibiting what I'm able to do with them, or whether they want to be with me. They haven't bought into that. The worst case was when I was at a restaurant trying to get to know someone, as you do, have some sort of meaningful, engaged conversation, and a middle-aged woman I'd never seen before came screaming up and shoved her mobile in my face and asked me to say hello to someone on the other end. *Hello?* Quite apart from anything else, I like my food and, like your average farm dog, hate to be interrupted when I'm eating! But most people in New Zealand are courteous and appreciative of a photo or autograph, and being able to put a smile on some young kid's face is pretty cool.

Once you're in the All Black environment, it's much more straightforward. There are only five key rules, non-negotiables. One of them is being on time — bang. The others are around dress code, recovery and post-match boundaries and expectations. We used to leave booze and women a bit grey, ask the guys to make good decisions. That's too open to interpretation, and what looks like a good decision when you've had a few is not the same as when you're sober.

So now we're more explicit. We don't say don't drink, but we do give a time that you've got to be home after a game. We want everyone home at three o'clock, say. And the expectation is that you're not bloody pissed and you don't make an idiot of yourself. So if you've had a couple too many and you're a little bit tiddly or whatever, no trouble with that. As long as you are home by three and you haven't made a dick of yourself or compromised your recovery for next week's training and playing.

We also say no women in our rooms or on our floors. That's a non-negotiable — wives, partners, whoever. If your wife or partner is staying on another floor, that's fine. Some days at the end of a campaign, we might relax the time thing and say, 'Look, it's up to you when you get back. Just remember you're an All Black.'

There's got to be some respite, of course. You've got to find ways of losing yourself, however temporarily. There aren't many avenues. An intense conversation. Family. Friends. Reading something engrossing. Music, although I'm not the guy with the iPod growing out of his ears. Hauling out the bagpipes for a blast might get me out of myself but isn't a great help to neighbourhood tranquillity. There's the 80 minutes of the game itself, and there's gliding, of course. But if you need alcohol to lose yourself, you're in trouble.

There's still always going to be the odd fall from grace, whatever you do. The team's reaction to that probably depends on the character of the guy in the firing line. Because there's so much pressure, it's got to be a pricks-don't-last environment, but sometimes a good bugger will fall over.

Jimmy Cowan, for instance, got charged with alcohol-related offences back before our first game of the Tri Nations and must have been close to getting the boot. I wasn't there that week when it all came out, I was at home injured, but he went to ground and wouldn't answer my phone calls, he wouldn't answer anyone's. He wouldn't even come out of his room apparently, poor bugger. He was in a bad hole there and when he eventually surfaced and put his hand up, we all tried to help him, because we think Jimmy is a hell of a good man. If he hadn't been like that, I think we would have just said, 'Piss off.'

He went to Sydney the following week, was on the bench when we got beaten over there and then, as luck would have it, he was the only fit halfback for the next game at Eden Park, where he had an absolute blinder against the Aussies and became first choice.

Sometimes when things go wrong with someone, you have to also ask whether we could have done better to prevent the situation, rather than blame him one hundred per cent for stuffing up. You look at guys who aren't performing and, yes, they have to do it themselves, but maybe also part of the problem is that we're missing something, there's something we can do to help them. I think that before you give anyone the heave-ho, you have to at least ask that question.

That 24/7 obligation is a tough one, particularly if there's a huge dichotomy between your public and private personas. If you're a different person behind closed doors, that's going to be hard to hide, as time goes on.

I don't think there's a huge difference between the public me and the private me: but — hopefully — there's a hell of a lot more of me that doesn't see the spotlight than does. I'll always want to keep a lot of myself to myself. That's just the way I am, where I'm from, the way I was brought up. I don't want to share my every thought with everyone — I'd as soon eat my own entrails as tweet — and I don't think there's a public right to know everything about me, just because I'm an All Black. Maybe that huge gap between the public Tiger and the private Tiger was Woods' downfall. If being promiscuous worked for him, that shouldn't have been anyone's concern, even in sanctimonious America. The problem was that he was also married and out there casting himself as Mister Family Values.

When Tiger Woods was single and winning majors by the handful every year, Greg Norman was asked what could possibly stop Tiger's inexorable march to beating Jack Nicklaus' record of 18 majors. 'Marriage,' said Greg.

I don't think even Greg imagined that his prediction would be quite that accurate!

Only those inside a relationship can know the truth of it, but by all accounts, Tiger had married well. It shows that you've not only got to be lucky in love, but also know it and respect it if you are.

Love isn't something you can find by focusing harder or by crunching numbers or making radical changes to how you go about things. Public recognition doesn't help: half the women run a mile and the ones who are attracted to that sort of thing are probably the ones I should avoid! Like everyone else, I've just got to wait until it happens, and like everyone else, I'll need a bit of luck to meet the right person. And to know it when I do.

The other thing that defines me 24/7 is my family.

My mother, Margaret, was born and raised in Mayfield, a little coffee shop, pub and garage town on the Scenic Route, Highway 72, near Mount Peel and Mount Hutt, where the Rangitata River comes out of the Alps and makes a dash for the Pacific. Her family, the McLays, are steeped in rugby. Her brothers, Bigsy and Peter, were both stars for Mid Canterbury and their father was a referee. Mum used to go to matches with him and walk up and down the sideline listening to all the comments and repeating them to her father at halftime. Maybe that was part of Dad's attraction to her — he did a bit of refereeing and organising refs on those Saturdays down in Oamaru. No wonder I like talking to refs and have my own interpretations of the rules — it's in the blood!

Dad was at the Canterbury Sports Awards one year and overheard Paddy O'Brien, in charge of referees for the IRB, talking to referee Steve Walsh. Paddy was commiserating with Steve about how difficult it was to referee 'that bugger McCaw' at the breakdown.

'The bugger's so bloody quick, we can't decipher what he's doing,' said Paddy.

'What am I supposed to do then?' asked Steve Walsh.

'We can't penalise what we can't see,' said Paddy, shaking his head.

We're very close, our family . . . With Dad, Mum and Jo at my 21st in 2002.

'That's encouraging!' I said, when Dad told me.

Mum and my father, Donald, met when they were still at secondary school, Dad at St Andrew's, and Mum at Rangi Ruru, in the same class as Dad's younger sister. They were friends for a long time before they got married — when Mum was 26 and Dad 28. I was born at Oamaru Hospital, up on the hill above the house where Janet Frame was raised, on the very last day of 1980, almost three years before my sister Joanna.

Jo turned out to be just as competitive as me, and Mum reckons the only reason we survived was because we weren't both boys — we'd have knocked seven bells out of each other. Jo played rugby and cricket with me on the back lawn. She's probably the reason I was useless with the bat and made the cricket team at Otago Boys' as a seamer, because she always wanted to bat and refused to bowl. She was always up for a game, and it's no surprise that she's done so well at netball for the Canterbury Tactix. The surprise is that the tomboy turned out to be such a beautiful woman.

We're very close, our family — you have to be when you're brought up in such an isolated environment. Selling the farm in 2002 was a big call. When Dad got an offer, he talked it through with Jo and me before he did anything. I know he found it hard to let it go, but he'd been having problems with his back for the three years leading up to that. He'd had one operation on a prolapsed disc which left scar tissue pressing on the sciatic nerve. He was in agony, couldn't even sit straight, couldn't sit in a car and was reduced to crawling around on the ground out there. That summer, I came home from school and drove the header, harvested the crops.

We had 500 acres in cropping and 600 in pasture. The Haka is demanding enough if you're able-bodied.

The back gave Dad a hell of a fright, he was really struggling and it forced him to start thinking about whether there was a life for him without the farm. It had been in the family for more than a hundred years and he couldn't bring himself to put it on the market, but when someone made an offer, he had to take it seriously. By then, I'd decided that if I was going to go farming, the Haka was too tough, cold in winter, dry in summer, with not enough water for effective irrigation.

The sale of the farm released Mum and Dad to have a life they couldn't have otherwise had. They're able to travel now and come to a lot of my games. If they're in town, and Jo is too, we have a ritual where we all meet at eleven o'clock for coffee on game day.

Like most families, when one of us takes a hit, we all feel the pain. Cardiff was hard on them. It's only now that a year has passed and the All Blacks have restored some mana that Mum and Dad and Jo fill me in on the details of their experience.

I remember being surprised when I got the word under the grandstand at Millennium after the game that Dad and Jo were at the players' entrance, but I had no idea how they'd managed to get there.

Mum and Dad and Jo and her boyfriend Sam had been sitting with Ben Blair, ex-Canterbury and Crusader and All Black and flatmate, who was playing for the Cardiff Blues. When the fulltime whistle sounded, Dad was trying to make all the right noises and said to Ben, 'Well, it's not that bloody bad.'

'It bloody is, you know!' said Ben. He was in tears.

Before they exited the stadium, Jo and Dad decided they couldn't go without seeing me. Dad reckons Jo just walked up to the security guys of the next section and told them who they were and why they needed to get to the players' entrance. Then, while the guards were processing the information, she bolted. Dad followed Jo and the security guards followed them both. When they got to the players' tunnel, they recognised Steve Tew and Jo yelled to him. Dad reckons he didn't know what to say to me, but knew he had to say something.

I was in a daze and not taking a lot in, but Dad's words stuck, the ones about the nature of sport. I'd forgotten the other thing he said to me: 'You're going to be judged on what you do from this moment on.' But that must have stuck too.

Mum's pretty forthright and Dad seems pretty laid-back, but Mum and Jo reckon he gets nervous enough for all three of them. Before that game at Cardiff, he had a bad feeling and hadn't slept much for three nights. He'd been to the Wednesday training and was disconcerted when two or three key players he knew, like Aaron and Dougie, walked past him, morose at being left out of the playing XV. Dad wondered what the hell the coaches were doing, but said nothing to me. Then, when he wished me good luck, apparently I said that I hoped we'd be following him and Mum and Jo to Paris, and not heading back up the M4 to Heathrow. That had worried him too.

At halftime, Dad went to get a hamburger and overheard an English fan saying that if New Zealand won this Cup, rugby was finished in the northern hemisphere. When Dad was watching developments in the second half, he wondered if the guy at the hamburger stand had got in Wayne Barnes' ear!

After they'd spoken to me, Mum and Dad went back to the Cardiff Blues clubrooms with the Welsh people they were staying with. 'We're used to losing,' they said to Mum and Dad, 'this happens to us all the time,' and got out the guitars and started singing. But later, Mum and Dad saw Raewyn Henry and the other coaches' wives. They were white with dread, wondering what was going to happen to their husbands when they got home. Wayne Smith's son was in tears.

Jo hit the town with friends from London and saw groups of Kiwis all round Cardiff, commiserating with each other. It was hard hearing some of the slagging, but she was among friends and kept her head down.

Uncle Bigsy was with a tour group, and, like Mum and Dad and Jo, they all had to make a decision to get over it, and they did, enjoying the rest of the tour by dint of sheer willpower. Dad reckons the upside was that he didn't get nervous in Paris before the semi or the final! It helped too that once Jo got on the internet, the media storm back home didn't seem as bad as they expected.

We can talk about all this now: it's still painful, but it hurts a hell of a lot less a year down the track, with the Central Otago sun on our backs and swimming and fishing with my old mates from school and Lincoln, and gliding to get stuck into, not to mention the Discovery Channel cameras arriving.

I've helped organise this show where league star Andrew Ettingshausen comes to Omarama and learns how to glide (as well as paraponting and aerobatic flying back in Australia) and we end up having a glider 'race'. Andrew's actually sitting behind Gavin in the twin-seat of course, but I'm doing loop-the-loops for real, with a lot of tuition from Gavin between takes!

It's a helluva lot more exciting than most promo shoots.

Being a professional rugby player means holidays aren't all downtime. You've got your schedule to keep to, so that you're where you need to be physically when you come back into camp. That's always in the back of your mind, and I like getting out and hitting the road. With my hat and glasses on, I get a few toots but no hassles.

The other obligation that doesn't sleep is work for the sponsors. You've got to be available, if needed. Sometimes, it's a trip to Germany for adidas, say, although that stuff is usually tacked on to the end of the northern tour.

When you sign up with the NZRU, you're effectively signing up to the All Blacks' sponsors as well, and it's the same with the Crusaders. Contractually, they don't own you as an individual, but they own you as a member of those teams. So anything I do to promote those sponsors, I do as part of my obligations to the All Blacks or the Crusaders, and there are obligations for, say, a minimum of three players to be involved in, say, a television commercial for an All Black sponsor.

Dan and me with adidas CEO and Chairman Herbert Hainer.

It can get more complicated than that with dual deals, though, because adidas, an All Black sponsor, also contracts me as an individual, so that they can put me out there as an All Black, in All Black livery, on my own. Same with Mastercard and Air New Zealand.

Then I'll have some personal sponsors on top of that, but with those individual deals, with Westpac or Versatile, say, I can't be Richie McCaw, All Black, I can only use my name. I can't use any All Black intellectual property whenever I'm acting as a Westpac or Versatile ambassador.

The obvious danger in all this is conflicting interests, between team and individual sponsors, which is why the NZRU has a veto. I can't go out there and promote a different airline, obviously, or sportswear, but if you're already signed up to one bank, say, as an individual before another one comes in as a team sponsor, that existing deal is allowed to continue. Theoretically, players in Super rugby could wear boots other than the sponsor's, because that's a tool of trade exemption, but that doesn't apply to me because of my individual deal with adidas. Complicated. But at All Black level, there are no exemptions: we're adidas all the way.

Despite the complications, it's basically common sense, because there's a limited pool out there for New Zealand rugby players as a generic group, and none of us wants to do anything to diminish that.

And whichever way it falls, the big rule for me is that it's not just about the money. That might sound a bit trite from someone in my position, but the big thing for me with the personal sponsors especially is the people involved and what they stand for. I need to understand what they do and be happy to stand by the product.

With the dual sponsorships, the likes of adidas and Air New Zealand and Mastercard, I don't have to do due diligence, that's all done by the NZRU before I get on board. But with any personal sponsors, my agent Dean Hegan, Warren Alcock's associate at the Essentially Group, and I are very careful. While Warren looks after my contract with the NZRU, Dean looks after the personal sponsors, deciding whether they fit, sorting contracts, and helping me with those relationships. I really rely on them and I'd be buggered without them.

The most critical part of the relationship with a sponsor, of course, is deciding whether you should have one. It's not always about how kosher the company is, though. Sometimes it's more a style thing. Back in 2004 when I had no personal sponsors at all, I was offered a television commercial for a prominent brand for very good money. I turned it down. They couldn't understand why. It was a style thing. I was worried about being the guy in such a relentless commercial. It's just not me.

Making a call like that probably comes back again to making sure there's not a hell of a lot of divergence between the public person or brand and the real person. I'm not that fussed about flash production values in a commercial — I need to feel comfortable with the style and content and the product.

I want to enjoy the association with any commercial partners and be there for the long term. Adidas, for instance, have sponsored me since I started and have been loyal and great people to work with.

A wise man once told me that you're pretty much protected from most people you come into contact with. The ones you are totally vulnerable to are your partners. So choose carefully, he said, in business, in life and in love.

That said, you probably still need a bit of luck in all three.

Start again

Every game-day mantra in my Warwick begins the same way: *Start again.* It's usually accompanied by other exhortations. *Get involved early. DMJ. Keep getting up.* They're reminders that what I did last week is history, that each week, the beginning of each game, is ground zero.

On the night before a test we have a stretch class at 6 pm, half an hour before dinner, and I use that to visualise what I'm going to do next day. On game day, we have something to eat about 3.30 for a 7.30 kick-off, then downtime in our rooms. I use that time too, to write down my mantras and to visualise.

Start again. Kick-off, where will I be? The ball is coming to me. How am I going to catch it? If it's our kick, what's my role, what will I be seeing? Defensive scrum. We've been through the sort of moves they're going to do, how am I going to get there? Don't take a first step forward, I want to go sideways first to get the space, then forward . . .

The same is true of each season. You have to start again. You hope to build on the things you set in place last season, but sport doesn't work like that. Every season is different. Even if you were able to perfectly replicate the attitude and fitness you had last season, it will still be different. Playing personnel will have changed, yours and the opposition's. Coaches and trainers and physios and doctors might have changed. Referees might have changed, and the latest bright idea from the IRB will definitely have changed rule interpretations.

You find yourself having to go back, not to ground zero, but to some indeterminate point that will only be revealed when the team gets together and starts playing.

Sometimes you discover you're not where you thought you were.

In 2009, that happens with the Crusaders.

As always, there are some new faces, notably Ben Franks' younger brother Owen. But it's the absence of a familiar face that strikes me when we assemble at St Albans: Dan isn't there — he's buggered his Achilles playing for Perpignan over the summer. Some sabbatical.

I know exactly what I've done. Medial ligament, against the Highlanders, 2009.

Todd Blackadder is the new coach, with Mark Hammett and Daryl Gibson his assistants. Hammer had put his name forward for head coach, but when he missed out he was big enough to sign on to help Toddy.

Toddy is the right man for the job — I had enormous respect for him as captain in my early Crusaders days, and the indications are that he'll make a great coach. He wasn't the biggest or most naturally gifted player going around, but maybe it's those players, the ones who really have to think about the game and how to get the best out of themselves, who make the best coaches.

Initially, however, things don't go right for Toddy or for me.

The Crusaders win the first game against the Chiefs. That's the end of the good news, for a while.

I get a knee in the head and blurred vision.

I miss the next game against the Brumbies, who win it in extra time when Stirling Mortlock nails a conversion from the sideline.

Then the Hurricanes come to Christchurch and beat us, first time for five years. I do time in the sin-bin.

Then we lose 6–nil to the Highlanders, the lowest-scoring game in Super Rugby history, the first time in Super history we've been held scoreless, and it's every bit as ugly and uninspiring as the score makes it sound. The ugliest bonus point ever earned in Super 14.

I might be biased about that. I get bent up pretty early. My ankle's up on a body and someone falls on the outside of my knee. It doesn't actually hurt that much, but by now I know the signs. I get up and the knee is wobbly. Sloppy. When the physio comes out and starts checking, it doesn't seem as bad as it actually is because the muscles take over and hold the knee in, stop it graunching sideways. But I know exactly what I've done. Medial ligament.

Going from super-fit to cripple in the blink of an eye is a tough mental jump.

I'm fine if I've got a plan, but if I just go day to day and it feels like nothing's getting any better, that's depressing. If every day is no different, I'd go mad, so the physios put a plan in place. If I can go, *Okay, I've got six weeks until I'm aiming to play again*, then I can work back from that.

The first week is just resting it, especially with a knee injury. If it's a bit wobbly, you've got to let it sit in a knee brace for a week or so. But if after that week you can start doing some rehab, some quad-strengthening exercises, say, you can work with that. It might be small stuff that you think is a waste of time but it builds it up, every day a little more, so you keep progressing little things. I can think, *Right, by the end of this week I'm going to be back on the bike*, and when I get on the bike I can think, *Okay, that's progress, I'm getting better.*

You're missing the team environment, but you've got to be really careful that you don't kill yourself off by hanging around too much. When you're captain you want to be there to help out where you can, but standing around just watching training can be bloody painful. It's best to take at least a week and get away from it. Or be there to help out early in the week, then make yourself scarce as they get closer to game day. Do your rehab and stuff and go home, because it's too bloody frustrating just watching.

I also get frustrated if rehab doesn't happen the way I want it to happen, if I don't hit the targets I'm supposed to hit. But you've got to have targets: I've got to know what I'm aiming for.

That's all well and good for the knee.

My head is the wild card.

When I got the whack on the head in the first game against the Chiefs, I was probably overcautious in taking the next game off. I didn't quite feel myself. I got a bit anxious about it probably. As soon as I decided I wasn't playing, all of a sudden I was feeling good again. By Saturday I was thinking maybe I could've played, but the right decision was to be overcautious.

The problem is that if you miss a game, you've got to say why. With my history, that's going to be news. That's shit I don't want to deal with, but you can't start making decisions, particularly about your health, because you don't want to deal with the media interest it will inevitably generate. So I took that week off when I probably didn't need to, but I'll always be ultra-cautious because of what I've been through.

In 2004, I was in a head clash during the game against England at Dunedin and missed the second test at Eden Park. I came back for the next test against Argentina in Hamilton, then a couple of days later I had a bit of a headache. I got worried about it and started to think about everything. Some days you don't feel that good anyway, and I do get neck symptoms which give me tension headaches occasionally. I think I got confused with all that, and there might have been a bit of delayed stuff too, and I started going around and around in circles, worrying about it. I was uncharacteristically short with people, particularly those who kept asking me how my head was!

By then I'd missed the first two matches of the Tri Nations and was never going to play the next two, so I decided to take a break from the whole series and work my way back for the NPC.

That's basically what happened, though I'd got myself in a state where I didn't know what was wrong in the end. It might've been the head knock, or it might have been me worrying about it too much, but I began thinking it was never going to be right. Then someone suggested that I just get back and get training, and when I did

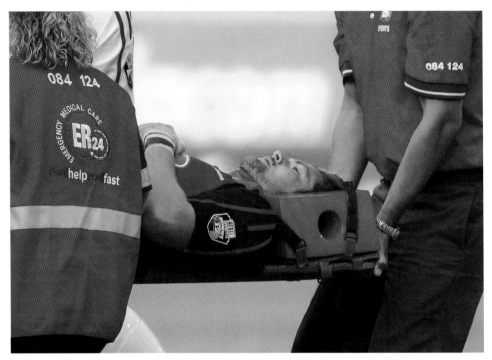

Stretchered off after my close encounter with Richard Bands.

that I felt fine. When it came to actually playing again, I still lacked confidence and didn't want to come back as captain, but that was when Aussie McLean and Steve Hansen told me I was playing as captain or not at all. That worked, forced me to think about the team, not myself. No further worries.

The following year, I got knocked unconscious at Loftus in a front-on tackle of Richard Bands, part Springbok prop, part Brahma bull. That was easier to deal with. I recovered pretty quickly and after a week or so I was feeling pretty good again. I just took it really easy to make sure I was right and stayed on the sideline for about a month. But it was a pretty spectacular hit and I was carried off on a stretcher, still out to it, so there was a lot of media attention, a fair bit of it urging me to give the game away, given my problems the year before. Things weren't helped later that year, on the 2005 end-of-year tour, when I got a head knock against Ireland and withdrew from the English test. It was a worry at the time, and you hope that you won't get any more majors, but it does mean that I'm very careful with any head knocks.

So when I got the bang against the Chiefs, I did the conservative thing and took a week off, even though by the Saturday I felt okay.

That's the thing. I'll never play if I have symptoms. People might say, 'But you passed the test.' Okay, that's the first stage, all the psychometric and other testing that the team doctor will carry out, and that of course is terribly important, not least because the team doctor is always there and knows everything about me. He or she will have a very comprehensive medical profile of every player for comparison purposes, particularly a player like me, who's been around for a while. The team doctor also has access to the huge research that has gone into head injuries from contact sport. There've been two big global conferences with leading people from all round the world getting together to share knowledge and experience about how best to manage this area. So I've got the benefit of all that. But even if I've passed the tests and my brain function and everything is fine, it doesn't mean I'm good to play — not if I still don't feel quite right.

That's what I've learnt: I know when I'm right. It becomes clear. You get that moment every time you get a knock. You might feel a bit funny for a day or so, then bang, you're good again. Although 'bang' might not be the best word.

Resting the brain — not reading or watching television — is definitely tougher than resting a knee.

The rehab goes well and by Round 10, I'm ready to come back against the Sharks.

Start again.

Todd Blackadder . . . calm, steely and great self-belief.

If you could pick someone to be standing in front of the team after winning one game out of the first six, including three losses in a row, Toddy would be that man. He's calm, steely, and his self-belief never wavers. It's not so much what people say in those situations, as how they say it. Some coaches can be talking up a storm about belief and you can see the doubt and panic behind their eyes.

After drawing the first game against the Force while I'm away, the boys manage to put together some results, albeit pretty scratchy ones — a three-point win over the Waratahs in Sydney, a six-point win over the Stormers at Jade, three points over the Bulls at Jade, before having the bye and taking stock.

We're eighth on the points table, but just three points adrift of the top four. We're on the cusp — the season is still salvageable if we win the next game against the competition leaders, the Sharks, but a loss will see us lose touch. Our defence has been pretty solid, but we're not scoring tries and we're not getting bonus points. We've lost four of our stars from last season — Mose's gone to Japan, and Dan and Corey and Casey are injured — but guys like Thomas Waldrom and Stephen Brett and Ryan Crotty and Tim Bateman are doing their damndest to step up.

But the biggest problem is yet another change in the referees' interpretation of the tackled ball rule. Correction: there has been no change in *interpretation*, officially, but there's been a change of *emphasis*.

Whatever they call it, there seems to be an annual rotation. Year One, the referees decide to make sure the attacking team gets just reward for its endeavours. Year Two, they decide to make sure the tackled ball is contestable for the defending team. This is a Year Two. Anyone who looks half on his feet seems able to have a go for the ball and is getting away with it. So instead of having just your really good fetchers getting into good position, anyone within cooee of the tackled ball can have a dig with impunity. I'm half expecting to see the ballboys and spectators join in.

The result is that there's no advantage in playing with the ball in your own half. Too dangerous.

So when we travel to Durban, we adopt a new strategy against the Sharks. Instead of moving the ball wide, we kick and try to keep them in their own territory, then pressure them in lineouts and breakdowns, and with suffocating defence try to knock them off their stride. It's not much fun — we prefer to play rugby with the ball, not without it — but it works. We get home by three points.

I have a good game, considering how long I've been out, and score a try off a Kieran Read assist. My base fitness — and the fact that my knee injury only stopped me running for about 10 days — allows me to see out the full 80. The lungs and legs are fine, but I get a blow to the forehead and have to get the medics to stop the blood.

We blow it at Bloemfontein a week later, getting beaten by the bottom-of-the-table Cheetahs 20–13. We forget the lessons of last week, try to run it at them after being encouraged by scoring early, and make a ton of handling errors.

Which makes the next match against the Lions in Jo'burg a must-win. But there's a problem.

Against the Cheetahs I collect another blow to the head, which opens me up above the eye. I'm named in the team for Saturday, but I'm still not feeling 100 per cent right at Thursday practice. It's not just the sore eye under the gash, but a familiar feeling that's difficult to describe, a kind of cloudiness. It's not bad, but it's not right either, so I follow my own protocols and withdraw, even though I know this latest withdrawal will precipitate speculation that my days in rugby are numbered.

I can't look that far ahead or allow the speculation to deflect me from doing the right thing in the moment. If I feel I can do the job right, I'll play. If I can't, then I won't.

As it happens, they don't need me. Jonathan Poff plays well in my place — George Whitelock is injured too — and it's one of our best attacking performances of the season. We get the win and the priceless bonus point, which takes us up to sixth on the points table, still three away from making the semis. We're still in the hunt.

By the time we get back to Christchurch I'm feeling fully recovered, and although I'm initially bracketed with Jonathan for the game against the Reds, there's no way I'm missing it.

The Reds have suffered decimating injuries, including Will Genia, whereas some of ours, like Brad Thorn, are coming right.

Making a break for the Crusaders against the Reds at Christchurch, 2009.

We belt them 32–12 in a cold, slippery southerly, get the bonus point and stay in the race. Toddy unloads the bench and I end up defending at first-five for the final minutes. I think it might be the only time I've ever played in the backs. Bet Dan, probably still on crutches, in front of a TV, is worried!

The calculators come out before our last game against the Blues at Eden Park, and the general consensus seems to be that we'll need another bonus point to make the semis. But we realise as early as the first half that it's not going to be a bonus point sort of game. It's all we can do to get the win.

We're down 13–12 with four minutes to go, when Rangi — Leon MacDonald — scrapes over a wobbly drop-kick. The media aren't slow to make the Cardiff comparisons. Neither am I. *It was a planned move, fellas.* And it's also Rangi's farewell to rugby in New Zealand, unless we make the finals.

The play-offs aren't decided until the ninety-first minute of the last game of the weekend, when the Bulls beat the Sharks 27–26 in Durban. That eliminates the Sharks and means the Chiefs finish second and play the third-placed Hurricanes.

Somehow, we've 'scrapped and scratched' — as one scribe puts it — our way to the fourth and last semi-final position. We finish with the same points as the Waratahs, but we beat them on points difference, courtesy of the best defensive record of any team. If defence is about attitude, that's us, but we're also second last on tries scored, and we have to own that stat too.

'Had anyone wandered through Cathedral Square in mid-March brandishing a wad of cash and daring anyone to bet against the Crusaders making the Super 14 play-offs,' writes Richard Knowler in *The Press*, 'they probably would have been wrapped in a blanket and gently asked just which institution they called home.'

But we've made it, against all odds, and have bugger all time to pack for the semi in South Africa, and go. John Miles, our logistics manager, does it tough when the turnaround is this tight — 100 bags of playing kit and luggage has to be packed out of his room at the back of the grandstand. Much easier for me: training kit, change of clothes, two pairs of new or near-new boots in the suitcase and, most important items, two mouthguards in my carry-on so there's no risk of them being lost in transit. Everything else can be replaced, even boots, but I won't step on the field without my mouthguard — particularly against the Bulls.

It's a pretty similar scenario to the 2007 semi-final, where we got stuffed: Hougaard kicked 27 points and Dan kicked 12, in a dour, bruising confrontation. As we fly across the Indian Ocean once again, we try to keep those terrible Yogi Berra words out of our heads — 'It's déjà vu all over again!' — because we're going to Pretoria and we know what we're going to get.

Some things against the Bulls never change. It'll be hot and dry and hard. Your throat will be stinging, your lungs bursting. It'll be an unrelentingly physical confrontation and you've got to be up for that. In my Warwick on game day, I write: *Courage on D and at breakdown. Keep coming. Keep getting up.*

You've also got to get ahead early and take the 50,000-plus blue horde up in the grandstands out of the game. The ball flies so much further at altitude that you can't give away penalties in your half or even 10 metres into their half. If you do, no matter if you're playing well, they'll keep the scoreboard ticking over and stay in touch, waiting for a chance to get territory, hold possession and start grinding you down. Once they get momentum, they're so difficult to stop.

That danger of penalties has been exacerbated this season by the way the tackled ball is being refereed. So once again we develop a game plan that goes against our instincts and is very different from anything we've used against them before.

When we watch the video of the teams that have done well against them, it becomes clear that you get a lot of reward for *not* playing, particularly in your own half. We figure that it'll be difficult for them to kick goals or get any front-foot if we kick deep, force them to make play from back there, or kick back to us. We'll only have a crack if and when they kick poorly. We realise that's going to take a lot of patience and discipline, because our natural tendency is to have a crack.

The game doesn't start well — we're seven points down after 10 minutes when Habana comes in from the blindside wing to take an inside ball and slice through under the posts.

But then we knuckle down, stick to the plan and it works — spectacularly. The Bulls kick badly, we force a ruck on their 22, shift it quickly by hand to the left and put Adam Whitelock over in the corner. *Planned move.*

Ten minutes later we hoist the perfect up-and-under and Kieran takes it on the full and smashes over close to the posts. *Planned move.* 20 points to 7.

There's an eerie silence in the stadium as we really climb into them, and I know that if we can make it to halftime without coughing up any points, we've got them stuffed.

But within sight of halftime we do exactly what we said we wouldn't do. Don't play anywhere near our own half, we agreed, keep putting it back and making them play.

Instead, a couple of guys try fancy-dan stuff in our own half. From the first, Akona Ndungane is put away on the left for a try in the thirty-second minute: 20–14. In the thirty-sixth minute Thomas Waldrom gets sin-binned. Thirty-seventh minute, Morne Steyn drops a goal: 20–17. Ditto what seems moments later: 20–20. Thirty-ninth minute, Jared Payne tries a chip-and-chase, the ball sits up for Pierre Spies, who runs 50 metres down the middle of the field to score under the posts: 20–27.

In eight minutes we've shipped 20 points and we go into halftime shell-shocked.

The second half's a struggle. We defend with huge heart, making twice as many tackles as the Bulls, but we can't get our game back. Meanwhile, Man of the Match Morne Steyn does what Bulls' fly-halves learn to do at their mother's breast — kicks a penalty and two more dropped goals. Tick-tock, tick-tock.

Two mistakes, deviations from the game plan, momentum gone, game over.

'A lot of the guys haven't been through an experience like this, and hopefully they'll be better next year,' says Toddy in his measured way after the game. He talks about the attitude of the guys through a season where we've had to battle back from a bad start, got to the semis without some of our stars, and, probably, got the best out of what we had.

Owen Franks — at contact training he doesn't know 50 per cent.

Some individuals have really stepped up. If last year was about the rise of Kieran, this year is about Owen Franks. He's such a strong young bugger and relishes contact. You'd get tired just watching him and his brother Ben in the gym, and sure as hell, if we're playing gentle 50 per cent contact at training and you get hit hard, it'll be Owen. He doesn't know 50 per cent.

There are in fact a lot of positives to be taken from what we've done as a team.

But not for me. For me, it's been an unsatisfactory stop-start season, which has just stopped again.

During the second half against the Bulls, I twist the same knee. I make it through the match, but when I get home the scan shows I've partially detached the lateral ligament on the outside of the knee. I'm told I'm lucky — it's close to being operation material, which would have meant a six-monther.

The following week I'm back in a knee brace — same brace, same knee, different ligament — as I watch the Bulls smash the Chiefs 61–17 at Loftus in the final of the Super 14.

The South Africans seem to have recovered from their World Cup hangover.

The game seems to have changed.

I try to keep my head up and commit to another rehab plan.

Start again.

Down

When Ted is interviewed before the opening 2009 Tri Nations match against Australia at Eden Park, he talks about his pride in our achievements last year — all the cups, the third Grand Slam in history on the northern tour, no tries scored against us, number-one world ranking, all of that. Then he says: 'We are likely to get beaten . . . I don't think that is going to be a bad thing.'

Whoa. I'm struggling back to match fitness after my knee injury and have been a spectator during the less-than-impressive Iveco series against France and Italy, but I don't understand why he would say that. It looks a bit like we're trying to get our excuses in first, and smacks of defeatism and just isn't the sort of thing an All Black coach says at the start of a season, even if it reflects the reality of the situation.

Ted's great at the big picture, but I'm obviously not seeing the same one he's seeing.

Two months later, it turns out that, if anything, Ted's looking through rose-tinted spectacles. By early September, we're at a nadir, our lowest ebb since Cardiff. The wheels have fallen off the All Black machine and we're struggling to figure out how to get them back on again.

It starts badly at Dunedin, where we get beaten 22–27 in the opening Iveco series match by what has been touted as France B.

Okay, we've lost a lot of players. Dan and Ali are still overcoming serious Achilles injuries, and Anthony Boric, Jerome Kaino, Brendon Leonard, Conrad, Richard Kahui and Siti are all out, joined by Rudi Wulf when he falls awkwardly at training on the eve of the match and injures a shoulder. Rodney's been ordered to take a break after a lacklustre Super 14. So we go into the test with some relatively untried combinations, particularly at loose forward, with Adam Thomson wearing the No. 7 alongside Kieran and Liam Messam. Nevertheless, as one train-spotter of a critic pointed out, we still go into that test with 360 caps against France's 342, and should never have been beaten to the hit for 80 minutes.

It seems we get smacked by the reality of test rugby every year. Last year it was England, but only for about 10 minutes. Smithy says Super 14 is Mars and test rugby is Venus, and we're still on Mars. Both might be warmer than Carisbrook. While part of our failure on a frigid Dunedin night could be put down to the inevitable transition from Super 14 to test rugby, it's made worse by the IRB's rulings about which of the ELVs are going to become permanent parts of the game.

In May, 10 of the 13 global experimental law variations were formally ratified into the rules of the game by the IRB rugby committee. Most of the ratified ELVs apply to scrums and lineouts and simply formalise what we've been doing for the best part of two seasons.

It's the ELVs the IRB decided to dump that hurt us.

The bent-arm penalty has been ditched, so the tap-and-go which had quickened the pace and kept the ball in play longer has gone. I still reckon if the bent-arm penalty had been reffed the way the IRB intended, where a full penalty was awarded if the offence was deliberate, it might have survived. But it wasn't, and didn't.

The other rule that's gone is the one allowing the defenders to pull down a rolling maul. That rule made the rolling maul easier to defend against — and therefore less often used — but the IRB thought that was a safety issue, so the old rule is back. The maul hasn't often been a strength of New Zealand rugby, but I'm glad it's back. It may contradict other basic rugby rules, like being allowed to tackle the man with the ball, and obstruction, but it's unique to rugby and, if done well, another weapon in the armoury.

An objective observer might ask why, however, when faced with rule amendments which simplify the game and lift the pace, the IRB has once again bowed to complexity and stasis.

Whatever, using Smithy's analogy, the rule changes leave us on Mars, where there are lots of tap-and-gos and virtually no rolling mauls, and Carisbrook turns out to be an unlikely Venus.

France take us on right up the middle, punishing us with rolling mauls and drives from lineouts. And, it has to be said, a level of aggression and physical commitment and relish for close-quarter combat which looks like it surprises a few of the new guys, as much as they've been warned to expect it. There are missed tackles, dropped pill, mis-kicks and intercepted passes that make it a wonder the All Blacks even get close.

BJ Lochore later tells Ted that the boys might have been ready for battle, but they weren't ready for war.

Neither am I, but I'm not far off, faithfully rehabbing my knee, following another bloody plan, hoping to be ready for the opening Tri Nations match. I'm frustrated as all hell watching these guys who stuffed us at Cardiff do us over again. They might have left a few hard men at home, but there are still enough familiar spectres on the team-sheet to get the blood going: Clerc, Traille, Heymans, Caveman Chabal, Szarzewski and, of course, leading them, who else but Dusautoir.

Big Bad Brad runs down winger Vincent Clerc to save a try.

I'm not really part of it, but it's easy to sense that things are a lot grimmer in the build-up to the return game in Wellington. Ted's almost jovial mood of the week before has evaporated, not helped by the loss to injury of Adam Thomson and Horey. But Jerome Kaino, who became a heavy hitter at test level in last year's northern tour, is back at No. 6, and with Kieran having his second game at No. 8 and Tanerau Latimer at No. 7, the back row looks better balanced.

It isn't a memorable test, but it has one memorable moment, when Big Bad Brad runs down winger Vincent Clerc in the sixty-second minute to save a try. That's the winning of the test 14–10 on a foul night in Wellington, made fouler by a strange

My first club game in eight years — Christchurch against Lincoln, July 2009.

rule that gives France the Dave Gallaher Trophy. *Eh?* We're the holders, and we've drawn the series 1–1. But it's decided by points difference across the two games. *Which Einstein came up with that one?*

One trophy gone.

I play my first club game in eight years that weekend and the knee comes through okay, but as one of us gets up, another falls down. Ali pulls his Achilles in the build-up to the test against Italy, and the poor bastard needs surgery. Our locking stocks weren't great anyway, apart from Brad. We have rookie Isaac Ross calling the lineouts and Bryn Evans on the bench.

There's bugger all at stake against Italy at Christchurch, and we play accordingly, winning unimpressively. They've clearly not come to play, but just to lose by as little as possible. Not for the first time, we find it much harder to break down a team with that mindset.

There's no relief on television either. On the same weekend we're struggling to subdue Italy, the Aussies give France a 22–6 thumping, and Dingo Deans says they couldn't have hoped for a better build-up and that 'this year's series is shaping as the most open in years'.

If we have any doubts about not being rated after Robbie's quote and Ted's comments about losing and our less-than-impressive form against France and Italy, they're dispelled by a column by ex-Wallaby great Andrew Slack in the *New Zealand Herald*, headed 'Rubbish All Blacks? Pull the other one'. We seem to have fallen so far in public estimation that Aussies have to reassure the New Zealand public that we're not crap.

I'm determined that the team make a statement at Eden Park, just as we did last year, when our win at Eden Park was the defining moment of the season. We've got Rodney back, and Siti and Conrad and Horey.

But the Aussies have us scrambling, opening with pace and width. Berrick Barnes scores early, selling Siti a dummy and stepping through Mils' tackle after an Adam Ashley-Cooper break. Not a great start. I'm rusty and make a few mistakes, and it's clear that Conrad and Rodney and Horey are all finding their feet again at test level too.

Meanwhile, George Smith is right on his game and Giteau and Barnes seem to have more rhythm and timing than we do, and their lineout dominates ours. At one stage, we're 10 points down. We're still losing at halftime, but not lost. Down 10–13, it should have been more.

In the second half, we start showing character. Our scrum dominates theirs. Their scrum becomes as bad as our lineout. With 20 to go, Jerome charges down a Giteau clearance, and Stephen Donald kicks the penalty to put us in front. From there, we dominate territory and possession and the last quarter of the game is our best. We grind it out and get there 22–16. It's not pretty, one try each, but neither are the conditions for running rugby.

Some guys step up. Kevvy and Kieran and Owen Franks make a difference when they come on. Richard Loe doubts that Owen's scrummaging is up to test level, but that's not what I'm seeing.

When we take off for South Africa next morning, I've no reason to believe that we're not on the up and up.

While we've been flailing our way through testing wintry conditions, the South Africans have been on a high, ramping on from the Bulls' demolition of the Chiefs in the Super 14 final to a three-test series win against an impressive British Lions outfit. That might have been a lot closer than the Boks were comfortable with, but the quality of the rugby was right up there, on hard grounds with the sun on their backs.

I'm hoping the travel will bind us together and the new environment will stimulate and lift us. We'd like to build on what we did at Newlands last year, even though it's a tough ask to travel to Bloemfontein and play at high altitude in the space of a week.

Some guys step up . . . me and Kevvy after beating Australia at Eden Park in 2009.

Down

That week in Bloemfontein I ask myself some questions in the Warwick that crystallise my worries and look for solutions:

When I struggle to get into the game and make an impact:
Get backs to set close target and give me something to hit.
Call drive so I can get involved.
Get in position early, run hard, demand the ball.
When ref is being inconsistent with his rulings. Especially when it is eliminating my effect:
Be calm when I talk to him.
Use right words — Can I speak when you have a moment?
Is that the standard for the game?
Put pressure on him.
Use short sentences which are to the point.
When I get taken out trying to get at ball at breakdown:
If they are putting one or two on me, must be opportunities for others.
Talk to others (8, 12, 13) and get them to do my job.
When I get taken out, identify who and why it is working.
When I'm planting and not getting shoulders on when tackling:
Why? Maybe I'm on the dancefloor too early. Leaving a little later will help.
Just keep going, and no worries about being stepped.
Big guys coming, get low and use shoulder. Just need to be confident.
NO FEAR.

We go in with the same pack, but bring in Brendon Leonard for Jimmy Cowan and Joe Rocks for Cory Jane.

We lose, but not for lack of effort or guts. Afterwards I tell the media that perhaps we weren't smart enough to play at the right end of the field. Euphemism. We play spiritedly, but dumb.

We set a target of not giving away more than 10 penalties in a game, but by the 30-minute mark, we've already given away seven. We give them away like a lolly scramble, inventing new and interesting ways to incur Alain Rolland's wrath. Some of them can be put down to Bok pressure, forcing us to try desperate moves in our own half. But two crooked put-ins to our dominant scrum? A miscued 22 drop-out by a prop?

Luckily, Ruan Pienaar's having an off-day with the boot and we grind our way back from 17–3 to 20–16 in the third quarter, after a couple of Stephen Donald penalties and a brilliant try by Conrad. We're getting some traction in the scrums and at the breakdowns, and despite Matfield's dominance of our lineout, we can hear them gasping. We hammer them in a series of drives, but when the ball is finally released, Piri throws it to Jaque Fourie. It's not the only inaccuracy which lets the pressure off, but it's a critical one.

Number-one world ranking gone. The Boks have it back.

We've got a week to sort ourselves before the return game at Durban. No excuses this time, it's at sea level and we should be acclimatised. We can't use the thin air to excuse our kicking, catching or chasing, or the lineout throws.

But we're worse, not better. We play reckless, panicky rugby, trying to run it when it isn't on. Joe Rocks neglects to force the ball or kick it, and instead tries to run it out from behind our goal-line. We play like we don't know each other. The Boks don't have to play a lot of rugby: we try to play enough for both teams. Certainly, we make enough mistakes.

The Boks kick better than us and Habana is a magnificent chaser, so they're always applying pressure through their kicks, whereas ours are mostly handing the ball back, either through inaccuracy or by giving them a lineout. One way or another, we give possession back more than 30 times. Heinrich Brussow is superlative on the ground.

Second trophy gone — the Freedom Cup.

We come home with our tail between our legs with 20 days to regroup before facing the Aussies in Sydney.

The only good news is that Dan has come through his low-key return to rugby, via a club game at his home town of Southbridge. So it looks like we'll have Dan back, but I'm not sure even he could have saved us from our worst run of results since I've been an All Black. Three defeats in six tests.

One more loss and any chance of retaining the Tri Nations will be gone, and the Bledisloe will also be up for grabs.

Is it a question of personnel? There are guys not playing well, for sure. Rodney is a worry — the respite from the Iveco series doesn't seem to have given him the fire back. You can't doubt Rodder's willpower, but the fierce joy for the fray isn't there yet.

Joe Rocks saved our arses last year against Munster by doing what he does best — running round or over people with the ball in hand. This season, either he's lost form or it's a different game. Instead of catch-and-pass, it's kick-and-chase: instead of doing one-on-ones at training, looking for speed and agility, Joe and the other wingers are standing under high balls. Joe might be a bit like the rest of us — unsure quite how the ground has shifted so quickly, from a ball-in-hand game to ball-in-air.

Back in May, Paddy O'Brien outlined the new tackle ball ruling endorsed by the IRB. Under this ruling, if the tackler or the first person arriving at the breakdown has their hands on the ball, they're now entitled to keep their hands on it even though a ruck has formed.

This has swung the advantage at the breakdown back to the defending team in a major way. We've been slow to acknowledge that. We've been trying to play an expansive high-tempo game with ball in hand. Time and again, we've been caught trying to run the ball back from Bok kicks. Time and again our runners have been nailed and we've had to scramble and have conceded kickable penalties.

In the face of criticism from the likes of Laurie Mains and John Plumtree, who've both coached in South Africa and advocate structure, field position and aggression, Ted's still saying that we're playing the right style of football. He admits that it's high risk, and difficult, particularly when you're living off crumbs. He believes that if we'd only nailed a couple of opportunities . . . Smithy agrees, saying that if we kick long against the Boks, it relieves the pressure for a few seconds, then the ball comes right back at us in the air, with great chasers arriving at the same split second.

We've got to play better, not differently, is the coaches' mantra.

Living off crumbs is inevitable if we can't win our own lineouts. The media pressure comes down on Shag. His remark about flushing a bad performance down the dunny gets a lot of blow-back.

The real worry is that Paddy O'Brien said back in May that there'd be no further changes to the rules until after the RWC in 2011.

Somehow we've got to figure out how to play our game under these rules.

The Aussies in Sydney aren't necessarily the best gauge of how we're going in that respect. At one stage we're 15–6 down, then 18–16 down with five minutes to go. Dan misses a drop-goal but we keep

We've got this lineout right . . . Kieran Read soars above Rocky Elsom at Sydney.

pressing and get a penalty in the seventy-eighth minute, which Dan nails with complete composure. Then we hold our nerve at the very end of the game when the Aussies lay siege.

No disrespect to Beaver — Stephen Donald — who always gives it everything, but Dan makes a hell of a difference to our kicking game and general confidence. His tactical brain and left foot keeps putting us where we need to be.

It's a huge relief to win, if only by a single point. We show real guts and character — that's been true of pretty much every game, even when we've gone badly. Ted should be revelling in going 5–1 up against Dingo Deans, but with the resurgence of the Boks, Ted vs Robbie has become the inconsequential sideshow it always should have been.

A win's a hell of a lot better than a loss — and we have again secured the Bledisloe Cup — but can we say any more that 19–18 over the Wallabies is a step in the right direction?

The Boks are the benchmark — they've already won the Mandela Cup for the

Got it! The Bledisloe, Sydney, 2009.

A try for me, but a shattering loss against the Boks at Hamilton.

series over Aussie — and we're determined to throw the kitchen sink at them on our home territory at Hamilton. We trail them by four on the points table. If we can come away with a bonus point victory, we've got a shot at retaining the Tri Nations championship. If we lose, South Africa takes it.

We prepare well. There's intensity during the week, a definite edge. *Physicality is the key*, I write in the Warwick. *Must have quality set piece. Positive mentally in how we're gonna play.*

I'm sure we'll have a big one. When the edge is there, we always do.

So what happens in Hamilton, the way it happens, leaves me as low as I've been since Cardiff.

It's not just about being beaten 32–29. We're comprehensively outplayed until the last 20. We don't win one of our own lineouts in the first half. Victor Matfield seems to know our calls better than we do. Francois Steyn kicks three penalties from inside his own half. You could do a word association which would be pretty consistent across almost every report of the game, including our own. Lineout . . . shambles. Ball retention . . . sloppy. Decision making . . . flawed.

The Boks are the Tri Nations champions. Another trophy lost from the cupboard.
Fans aren't happy. The media aren't happy. We're not happy.

'Surely now the lineout has become intolerable?' writes Gregor Paul. 'If Steve Hansen can't fix it, should someone else be given the chance?'

Larger questions are looming, not just in our minds. We've lost four tests out of eight.

'The time has come,' writes the same scribe, 'to ask whether, two years out from the World Cup, it's time for a rethink — have the coaching team lost the dressing room?'

The answer is no. The coaches haven't lost the dressing room. But the dressing room is in danger of losing itself.

We — I — might be almost at a lower ebb than Cardiff. Different, would be a better way of describing it.

In Cardiff, even after we'd lost, I still felt we were the best team there. That's what made the loss so frustrating. We didn't play to our potential.

This time, for the first time, I have a thought in my head that I can't remember ever having before about any All Black team I've been in.

Maybe we're not as good as we thought we were.
Maybe, no matter what we do, we're not actually good enough.

Keep getting up

If a week is a long time in politics, it's an eternity in sport, particularly after a demoralising loss. We fly to Wellington on Sunday, and it's a difficult day; I'm just hating it. That night I don't sleep, and at 6 am on Monday morning go for a walk around Oriental Bay to try to clear my head, sort myself.

Need to be positive, I write in the Warwick when I get back to the hotel, *and keep belief with boys in what we're doing.*

There's a shit-load of criticism coming down on the coaches, and a lot of agonising over the course of the week leading up to the final test of the Tri Nations against Australia.

It might be sheer desperation that drives a performance which turns out to be more than enough.

We whack the Wallabies 33–6 in Wellington. The edge we felt in training last week before the Boks is delivered on the field this week, and we hammer the Aussies in the breakdown, but also in the set-pieces. Even our lineout delivers, with Tom Donnelly featuring, having been brought in for this test.

Tom's great virtue is that he hasn't been infected by the loss of confidence that pervades the rest of us. Tom has a ton of experience, is a pretty phlegmatic individual and has an expectation that if he does what he's always done, he'll win most of his ball. Simple. And that's exactly what happens, apart from the first throw which goes over his head and has the rest of us a bit jittery, including Reado who's now making the calls. But Tom isn't fazed and the next throw goes to hand and we're away. It's gratifying to see Tom play well. He played against me for Rotorua Boys' in the New Zealand Schools First XV final in 1998, and he's a great example of someone who stuck around to pursue his All Black dream when he could easily have gone overseas.

If defence is about attitude, we have it in spades. It's also my best game of the season, which helps.

But we wonder how much can be read into the win. It must be the lowest moment of Robbie's tenure as coach, as his players 'capitulate' — his word. There's

Sheer desperation against Australia at Wellington in 2009. Wallaby tackler is Mark Chisholm.

now a feeling that the Aussies, while always worthy test opponents, are no longer the gold standard in terms of their physicality and tactical approach. On what we've seen this season, there are two sides we've got to benchmark ourselves against. One is obviously the South Africans and the other, on the strength of what they did to us in Dunedin and Wellington, is the French.

We don't play the South Africans again until next year, but there's a game against France at the end of our impending end-of-year northern tour.

That's the game we decide to target. Beating a full-strength France in Marseilles would finally put Cardiff 2007 to rest. We'd like it to be the first step towards RWC 2011.

We know we have to start looking forward, not back, but before that we have to put the Aussie win in context, look at our abysmal season and make some clear-eyed decisions about how much that test really meant, and where we're at.

We might have retained at least one cup in the NZRU trophy cupboard, the Bledisloe, probably the one that means the most to us after Old Bill, but losing four out of nine tests is never going to be acceptable for any All Black team. Chief Executive Steve Tew voices a common concern when he says, 'I guess we can all live with defeats if the performances have been good. I think we can all see they haven't been up to the standard we have achieved in the past.'

That hurts, but we have to suck it up.

Ted's quoted after Hamilton saying there are no plans to change the All Blacks' tactics. But at a leaders' group meeting in early October at Clearwater, just to the west of Christchurch, everything is up for grabs.

We look at ourselves first. A lot of the senior players were out for the first couple of tests, so the leaders didn't set the direction of the team and lead it properly. Then when we rolled back in, perhaps we thought it was just going to happen. We agree that we haven't been playing as well as we could have, and we haven't really been tight and driven the team like we should have. It's been the coaches doing it because they had to do it, and we just allowed it to happen rather than saying we're driving this team too.

We feel we need to get right back to basics and drive the team, and have good conversations with the coaches, so we all really are on the same page — no doubts.

We pick apart the season from an individual point of view, then look at the team environment and issues.

The same things keep coming up for both coaches and players. That sometimes we feel we're on a treadmill, not getting the same enjoyment as in the past, we've got a bit stale.

How do we get the meaning back, so it isn't just the same old stuff?

We might have found one of the keys to that in South Africa after our losses to the Boks in Bloemfontein and Durban. They were playing with great character and heart, so when they invited us to their changing rooms for a beer after the game in Durban, we said too right. As much as we appreciated the beer, the coaches also wanted to read what they had on their walls and generally have a wee nosey. It soon became apparent to us that the South Africans were playing for transformation, they were playing to advance the cause of the Rainbow Nation, they were playing for something bigger than themselves.

For Ted and Smithy and Shag, it reinforced the need for us to meet them emotionally. The Boks were putting their bodies on the line for something other than the game, whereas we were very task focused. So we began talking about using emotional triggers for big games.

I've got to say that when it was first touted, I had some doubts about this. I believed that All Blacks should be able to find sufficient motivation within themselves and from the All Black legacy. People say that they're playing for their country or their family, and yes, I do that too, but mostly I play for me. It might be really selfish, but that's what I do. I know that if I do that, if I live up to my internal drivers — pride in myself and my performance — then I'll also serve the team. I was also worried about what happens when you've used up all your emotional triggers. What happens when you roll them out the second or third time?

However, part of being in a team is recognising that not everyone works the way you do, and most of the other guys thought it would be helpful to give it a try.

The coaches have also come up with a radical change they want to run past us, and get our buy-in. They tell us they want to change roles: Ted from defence to the forwards, Shag from forwards to back attack, Smithy from attack to defence and counter-attack.

We're a bit thrown to begin with, but can see the logic once they explain to us that while they were putting a lot of pressure on players to make personal improvements, to get up every day and try to be the best in the world, they felt that they themselves were stagnating a bit, plateauing. They felt that by changing their roles, they'd force themselves to learn again, and to work harder on getting better.

The coaches are aware that the role changes will provoke all kinds of speculation — as indeed they do, one journalist inevitably hauling out the hoary old 'changing the deck-chairs on the Titanic' cliché — about who had precipitated the changes, whether they had been mandated by the NZRU or whether they're an indication of player power. What I know is that player power is a product of the changes, not a driver of them.

Ted hasn't coached the grunts for a long time and that means me and Horey and the guys all of a sudden have to really make sure we know what's going on, rather than just meandering along. When Ted sits us down and starts quizzing us on different aspects of the forward effort, we start talking about things we'd just taken for granted. Details, assumptions. What are you trying to do there with that lineout call? Where is the space? Where'd you think it would be? His questions force us to re-evaluate, and take more responsibility for the solutions.

Once we've been through that process, we feel like we have more ownership, which is hugely important.

Ted and me at training. He hasn't coached the grunts for a long time . . .

It's the same for the backs with Steve, who himself played at centre.

Defence won the Crusaders two Super championships back in the late nineties, and it was Smithy who'd set up those systems, so he was delighted to be back in charge of that aspect of our game and throws himself into it.

The big question underlying all that is said and done at Clearwater is how do we play South Africa? How do we combat their game plan? What is broken and needs changing? What isn't broken and is worth keeping?

Clearly, we aren't that good at a kick-and-chase game. That's where we've come to grief. The Boks were putting bombs up, chasing like hell, forcing us to cough the ball up in our own half. Once they got the ball back on the front foot, that's when their big guys got into the game. Then we were defending, and in desperation were giving away penalties too easily under the new tackled ball rule interpretation. Pretty bloody simple to analyse, but difficult to combat.

Our strength has always been to use the ball. We want to counter-attack; we want to have a crack. That's fine when it's on, but what we're not getting right is timing — when to counter. Dan and I are pretty pragmatic: we want to do whatever it takes to win, and it's clear that throwing it around willy-nilly won't work. But the coaches want us all to be aligned and for that alignment to be around keeping the faith in our traditional game of athletic, running rugby. Yes, we have to be able to mix up our game, play a bit of their game, but still be able to take our opportunities with the ball in hand. They urge us not to get too bound up in changing our game to meet the current interpretations: they have an inkling that despite Paddy O'Brien's assurances that there won't be any changes before the RWC, rugby globally has become so stodgy and kick-dominated that there'll have to be changes.

Sometimes the opportunities to play the way we aspire to play weren't there because our set-piece wasn't good enough. We couldn't rely on winning our own ball at lineout. That really stuffs up your ability to work to any kind of a game plan. We've got to fix that. And we want our scrum to be feared.

What's the formula for great All Black teams? I write in the Warwick. *They dominate physically up front. They have great decision makers, and they have the pace and power to kill teams if the chance comes.*

For all the talk-fest, it's Brad, never a man for over-analysis, who provides the biggest moment of clarity. He's been marking Bakkies Botha at the front of the lineout in the Springbok tests. I'd been giving Brad a bit of shit that he was Bakkies' twin, and they do have a certain resemblance, helped by their reliance on God, presumably different incarnations, to bless them in creating mayhem against one another. But Bakkies is an even bigger man than Brad, maybe five centimetres taller, and yet Brad relished going up against him. Absolutely loved pitching himself in there, and had done reasonably well winning his own ball in an otherwise dysfunctional lineout.

At Clearwater, Brad decides he's had a gutsful of what he's hearing. 'We're always talking about how good the bloody opposition are,' he rasps. 'What about us? I reckon it's about time we started talking about how good we are. *We're* big, *we're* strong, *we're* skilled, *we're* fast. Let's talk about that.'

So we do. It's a moment of clarity that helps change our mindset before we embark on the end-of-year tour.

When the team gathers at the Heritage, I'm conscious of the lack of direction earlier in the season and get them together at one of the meeting rooms, lay out an All Black jersey on the floor in front of us and ask them a question:

Will you do what's expected of you as an All Black?

Maybe some of us don't know exactly what that is. Or why there are expectations of this team.

It's simple. Over time, the All Blacks have been the best, the winningest team in rugby, setting the standard for the world. There've been some great men who spilt blood for this jersey, made sacrifices, dating back to amateur days when pride was all they were playing for. We can look at that legacy in two ways: as a burden that inhibits us, or as something we can embrace.

The great thing is that this group has an opportunity to add to this proud history, to be a part of it. I'd be bloody disappointed if our own expectations of ourselves and each other were anything less than that.

How do we ensure we do that? What does each of us need to do each week to ensure this happens?

I talked last year about toughness and the state you need to be in when you turn up to play. Bone-deep preparation, not skin deep. You can turn up and do your thing, do what you have to do, put in another day at the office. Or you can put your body on the line, empty the tank. Or you can go one step further, spill some blood, have one of those big, big days, and leave a piece of yourself out there.

For this team to perform, we need the whole team to empty the tank each and every time they pull on the black jersey. Four or five of us have to go that step further. It won't be the same guys every week.

That's where we have to be.

That's not where we've been these last three games.

You might think that's an unreasonable expectation, but there are plenty who'd be willing to give that. We're the lucky ones who have been chosen to wear the jersey.

When you look at that black jersey with the silver fern, yes it's unique, but it's just a piece of cloth sitting there. It only becomes something special when it's filled by men who have the right to wear it, men who are prepared to do things that others aren't prepared to do.

This jersey will show up the frauds, the imposters. It'll squeeze those who look for short cuts. You won't last in this jersey if you're not prepared to do the things you need to do to fill it.

What we've done well in the last three games is learn our roles, get structures right, done our homework. But that's only 20 per cent of it.

It's the other 80 per cent that we need to deliver. The toughness, ruthlessness, power, pace. The want. That's got to come from within, that inner desire to spill some blood if that's what it takes.

That's how the All Blacks have been successful, that's how trust in each other is earned. You've gotta know that when you go to the well, your mate beside you will do the same. Every time you pull that jersey on. That's what filling the jersey is about.

It's not about wearing this jersey, it's about filling it.

Love every minute of it.

Tokyo is this year's joint All Blacks/Wallabies fund-raiser venue for the NZRU and the ARU.

Tokyo, Hong Kong, Milan, Paris . . . to some extent, exotic and unique venues are wasted on us: we move from the inside of a hotel which is much the same as international hotels everywhere, to a training venue which is much the same as training pitches everywhere, and back to the hotel, staring out through the windows of the bus at a world which we can't get out and lose ourselves in. We have some downtime and go for walks in the vicinity of the hotel if it's safe, and sometimes we're taken out by locals to see the sights, but you never really forget the count-down to the job you're there to do, when you take the bus to a stadium of light, where you've got to deliver.

There are a lot of places I'd like to go back to when I don't have to be preoccupied about team dynamics and delivering a performance.

Which we do in Tokyo. Fired by Brad's words, we challenge in the air, attack the Aussie lineout, and reduce it to indecision and errors. Apart from a shaky 10 minutes before halftime, when Siti gets sin-binned and the Aussies score their first try against us in 260 minutes, we're better than solid. 32–19 is a bit of a walloping and makes it seven in a row over Australia. So far so good, but that doesn't tell us anything we didn't know after Wellington six weeks ago.

The following three weekends in Europe are a better indication of where we're at: frustrated.

Courtesy of Smithy, we've put out a stifling defence in each of the tests against Wales, Italy and England — extending our European clean sheet from way back in 2006 — but we've been stifled in turn.

Wales are tough, but we manage to keep our noses in front from go to whoa, and there are good signs in critical combinations, like Ma'a's power and Conrad's nous in the centres. They're now being talked about as the best in the world. Kieran starts at No. 8 over Rodney, and with Jerome at No. 6 and Adam Thomson doing well in Tokyo, the loosies are starting to gel as we play together more. Which means the end is in sight for Rodney, who hasn't been able to get the fire back.

There's a real sadness over the demise of Rodders. He's had a lot of injuries and is fighting a neck problem that won't go away, and he's fighting the rise of Kieran. Rodney's been one of our best for so many years, always combative, super-fit, tough. I've become used to him being there and doing what he's always done. It's been a surprise that, like Jerry, he's hit the wall so fast. It's not through lack of willpower, but sometimes the conscious mind seems unable to force the unconscious mind to go to the painful places any more. I hope that if that time comes for me, I'm the first to see it.

Italy turns out to be another painful place for Rodney, when he captains the side at San Siro, the great stadium in Milan which serves as base for AC Milan and Inter Milan. The game is supposed to be a showpiece for rugby in front of 80,000 Italian fans, but it turns into the worst possible advertisement for the game. Ref Stu Dickinson allows the Italian tighthead Martin Castrogiovanni to bore in on Crocky and for minutes on end the game stalls as scrum after scrum collapses and has to be reset on a pocket handkerchief of turf near the All Black line. A complete waste of time and opportunity, and Paddy O'Brien does the right thing by publicly lambasting Dickinson.

England at Twickenham isn't much better, and we're held to 6–6 until close to the last quarter, before we get away on them.

'Defence is now the measure by which this team should be defined,' writes

Ma'a's power and Conrad's nous, against Wales, 2009.

Gregor Paul. 'They are not the swashbucklers of old — this is a team built on the most basic principles of test football.'

Which is a lot kinder than Peter Bills, who, after the England game writes: 'Silly, elementary errors, poor wobbly finishing and a lack of composure, even from Daniel Carter for long periods, this was an unrecognisable New Zealand team.' And the ultimate condemnation: 'It was like watching England play.'

That bad?

And this: 'The UK media was full of lament, mourning the death of running rugby. There was a genuine sense of disbelief that there was no champion of the beautiful game any more.'

And this: 'The game plan was all about field position and ball security. Defence was the crushing weapon, with the ferocity of the tackling pressuring opponents. The All Blacks lived off other team's mistakes more than they ever had.'

That's more by necessity than design. We still have every intention to have a crack when we can, but our execution lets us down. For all that, we were up against a big brutal English pack, and it took us 60 minutes to take their legs and lungs away from them. We got over the top of them in the last quarter and won comfortably enough and, for my money, we played smart rugby.

Barking out instructions at Twickenham . . . It took us 60 minutes to take their legs and lungs away from them.

We're knackered, on our last legs, but we know we've got one more game in us. We're trying to play the game we aspire to, we're trying to stay aligned to the coaches' vision and keep the faith, but it hasn't quite happened yet. I have a feeling that we're just a game away from getting it right and playing the way we envisage we can, if we can just hold it together long enough. We back off training, take it carefully, as we head for sunny Marseilles.

That week when we do our priority planning, I tell Smithy we won't need any defence this week. Smithy's really uncomfortable with that, but I'm sure that we don't need to, we haven't had a try scored against us in the last three matches and the boys are highly motivated. Trust us. Smithy does, and that week he works on our attacking game, running the drills he knows so well from his previous role, so that Ted and Shag can coach from behind.

That's an illustration of the coaches being flexible, and an illustration of the power of imagination and attitude. We're developing to the point where we don't have to smash each other physically as much as we used to, particularly on tour: we used to have mouthguard sessions for 40 minutes, sometimes 50. That's come down to five or eight minutes. The rest is accuracy and execution — and imagination, like the way I work on my drills by myself.

Before the tour began, we'd targeted the last game against France, and we're hoping we can finish a particularly difficult season on a high note. And get at least one of our cups back, the Dave Gallaher Trophy.

There's also another, entirely unexpected prize on offer — the number-one world ranking is up for grabs, after South Africa get stuffed by France and Ireland (not to mention their midweek side getting beaten by club sides Leicester Tigers and Saracens).

We decide that this is the game where we take our first step towards Auckland and 2011, and leave Cardiff and 2007 behind. Look forward, not back. And yet . . .

There's a weird sense that this is where we should have been playing our quarter-final in 2007, here in the sun of Marseilles, not the gloom of Wales. Marseilles feels familiar — this is where we began our 2007 RWC campaign against Italy, and, unfortunately, played as well as we did at any stage of that tournament.

We're looking for some sort of step up, a shedding of the stifling shell we've been playing in. Maybe it's the perfect place to shed the remnants of the Cardiff legacy too.

I look at France's team-sheet and feel the familiar names bite home. Traille, Clerc, Heymans, Jauzion, Bonnaire, Chabal, Lionel Nallet, Sylvain Marconnet, William Servat, Szarzewski, along with some we're still getting to know, tough front-rowers like Fabien Barcella and Nicolas Mas. And, of course, the conductor, Dusautoir . . .

New coach Marc Lievremont appears to be putting together something special for 2011.

They did us at home in Dunedin and almost got over us in Wellington. Just a couple of weeks ago further along the coast at Toulouse, they dismantled our nemesis, the Springboks. The score was close enough, 20–13, but they bashed the

Skits night on the end-of-year tour, 2009. Rodders and I are the wannabe counter-terrorists.

Boks at their own brutal, physical game. We never got close to doing that to the Boks this year.

On a cool clear night at Stade Velodrome, we know we have to make a statement. Our recent history gives us any amount of edge and emotion for this game.

We're in the wrong jersey again, white, because France have gone for their dark strip, but that's the only thing wrong with tonight's picture, in front of 60,000 Marseillaise.

Marconnet and Barcella give us the big face-off after the haka, and bring real attitude to the first scrum, splintering us. Penalty. Three points down. But this time we're absolutely up for it, our lineout's working, we're hitting holes, and Dan's got his dancing shoes on. He's electric, taking it to the line and giving Ma'a and Conrad space and time. It doesn't immediately pay off, but soon we're able to put Siti away on the left and he goes round Clerc to score. But Julien Dupuy goals twice from penalties, and we're still down, 9–7.

There's a difference in approach from France: they've come to play. They believe they can beat us at our own game. They've brought their Toulouse tactics, not their Biarritz. That suits us. In the twenty-third minute we score from our own 22, when Mils sees some space on the counter, and puts Siti away. Fifty metres later, Siti finds Mils backing up inside and Mils is over. Try.

The signature moment comes shortly after, when Reado breaks their line, but we knock on. They have the put-in to a scrum in the shadow of their posts, but this

Life couldn't get any better at the end. We've whacked the French 39–12, got our number-one ranking back, and I've just won my second IRB Player of the Year Award.

time it's France who splinter and Jerome scores. Marconnet and Barcella have gone from roosters to feather dusters. If you put such store on face, what do you do when you lose it? From that moment, we feel like we've got them.

In the second half, we play with the pace and precision we've been looking for all season and we blow the French away five tries to none: 39–12. Even Dusautoir can't get into the game.

We've made the statement we wanted to make, needed to make. Reassured ourselves that we can still play, kept the faith with the coaches that if we create a solid platform, we can elaborate on that, build a game with so much width and pace that no one can live with us, even under the existing rules.

'That's the way you play the game,' I tell the media conference. I believe it. There've been so many moments of injury and doubt and difficulty this season, but in the end we've managed to play the way we've always aspired to play. And Smithy shakes my hand after the game and agrees that the defence was magnificent.

Dusautoir in defeat is as unreadably polite as he is in victory. Kipling may have been thinking of a Victorian Englishman when he wrote about meeting those two imposters, triumph and disaster, and treating them the same, but Dusautoir seems to fit it perfectly. He doesn't seem to sweat it, no matter what happens.

We've got the Dave Gallaher back. We've got the number-one ranking back. And I've won my second IRB Player of the Year Award.

But, more than that, we've now got more genuine world-class players than we had at the start of the year.

Cory Jane came in to the wing to replace Rudi Wulf as a converted fullback. But he's been a revelation, balanced, agile, very good with the ball in the air, receiving and kicking, the perfect modern wing. Ma'a's cemented his place alongside Conrad, after experiments with Dan and Beaver didn't work, and the Ma'a/Conrad double act is acknowledged as being up there with Jean de Villiers and Jaque Fourie as the best centre pairing in rugby. And it's been gratifying to see Jimmy Cowan really start to deliver consistent world-class performances week after week.

Kieran has been magnificent. Jerome has finally found his feet at test level and is delivering the explosive defence and attack that lifts him above the usual tight/loose No. 6. Tom Donnelly, so-called journeyman lock, has given us aerial stability and tough-mindedness in the second row.

Neemia Tialata's knees can't handle the volume of work needed to make him an effective force around the field for 80 minutes, but that scrum under the French posts showed he's still an international tighthead where it counts. And behind him there's Owen Franks, who hasn't followed the usual academy route to international rugby, but has come through the school of hard knocks, propping in senior club rugby when he was 18. *The Rise of Owen* might even make the constant calls for *The Return of Zarg* (Carl Hayman) redundant. At 21, Owen will come back next year older, wiser and even stronger. Then there's Ali, at home, recovering from his Achilles. It'd be great to see Spiderman fly again.

When you start weaving those guys into the 'veterans' who are still delivering, like Woody and Horey and Kevvy and Brad and Dan and Mils and Siti and me, there's the making of something special.

We've come a long way since a cold night in Dunedin in early June, a long way since a cold night in Cardiff two years ago. Gilbert Enoka reckons two years is often a significant marker in processing loss. It certainly feels like we've taken the step forward we needed to take.

No more looking back.

Bugger France 2007.

From here on, it's about New Zealand 2011.

Bring it on

A recurring theme at the leadership group back in October at Clearwater was staleness. How it all began to look the same: the games, the grounds, the opposition, the hotels, the departure lounges, the stadiums, the people, the places. We looked at ways of changing things.

You should be careful what you wish for.

In high summer, I fly up to the Tasman Glacier to Mount D'Archiac, right at the top of Lake Tekapo, the northern way-point of my first solo 500-kilometre flight. I've been lucky, got on to one of those nor'wester waves crashing over the Alps, so I'm surfing along the front edge of the lenticulars at close to 20,000 feet, on oxygen, as the GPS counts me down, keeping the speed up, looking ahead for the best place to turn, the vario bleeping or moaning in my ear as I gain or lose height. As I hit the way-point and turn east before heading back south, I can see across the Canterbury Plains, past Mayfield where Mum grew up, past the Rangitata, north to where the sun glints off the silver braids of the Rakaia and Waimakariri as they work their way across the plains. Between them, as they meet the coast, sits Christchurch, nestled into the crook of the Port Hills, the beginning of Banks Peninsula, fingering out into the blue Pacific.

When I shifted to Christchurch in 1999, I thought I'd made a big mistake. I was away for the first four or five weeks of term with the New Zealand Under 19s, and when I got back to Lincoln I felt left out. I had some mates who'd come up from Otago Boys', but most of my friends had gone to Otago Uni and had been having a huge Orientation Week, which seemed to go on for a month.

I was in a hall of residence with other sports scholars at Lincoln, but once I got through the first semester, I realised that I had four or five old mates in other halls, two or three I'd gone to school with, one even going back to North Otago age-group rugby. And I gradually made new friends, some through contact with Lincoln, my classes and the halls, some through the rugby academy, and some through my decision to play for the Christchurch club.

That was a biggie, because most of the guys on the rugby scholarship were playing for Old Boys, but Dad's brother Ian had played for Christchurch, and Bryan Mustchin, who was on the committee there, rang me before I went away with the Under 19s and showed me around the clubrooms. When I got back from Wales, I was in two minds what to do, and thought maybe I should just go with the other guys to Old Boys, when Bryan rang me and said, 'Training's on Tuesday.' So I went along to the Christchurch club to play with their Under 21s, met a whole new bunch of people and really enjoyed it.

I didn't quite finish my Bachelor of Agricultural Science degree at Lincoln — I'm three papers short, a semester's work, effectively. There's a certain regret about not finishing it off, because while I was there I worked hard for it, and Lincoln bent over backwards to help me cope with the increasing demands of professional rugby.

There was always an aegrotat option for exams I missed through rugby, but I didn't want any aegrotat passes on my results transcript, I wanted whatever grade I deserved, so I ended up sitting special exams. Lecturers would set different papers for me because I was sitting the exams after the rest of the students, whenever I got back from touring.

Despite my best intentions, the grades started slipping, A grades the first year, then the odd B would creep in, and then a C or two by the time I pulled the pin in the first semester of 2002. It got too difficult trying to keep all the balls in the air. Whenever we got a bye week, I'd be out until midnight or later every night until game night came round again. I wasn't doing myself justice and even though I was passing the exams, I wasn't actually learning anything. I thought, well, I can always come back to it. Maybe I will one day, or do a different degree. I enjoyed the academic challenge and kind of miss it.

It was leaving Lincoln that opened up flying to me, really. When rugby was all there was, I found I needed something else to challenge myself, so I began flying at the end of 2002.

Walking away from my degree was the right decision at the time, but you have to be careful about narrowing your world too much. If you want to get to the top in professional sport, it's easy to develop tunnel vision, seeing the world around you as a means to an end. To some extent that's inevitable because you've got to be selfish, in the sense of making sure you do whatever it takes to get the best out of yourself week after week. But there's a danger that soon your whole world ends up inside that tunnel, and you lose your friends from outside the sport who see the world through different frames of reference. I've been fortunate to keep old friends from school and university, who have that outside perspective.

Although, in saying that, keeping my old friends isn't just a matter of luck. Once I got really embedded in professional rugby, I made sure that I kept up those friendships outside rugby, not let them slip. I was often away, but when I was at home I'd make contact, because I realised it would be easy for them to start thinking, 'Ah well, he'll be busy,' and not bother. I've still got a bunch of mates who are hugely important to me. They're the ones who'll give me shit and tell me to pull my head in if they feel I'm getting carried away with myself.

The longer I stay in Christchurch the more I realise what a good decision it was to come here rather than stay in Dunedin. I'd done my time at school and it was an opportunity to move on to something else, and I've ended up with a great mix of friends around me, not to mention family.

Mum and Dad both went to school in Christchurch, so it was always more familiar to them than Dunedin, and when they sold the farm in 2002, they bought a lifestyle block to the west of the city and settled there. Jo and Sam live close by, and in 2008 I bought a townhouse close to Crusaders HQ in St Albans, and finally gave away the flatting to live more or less on my own, apart from Hayley and the occasional house-guest like Spiderman. I can — should — walk to work, though I seldom do.

Christchurch has become the centre of my world, for all those reasons and also because it's easy to get from there to the other places that are also important to me, either by driving one of the great roads of the world, from Fairlie across the Mackenzie Basin to Omarama or on over the Lindis Pass to Wanaka, or by flying myself down there.

In winter I usually bring the Discus back to Springfield airfield, about 25 minutes from Mum and Dad's, and get to glide around the foothills of the Alps and look out at the city that's become home.

In 2010 the pre-season preparation and housekeeping at St Albans for the Crusaders falls into place easily enough. Jacko has returned to claim the back seat of the bus alongside Brad and Corey, I've got a great leaders' group around me — Reado, Andy Ellis, Brad, Jacko, Ti'i Paulo, Corey and Dan. Owen and Corey share the sheriff duties, Colin Slade and Kahn Fotuali'i are the timekeepers, video entertainment is courtesy of Andy, Adam Whitelock, Tom Marshall and Isaac Ross, music by Kade, Sam Whitelock and Dan Bowden, Ministry of Perks and Lurks under Crocky (mentored by Toddy), Ministry of Information under the control of Pete Borlase, Robbie Fruean and George Whitelock, team song by Tim Bateman and Isaac, refreshments organised by Sean Maitland, Ryan Crotty and Zac Guildford. These are the off-field components of a team which expects to do the business on the field.

And we do, for quite a long time, despite getting thumped by the Reds at Suncorp in Round 2, where Ewen McKenzie is making his mark with a talented young inside back pairing of Will Genia and Quade Cooper.

I've been given leave to miss the first two games (and the pre-season stuff) so that I can recover from last year, and come off the bench in Round 3.

We put together a couple of bonus point wins at home over the Sharks and the Blues, before travelling to Hamilton to beat the Chiefs, and then beat the Lions for another bonus point.

Leading the Crusaders out for my 100th game of Super rugby, against the Stormers at Cape Town, 2010. Shame about the result.

By the time we get to Round 7 and the bye, we've won six out of seven, got the benefit of a swag of bonus points and are looking good for a home final.

Inevitably, the other team that is travelling really well and collecting even more bonus points is the Bulls.

A draw against the Canes in Wellington is okay, and we manage to cream the Cheetahs at home, but our trip away is an unmitigated disaster.

We lose all three, going down to the Force, who always seem to present problems for us in Perth, then get utterly hammered by the Stormers 14–42, when Stu Dickinson, never my favourite referee, whistles up his own storm. It's my 100th game of Super rugby, so I'm up for it and even though we didn't play that badly, we just get smothered.

Despite the loss, there are two uplifting moments in Cape Town. One was a present from Schalk Burger for my 100th game, a case of wine from his family's vineyard. The present cements a friendship that developed through playing together for the Baabaas at the end of 2008, and epitomises one of the wonderful contradictions of rugby, that such fierce rivals — and there are none more ferocious than Schalk — can drop their guard off the field and be mates.

We stayed on a few days after the Stormers game before heading up to Pretoria, and the Force were staying in the same hotel. I took the opportunity to meet veteran Aussie lock, Nathan Sharpe, about Players' Association business. The business chat took half an hour, then we sat and talked for another two. Really nice guy. I'd been playing against him for about eight years, but had never got past 'G'day'.

The following week we go down narrowly and desperately after the hooter against the Bulls 35–40. That really hurts — we're almost home, and succeed in charging down a Morne Steyn drop-kick, but the ball goes loose and, bugger me, they score from a marginal forward pass. When your luck's out . . .

That loss really costs us, because a bonus point win against the Brumbies comes too late. We make the semis, but two South African teams, the Stormers and the Bulls, have taken the top spots and no prizes for guessing who we've drawn. I pack the boots and the mouthguards and board the plane for the trek back to South Africa, trying not to hear Yogi Berra chortling in my ear.

Loftus Versfeld is being readied for the Fifa Football World Cup, so we play at Orlando Stadium in Soweto, which is different, particularly when we get delayed in traffic. The saving grace is that the ref, Stu Dickinson, is even later. The atmosphere is different too, particularly when the crowd start practising their vuvuzelas. But nothing else changes, when for the third time in four years, we go down to the Bulls in a semi-final, this time 24–39. We get a sniff of it early in the second half, at 17–23, but Matfield and Fourie du Preez are immense. Du Preez takes the game away from us by reacting quickest to a screwed defensive scrum and scoots down the blind. A shame, not least because Owen Franks, now 22, has shown, particularly in the two Bulls games, that he can deal to the best of them at tighthead.

The Stormers thrash the Waratahs in the other semi, and the Bulls win the final narrowly at home.

I'm hoping that Super 14 form doesn't equate to test triumph, because if it does, the All Blacks are in trouble.

While the Super 14 might have ended in what is becoming an all too familiar disappointment, the All Blacks come together really well, and in the June tests, renamed the Steinlager Series, we seem to be ready to kick on from Marseilles, rather than have to start again.

In May of 2009, Paddy O'Brien said there'd be no more rule changes before the RWC. But 2009 was such an appalling year for the game globally that even the northern hemisphere sides wanted changes to the interpretation of, you guessed it, the tackled ball rule. So that inkling that Ted & Smithy & Shag had last year that the rules or interpretations had to change has proven to be well founded.

This year, the tackler has to get out of the way and any potential snaffler has got to be on his feet supporting his own body weight to win the ball. The refs have license to be harsh on the tackler, who used to be able to lie there and passively obstruct, and also on the guys who were having a dig when they're half on their feet and half not.

The other change is to the 10-metre exclusion zone around the kick retriever. The chasing team used to be able to put an umbrella defence around the catcher, forcing him to go forward, but now that zone extends in a line across the field, which gives the catcher a few more options.

That really changes the game back to one where it pays to have the ball in hand; it pays to play with the ball rather than without it. All of which helps us in the development of the game we want to play — and puts us a year ahead of the opposition.

These changes are seized upon delightedly by Ted & Shag & Smithy, who have clearly been putting the preparatory work in during the Super 14. To that end, they've decided to change roles again, with Ted going to attack and strategy overview, Smithy keeping defence and counter-attack and Shag moving back to the forwards.

The first test against Ireland at New Plymouth turns out to be a bit of a romp after their No. 8 Jamie Heaslip gets red-carded after 15 minutes, then Ronan O'Gara follows him with a yellow shortly after. By the time O'Gara comes back, we've put 38 points past their 13 men and the contest is over. Notwithstanding that, we're intense and focused until the last quarter when we lose our shape — not helped by my gifting an intercept to Tommy Bowe. Israel Dagg and Sam Whitelock have notable debuts, and others like Kieran and Conrad and Jimmy have fine games, and Cory Jane once again looks like the complete package at right wing.

We make only one change a week later against Wales, which is supposed to be our last test at Carisbrook. After a quiet first 40, we thrash them 42–9. Part of that is due to Dan, who's been subdued during the Super 14, taking on the line again — and breaking it, spectacularly. It helps that he's got Jimmy playing so well inside him, and Conrad taking leadership outside him.

I've got Welsh fullback Lee Byrne in front of me as I size up the options against Wales.

By the following week in Hamilton, Wales are more defensive. Sometimes you get the feeling, particularly with northern hemisphere teams, that they've decided to go out there and keep it as close as they can, stay in the hunt, then see what happens. By our lights, that's an impoverished sort of ambition, but it works in so far as they lose by 19 points instead of 33.

We seem to do better against teams that come to play. It's strangely counter-intuitive that we have a better chance of slamming a team that genuinely believes it can beat us by playing footy than a team that doesn't believe it can do that and shuts up shop.

I'm very aware that we've been beaten at critical times in the past by teams that have a perverse combination of those elements: they believe that the only way they can beat us is by not playing, just spoiling.

Like France, when they go the Biarritz way.

Like South Africa almost any time at all.

The 2010 Tri Nations begins with two home tests against the champions, who did us 3–0 last year.

'If all the Springboks do during this Tri Nations is pretty much keep the ball amongst their heavyweight forwards and rely on Morne Steyn's boot to retain the trophy, then the game worldwide is in serious trouble,' writes Peter Bills. He also opines that the South Africans 'have the strongest and best squad'.

Last year after Hamilton, I might have agreed with him. I don't any more.

Ted's been assembling the big picture during the Super 14 and the Steinlager Series has been a good shakedown. We go into Eden Park with no major injuries and a determination to really take it to them. The night before the game I note in the Warwick that I'm looking forward to *another great day doing what I do*.

And it is a great day. The Boks look as lost this year as we were last year. It becomes apparent early on that they haven't adjusted their game to the new 'interpretation' and expect to make hay with the same old same old. But it's not just the tackled ball interpretation that's different. We're different, in mindset and strategy.

We smash their double runners back with huge defensive hits. That takes guts. Reado and Jerome are immense. We've also learnt to catch and compete in the air, both at lineout time and in general play, and this year we're able to launch counter-attacks and recycle quickly and securely if we get stopped.

There's one of those signature moments midway first half, when Mils, who's been out with injury and needs a good game after Israel Dagg's debut, takes a Ricky Januarie up-and-under beautifully. Joe Rocks gives Mils a heads-up that he has room and Mils rips them apart on the counter. Seven points. We're able to breach the gain-line through Ma'a and the loosies, and keep the pressure on them in the set-pieces. It's true that we try to avoid kicking the ball out, to give them as few lineouts as possible, but when we have to go there, we do the business. Elsewhere, in scrums and breakdowns, we're brutal and we feel we've got the wood on them.

Backing up a performance like that has always been problematic.

John Smit admits their minds 'weren't in the right place'. There are reports that the Boks were still jet-lagged after getting into Auckland too late, that key players were still wandering around yawning on game day. Maybe Bakkies was sleep-walking when he assaulted Jimmy and got sin-binned. It was so crass that you had to wonder what the hell he thought he was doing.

If that game doesn't wake them up, nothing will. We're expecting a backlash, if that's the right term for a team that relies on strangulation. John Smit is reported as describing his team as a malevolent hybrid of python and green mamba that

Another great day doing what I do . . . against South Africa at Eden Park.

constricts the life out of its prey and then delivers deadly strikes when its prey's limbs are limp. I can't compete with that. We've got the odd boar and a tiny poisonous spider that might give you a nip if you sit in the wrong place on a sandhill, but the thing that kills more people than anything else in our bush is the weather. Hypothermia doesn't really stack up against pythons and green mambas, but you can usually count on Wellington to do its darndest.

This time, though, Wellington serves up a clear night. Danie Rossouw replaces Bakkies and also replicates his yellow card, for an attack on my head with boot and fist, neither of which impresses Richard Loe: 'It wasn't a kick, it was a nudge, and the punches weren't up to much either.' That's a relief — I shouldn't have felt a thing.

We score a point a minute for the 10 that Rossouw is gone. It gets tough before halftime, and midway through the second half, where they get some possession and drive and the game might be in the balance.

The way we deal with those moments, the brutal defence we put in, and the way we keep our confidence in the game plan, are as satisfying as anything else. We're 14 months away from the RWC and we know that it's those moments, when we're under the cosh and keep our shape and composure, that will determine whether we're winners or losers.

Kieran is mighty again, Jerome's not far behind him and it's hard to find anyone who didn't have a good night. Piri's Man of the Match in some people's estimation and shows such startling pace when he scores his try that he's described by one journalist as 'a runaway fire hydrant'.

Two weeks later we cream Australia in Melbourne, 49–28.

'This was shock and awe rugby . . .' writes Gregor Paul. 'This was the Russian tanks rolling into Prague . . .' Not sure about that, but we are pleased with ourselves. A more satisfying reference by the same writer is to the great Dutch team of the Johan Cruyff era that was known for playing Total Football, where defenders could attack, and everyone in the team had a plethora of skills. Paul points out that it was Dan who won the turnover for Mils' first try and it was two tight forwards, Kevvy and Brad, who then 'pulled off the neatest and slickest of interchanges to get the ball to the wing'.

Wallaby legend John Eales proclaims we're on the verge of a great era.

And it is starting to feel special. The team's fizzing, I'm fizzing. Seven tries against Australia at home ain't bad.

A week later, we host a much better Aussie team in Christchurch. Their forwards are able to hang on to possession for long periods and really test our defensive structure and faith in one another. A different sort of test for us, but no less valuable, forcing us to work hard for everything we get in a 20–10 win. It's a different type of game, where we're in control on the scoreboard, play smart and shut it down. Conservative by our standards, but effective. We need to be able to play like that too.

Shock and awe rugby . . . dotting down against Australia at Melbourne.

Robbie's homecoming might be miserable — the win secures the Bledisloe for another year and is our ninth consecutive win against Australia, all since he took over — but at least he can look across the AMI Stadium at the new Deans Stand.

We invite the Aussies into our changing rooms for a beer, but they've got a bus or plane to catch. After the match in Melbourne, when we were disappointed not to be invited by them for a beer, there's a growing perception on our part that Robbie wants to keep the Aussies from fraternising with us. Okay, we can appreciate he's just lost his ninth test in a row to us and is under a fair bit of pressure, but even so, he's back in Christchurch, his home town, with a lot of us across the corridor who know him and would have welcomed him.

The difference between the Boks and the Aussies seems to be that once the game is over, the Boks are ready to drop their guard and have a beer with us, so I've been able to get to know articulate, worldly guys like Schalk Burger, Victor Matfield, John Smit and Jean de Villiers. The du Plessis brothers are formidable opponents but are great mates off the field with Horey, and I've got to know them a wee bit through him. I've always had a lot of time for George Smith and I got to know and like George Gregan when we played together in the Baabaas, but apart from Nathan Sharpe, I can't say much about many of the current Aussie team because I don't know them.

Bring it on . . . at the National Stadium, Soweto, 2010.

We're happy to be where we are, and our mindset for the trip to Johannesburg for the third game against South Africa is *Bring It On!* At a leaders' meeting on Jo'burg we talk about what that *BIO* mindset means in terms of clarity and intensity. A win will confirm the Tri Nations for us, but it's also the last time we play these guys for 12 months, and we want to leave them stewing on as many doubts and troubles as possible.

We take it easy early in the week and keep trainings short and sharp, so we're well acclimatised by the time we take the field at the amazing National Stadium in Soweto. The Fifa World Cup has been and gone but it sounds like every one of the 94,000 crowd has held on to their vuvuzela. The Boks come out after two losses with big attitude. The physicality and intensity they bring to the game is a big step up from anything they showed us in Auckland and Wellington.

It's one of the most satisfying tests I've ever played in. The Boks have us under the cosh for much of it, determined to send us a message, and partly due to Dan having a bit of an off-day by his standards we're 17–22 down with a couple of minutes to go. We have to score twice to win, and one of them has to be a try.

I'm disappointed that we've given the Africans what looks like a winning lead, but behind the scenes, we've been doing a lot of work with Ceri Evans on how to

Celebrating with Cory Jane after just getting over for the try at Soweto.

handle the psychological pressure in exactly this sort of situation, and there's part of me that relishes the opportunity to find out if we've learnt anything. Evans is a former All White defender who's now a consultant forensic psychiatrist and Clinical Director of the Canterbury Regional Forensic Psychiatric Service.

We keep believing. From a penalty, we take the tap-and-go, and I find myself out on the touchline with an overlap. It's a case of putting my head down and going for it. Maybe I'm lucky, because the video replay can't say definitively whether or not my foot is in touch when I drive for the line. But as we wait for the video ref's decision, instead of sweating on the decision, we talk about what we need to do next if the call goes against us and we go to a defensive lineout. As it happens, the try is awarded: 22–22. Dan lines up the conversion to win the game . . . And misses.

It would be easy to settle for that. We don't, that's what's really pleasing. Despite the supposed disadvantage of altitude, we feel we've had the Boks on the rack in the last 20 minutes and the desire is in us to press for a win rather than settle for the draw. From the last move of the game, Conrad and I get a turnover in a defensive ruck and Ma'a attacks John Smit's right shoulder, makes the break, losing a boot in the process, and throws a wide flat ball to Israel Dagg who goes over in the corner.

John Smit, in the last minute of his 100th test, lies on the ground clutching Ma'a's boot, watching Israel score the winning try. 'It's a cruel game,' says John, as we walk off the pitch together. What can I say? *Yep*.

'It doesn't get any bigger than that,' says Ted afterwards, 'that was a huge game of rugby.'

While I can understand Ted's sentiments and how great it feels to seal the Tri Nations championship, we know it does get bigger than that: it's going to get much bigger than that in 13 months' time.

My only worry is how long away that is. The Boks have gone from Tri Nations champs to chumps in the space of 12 months. The pace of change year on year is disconcerting. If there's a worry, it's that we have to hold the advantage we've got until the end of next year. We were ready a year early before the last RWC too, playing our best rugby in 2006, which we weren't able to reproduce for one reason or another in 2007, when it mattered.

We're ready now. AMI Stadium is ready. The fans in Christchurch are ready — there's a palpable excitement about what's coming next year.

On 3 September the front page of *The Press* reports that Christchurch hoteliers are expecting a rush on rooms for next year, and have already finalised $60 million worth of accommodation for players, officials and VIPs at the Rugby World Cup.

I know in my bones that come the extreme pressure of RWC knockout phase, there's going to be a moment when everything is on the line.

The only RWC when that didn't happen was the first, in 1987, when the All Blacks were never really pressed. The lesson from every other RWC is that the winning team will at some stage during the knockout stage need to survive a moment which tips it one way or another. The winning team has often needed some luck in that tipping moment, but you can't count on luck, and what I want to make sure of is that when that moment comes, we are able to manage it without freezing.

In the past, we've maybe downplayed that pressure, taken the attitude, *Hey, we're tough, we're All Blacks, we can deal with it*. We thought that if we didn't talk about it or make a big thing of it, maybe it'd go away. This time around, we're going to do it differently: we decide to acknowledge that pressure and try to develop some tools to deal with it.

To that end, we work with Bert and with Ceri Evans. When Ceri analyses what happens to the brain under extreme pressure, it makes a lot of sense to me in the light of events in Cardiff. He explains that underlying pressure comes from expectation, scrutiny and consequence. If you play for the All Blacks you've got expectation, people are watching and the consequences for not winning are huge, particularly given our history in the RWC.

Acute stress comes when the brain perceives a threat, either predicted (opposition or individuals do something you've planned for) or unpredicted (they do something you haven't planned for). Either is okay, as long as it's not accompanied by a feeling

A happy bunch with the Tri Nations trophy after our win in Soweto. With me here are Woody, Ma'a, Sam and Kevvy.

of helplessness. That's when adrenalin-fuelled responses overwhelm the individual, and you get aggressive, or you try to escape, or you go passive — so it's fight, flight or freeze. I know that I end up becoming passive.

When any of those things happen, decision making becomes muddled, clarity is lost and accuracy is compromised. If you go into freeze mode, your reactions are dulled, you go through the motions, lack coordination, become indecisive and withdrawn, you don't hear people around you, you don't see what's in front of you any more. You become captured by bad-experience pictures from the past or fear of future consequences.

Ceri calls that state, when you lose contact with the present, getting trapped in the Red Zone: that glazed look that I saw on those All Blacks' faces standing under the posts in '99 and that I saw around me — and was part of — after Traille scored in 2007. Where you're staring but you're not seeing what's in front of you any more.

To get out of the Red Zone and move to what he calls the Blue Zone, you need to somehow retain situational awareness so you can make decisions and be able to execute on those decisions.

Ceri gives us exercises to help us make that transition from Red to Blue. Breathing slowly and deliberately, nose or mouth, with a two-second pause. While breathing, hold your wrist on the out-breath. Then shift your attention to something external — the ground or your feet, or the ball in hand, or even alternating big toes, or the grandstand. Get your eyes up, looking out.

You've got to use deep breaths and key words to help yourself get out of your own head, find an external focus, get yourself back in the present, regain your situational awareness.

The other thing you've got to do long before you get into the Red Zone is plan for the unpredictable, so that when it happens, it's expected and you don't feel helpless.

Ceri and I look at scenarios that might engender the feeling of helplessness I had at Cardiff, when we didn't have a play to go to that was specific for the situation we found ourselves in. How to deal with that, how to change momentum when you feel the game plan is not working. It's not about having or implementing a Plan B, it's not about turning things round by scoring a spectacular try in the corner, so much as having really specific, practical plays to fall back on to take us through the next minute or two in order to change a particular element of the game. For instance, if we haven't had the ball for a while, and when we do get it, it's deep in our territory, what do we do? Hold on to it or kick it? My task is to work through these specifics with Ceri, then translate them into calls or plays that everyone will understand, so we're all on the same page when we need to go to them.

But no matter how much you plan, in rugby or in life, not everything is predictable. Some things no one can see coming. They are the unforeseen tragedies which test the human spirit in the most fundamental way possible.

Blue Zone

At 4.35 am on Saturday, 4 September 2010, a 7.1-magnitude earthquake strikes Christchurch.

I'm oblivious, asleep in Auckland, staying at Ali's place, ready for a leaders' meeting before the team flies out to Sydney for the last Tri Nations match of the year. When I wake at about seven and switch on the mobile, it lights up with messages, all variations of 'Are you okay?'

Ali's girlfriend Casey tells me that there's been a big earthquake in Christchurch. When I try to ring Mum and Dad I can't get through. While I'm trying, I see on the internet that the epicentre was at Darfield, south-west of the city, not far from my parents' place.

On television, there's something both familiar and unreal about the pictures coming through. They're much like disaster stories of fire, flood and earthquake you've seen before — of Civil Defence no-go cordons, cracked or shattered inner-city buildings, impassable roads, gashes across the landscape, streets under a sea of mud — but this time the streets and surroundings are your home town, buildings you recognise, that you might have been walking past yesterday. The Deans family homestead, Homebush, quite close to Mum and Dad, is semi-upright rubble, with rooms gaping open to the sky. Reports come in that there are no deaths — luckily, the badly damaged inner-city bar and club precinct was largely deserted at that hour of the morning.

When I do get hold of my parents, Dad says the force of the quake threw him out of bed, but he and Mum are otherwise okay, and their comparatively modern home hasn't suffered any damage that they can see. Then I get hold of Jo, and she's good too, and later in the day she goes round to my townhouse and reassures me that there's no obvious damage.

The leaders' meeting is cancelled and it's decided that the players will fly straight from Wellington, Auckland and Christchurch — when they can get out — direct to Sydney. Until my afternoon departure, there's nothing to do but wait and watch the coverage on television.

Firefighters battling a blaze in Worcester Street in central Christchurch after the September 2010 earthquake.

More than a hundred commercial buildings have serious or potentially serious damage, and a large number of inner-city and Lyttelton heritage buildings have suffered a variety of damage, especially to old towers and turrets and chimneys, though the Cathedral seems relatively unscathed. Some suburbs have been badly hit, particularly around the Avon River — Avonside streets have gaping cracks and are covered in mud, and there are these mini volcanoes of liquid silt bubbling up in the ground. Liquefaction — where the soil behaves like liquid — is a word I've never heard before. It mixes with broken water and sewer mains and turns Avonside and some of the eastern suburbs like Bexley into foul-smelling swamp. Hundreds of people with damaged homes turn up at Civil Defence centres like the Burnside High School gym, not that far from my place.

The stories coming from rural residents around the epicentre are like Mum and Dad's: kitchen floors covered with smashed crockery and food, but surprise at the lack of damage, considering their proximity. For all that, some roads are buckled and closed and there are a lot of power and water outages. At one stage, there's an aerial shot of the gash across the plains left by the newly discovered Greendale fault, showing shattered roads, broken water races and shifted shelter belts and fences. One of the more colourful reports says there were three different earthquakes, which 'unleashed the energy equivalent of sixty-seven nuclear bombs speeding into Christchurch'.

As much as I try to understand it all, I really don't. I wasn't there and I didn't feel the force of it. Even when Dad told me he was thrown out of bed, I was thinking, *Oh, yeah, he's probably exaggerating just a wee bit.* Which makes it much easier for me to put it out of my mind and concentrate on the test.

The eight Canterbury-based players in the All Black squad, plus Smithy and Shag and manager Darren Shand, are a day late getting out of Christchurch, and there are a few war stories when the boys gather in Sydney, mainly of the sounds of the quake: of thunder or a train roaring through the house, creaking timbers and plaster falling out of ceilings and the contents of shelves and cupboards smashing on the floor. Kieran had been pretty freaked, taking shelter under a doorway with heavily pregnant Bridget. Some, like Brad and Corey, had to leave partners and young kids. Most of them have some damage to their houses, but the worst hit is Steve Hansen, whose house at Tai Tapu on the city fringe is close to collapse. He's got a young family and his elderly father living with him.

None of us knows about aftershock patterns — one is 5.6 — and as the week goes on and we hear from those left at home about the continuing shocks, the phone bills skyrocket and it must be bloody difficult for some to keep their minds on the job, as fearful partners describe what they're going through. Steve gets a call from an engineer to say his house is 'stuffed'.

We try to talk about it as a team without letting it throw us off course. Steve tells us that we better do a bloody good job, to make the time away from the people we love worthwhile. 'Hopefully, if we put in a good performance we can put a smile on some faces back home.'

That smile doesn't look likely when we're 9–22 down and the Aussies feel like they're finally getting over the top of us. But we know that they've just flown back from Africa, where they had a big win at altitude in Bloemfontein, and we have an inkling that if we can get field position and exert pressure, the travel factor might tell in the last quarter. We decide to change the attack, go narrower with pick-and-gos, bring it back to our forwards and see if we can beat up on the Aussie pack, take their legs and lungs away. That works: Kieran and I are able to work a move off the back of the scrum to get us to 16–22 with 14 minutes to go, then Kieran smashes over to score the winner in the seventy-third minute.

Okay, it's not ideal, but it's hardly surprising given the events of the week that the boys take so long to get into the game. Once again, our composure is tested, and our leadership gets us home. Even though we lose Kevvy, who exits early with a calf injury, Corey steps up in a rare 70 minutes, despite his worries about what's happening back home.

But the biggest 'learning' from the game is easy: we miss Dan. This game proves that if we have an Achilles heel, it's Dan's. The niggling ankle that's been troubling Dan all year has been operated on to remove loose material from the back of the joint, so Aaron Cruden is the latest to get to pitch for the Dan Carter Understudy role. But Aaron has a difficult debut, not least because our pack is beaten for the first 50 minutes. Aaron's replaced by Colin Slade early in the second half, and he shows a lot of composure in his first test. Opposite him, Quade Cooper starts his first test too, and shows a surprisingly heady kicking game.

But the kicking hero comes as a bit of a surprise, certainly to me after seeing him spray them all over the park in a practice session the day before. Piri Weepu nails five out of five, while Matt Giteau misses four of his seven attempts. That's the difference.

My first view of Christchurch is reassuring, as I give Corey a lift home from the airport. I'm prattling on that there's no way you'd know there's been an earthquake, when we pass an empty lot on the corner of Cranford and Westminster streets. Ten days ago there was a fish-and-chip shop and milk bar, now it's a pile of rubble. It was badly damaged, says Corey, and they've had to bowl it. *Oh.*

Once I start looking, there's toppled chimneys and collapsed brick walls. I've read that Canterbury Hockey has lost its artificial pitches at Porritt Park in Avonside, and the rowers have lost most of the buildings at their Kerr's Reach facility. Luckily, Rugby Park seems pretty much unaffected, though you can stand there and see over the back fence to where a chimney has broken off and is lying on a roof.

Cups and trophies from the sideboard are strewn all over the floor at the townhouse, but that seems to be the extent of it. I decide to put in a claim for damage assessment on someone's advice that there could be stuff I can't see, but in the ensuing days, as the aftershocks come in, I'm not that fazed. They're 5 in magnitude or below, and while I read somewhere that a 6 magnitude is 10 times more powerful than a 5, it doesn't really register, and part of me wonders what all the fuss is about. People are buying survival kits, but I don't bother. Meridian Energy sends a wee transistor that you should have in your survival pack and I'm thinking, *A bit after the fact, isn't it?* GNS Science is quoted in the paper as saying that there might be a couple more aftershocks of 5 magnitude or higher, 'but the risk of a bigger earthquake is fading by the hour'.

That's good enough for me. I do a safety and hygiene video for Red Cross and visit a couple of badly affected schools, and my message is that if that's the worst of it, we can cope, we'll be okay . . .

So I think, bugger the aftershocks, and plough back into training for the end-of-year tour. Over an intense nine-test programme like the one we've just completed, you're obviously match-fit but you lose a bit of base because there isn't the time to do a lot of individual work. So I try to build my base fitness back up, following All Black trainer Nic Gill's schedule. There's greater emphasis this year on shuttle work and change of direction because the game is more ball in hand. I do a lot of this shuttle type running and we get tested with a yo-yo, which is a modification of the old beep test, 20 metres down and back, with a 10-second 'rest' to get back to your mark, getting faster and faster until you can't get back to your mark on the beep and you're out.

I hit it hard because I know we're going to try to lift the pace of our game. By the time we gather in Auckland to fly out, I'm posting figures as good as I've ever done.

The big news around the naming of the All Black squad is the selection of Sonny Bill Williams. I've been watching SBW play for Canterbury in the ITM Cup and, gee, yeah, he's an impressive physical specimen. It's clear he has a lot to learn about when and where to best use his pretty outrageous talents, like offloading, and the different lines he has to run on attack and defence, and the complexities around the tackled ball. But the most impressive thing is that he listens and clearly wants to learn, and when I look closely at what he's doing at the breakdown, for instance, I can see he's struggling with timing, knowing when to commit and that sort of thing, but when he does commit, he gets his body position right and is brave and strong over the ball.

Dan's back from his ankle op, and it's decided to take one understudy, Stephen Donald, and leave the two younger men, Aaron Cruden and Colin Slade, at home. Big call, but that's what the selectors are there for — and Beaver's been the strongest in the provincial ITM Cup.

There's no particular discussion of the Christchurch situation before we fly out. The talk is all about housekeeping and objectives, particularly another shot at a Home Unions Grand Slam and the chance to set a new record for the most consecutive test wins amongst the top-tier nations. We're sitting on 15, and wins against Australia, England, Scotland, Ireland and Wales will take us to 20, and break the current record of 17 held jointly by the All Blacks and South Africa.

SBW . . . he's an impressive physical specimen.

That objective lasts as long as it takes us to fly to Hong Kong and play Australia. We've got the game in the bag at the 60-minute mark after another lethargic start. Our early mistakes put us 12 points behind, but we get back to 17–12 by halftime and are out to 24–12 before Dan goes off and the wheels of the All Black machine seem to fall off with him. Dan might have been okay to play through, but he's coming back from the ankle surgery and we don't want to risk him. So on comes Steve Donald for a cameo that does his stocks no good at all.

It's not Beaver's fault that Drew Mitchell scores within minutes of him replacing Dan — it's another replacement, Ice, who slips over and gives Drew a clear run at the line. But it's Beaver who misses a straightforward penalty that would have given us an eight-point lead with five to go, and then it's Beaver who doesn't find touch with a goal-line clearance, and gives Kurtley Beale a chance to run it back in

With Conrad and Ma'a on the way to training in Hong Kong, 2010.

Beaver (front) and Ice after the final whistle in Hong Kong.

broken field. If he'd kicked it into the grandstand, a lineout would have taken up time and allowed us to re-set our defence. Young James O'Connor converts his own try and breaks a 10-match sequence of Aussie losses to us. It would be easy to look at Beaver's mistakes and say they cost us the game — and they certainly didn't help — but we all needed to take some blame for letting them get back into the game.

It irks me that we haven't managed to close the game out from a position of such strength with 20 to go, and keep our foot on the Wallaby throat. The way we lost momentum at a time when we usually grab it. And Quade Cooper giving me a shove and a spray after they score the winner doesn't help. Some people have natural charm and grace: Quade ain't one of them. But he is one of a really potent Australian backline, alongside young but maturing talents in O'Connor and Beale and, particularly, Will Genia, who is already world-class.

You can see those players improving with exposure to test-match pressure, and we've got to hope that the same will be true of guys like Beaver. And, if in order to advance that, we had to choose a game to lose before the RWC, this would be it. We've won six in a row in the Tri Nations, and this is a timely reminder that it won't just happen: to win a test, you've got to turn up and get it right. Every bloody time.

The loss fires us up for the Grand Slam, although in saying that we hardly need firing up to play England in front of 81,000 fans at Twickenham.

It's Sonny Bill's debut and there's a big buzz around that, but Sam Whitelock's first run-on test is at least as important to us. Sam's got the size for an international lock, and has earned his shot with a great work ethic. He's also got an old head on

Sonny Bill's trademark offload on show against Scotland.

Sam Whitelock, who got his first run-on test against the English in 2010.

his young shoulders, knows where he needs to be, has the athleticism to get himself there, and enough mongrel to make his presence felt when he does.

The game is a much better spectacle than last year, and England play their part in making it so, despite their defensive coach Mike Ford saying before the game that tests should be low-scoring grinds. Hosea Gear and Kieran score in the first half and we're out to 17–3 by halftime. Maybe England are so far behind they're forced to change tactics, but after a couple of Toby Flood penalties — we're getting murdered by French ref Romain Poite in the scrums — they start running at us and stretching us wide. Jerome gets sin-binned and we play out the last eight minutes one man down. In the end, 26–16 is probably a fair result.

The same weekend, Australia beat Wales comfortably, and the Springboks keep their own Grand Slam hopes alive by beating Ireland narrowly.

Sonny Bill has a stellar game the following week against the Scots, moving Toby Robson to write that he's 'dominated a test in a way not seen since Jonah in his pomp'. The Murrayfield Massacre is a 49–3 thrashing, our biggest win over Scotland in 105 years, and Sonny certainly shows his stuff — six offloads in the first 20 minutes and a big hand in four of the seven tries. But it is only Scotland, who on the evidence of that outing don't have a hell of a lot of the old Scots rip-shit-and bust about them.

It's hard to assess whether we're that good — we're certainly playing a brand of pace and power rugby that is light years ahead of what we did last year up here in the UK — or whether the opposition is really bad.

The other southern hemisphere teams' results might be a clue. That weekend, there's a headline I've never seen before: 'Wallabies Fall to Dazzling England'. Can't say I ever expected to see 'England' and 'dazzling' in the same sentence, but maybe that's an indication that it's more a case of what we're doing well, not what the opposition is doing badly. That's confirmed by a narrow 29–25 win by the Boks over Wales, as they edge towards a Grand Slam too.

Back home, a couple of severe aftershocks rock Christchurch, 4.8 and 4.9, but, as far as I can tell, the guys seem pretty blasé about it by now. Modelling by GNS Science predicted between five and 17 aftershocks of between 4 and 4.9 magnitude could strike Christchurch this month, so it seems more or less in line with predictions — a pattern of diminishing aftershocks and no more major damage. That makes it easier for the Canterbury boys to focus on Ireland, which ought to be a better test.

And it is. The Irish play well against us in Dublin for all but three minutes of the 80. It could have been an arm-wrestle. On the field it was. On the scoreboard it wasn't. In three minutes we score two tries and the game changes from a tight 19–13 test match to all over. What's most encouraging is our ability to punish opposition mistakes or loss of concentration, no matter how fleeting.

'When the numbers don't match, the All Blacks pounce,' writes Toby Robson. 'When a kick is slightly inaccurate or a chase is weak, they make teams pay . . .'

Some of the kudos we're getting from the press about our Total Rugby concept is music to our ears, I must admit. 'The backs clean rucks with the forwards and the forwards can throw passes off either side like backs . . . Unlike the South Africans, the All Blacks often unload in the tackle, and, unlike Australia, the pack are happy to indulge in an arm-wrestle if the weather or pitch conditions dictate.'

A better indication of our prowess might be that the same weekend we destroy Ireland, the dreadful Scots beat South Africa 21–17 and stymie their bid for a Grand Slam.

It's my record ninety-third test for the All Blacks, Mils too, overtaking Sean Fitzpatrick. Given that, I might have been a bit mean in turning down an opportunity for Dan to kick an easy penalty to set a world record for the number of points in a test. I didn't know until someone tells me after the game. I look at Dan. 'Oh, mate. You knew?' He tries to make out he didn't, but he did. Ah well, there's always next week.

Brad's not as phlegmatic about missing the Irish test due to a tweaked hammy, because it would have been his fiftieth. Bloody incredible, when you consider what else the man has done! He's pretty dark until the hammy holds up through training and he's chosen for the test XV against Wales.

Once again, it's difficult to stay focused on one more game, when the feet are screaming out for Jandals and you start dreaming of sun on the face. Wales seem a bit distracted too. After a dismal draw against Fiji, their coach, Warren Gatland, stormed into the Welsh dressing room and sacked his captain, Ryan Jones, a big tight-loose forward who'd impressed with the 2005 Lions.

Ninety-three tests apiece. A new record for Mils and me after the test against Ireland.

Two days after the Irish test the news comes through about the Pike River mine tragedy. Twenty-nine missing. New Zealand's two degrees of separation kicks in: my old flatmate Ben Blair, now living in Cardiff, played club rugby with one of those missing. John Sturgeon, NZRU president, on tour with us, an ex-West Coast coalminer with friends among the families of those lost, fronts the media, tries to stay upbeat. Privately, he's really shaken and tells me: 'These sorts of things don't end good.'

Wales is a country that understands what goes down in mines. After the first explosion, we all bow our heads and say a prayer for the missing, or just hope that they'll be saved. By Wednesday morning, a second explosion has ripped through the mine and Sturge shakes his head. We watch the internet and television pictures of the Paparoa Range on the wild West Coast, but this time it's not a tourist promotion. We feel a long way from home.

This year, the coaches have given me more responsibility towards the sharp end of the week, and I take it carefully. It's our fourteenth test of the year and the last thing anyone needs is any gut-busters or big contact.

At the beginning of the week, it's 80/20 the coaches driving things at practice, but as we get closer to the game, the ratio reverses because we're the ones who have to drive it during the game. Thursday training is a bit of a mix: the coaches set out what we're doing in broad terms, and they run some drills, but instead of them saying I want you to do this move and practise this one, we're just told, 'Scrum there, do what you need to do and if it doesn't work, you figure out why.' Replicating

White armbands for Pike River . . . prior to kick-off against Wales at the Millennium Stadium, 2010.

game day. They'll step in if there's a glaringly obvious hole in what we're doing, or they'll throw in what they call 'unpredicted events', to try and get some problem solving, or even try to upset us and force us into the Red Zone. Sometimes the coaches take that to the extreme. Whereas before we used to go through everything the next opponent was likely to throw at us on video analysis and then prepare for it, the coaches have started holding some of that stuff back from us. They won't tell us what they've picked up, then Smithy, say, will dump the move or situation on us at Thursday training, hoping that it'll work, that it'll break us. The theory is that what breaks us on a Thursday will never break us on a Saturday. We'll work it out and cover it.

This methodology has often made training a bit messier than it used to be, because we only ever get one go. Even if Smithy pulls a stunt like that and we ask if we can have another look at it. Nup. Then he'll pull something similar out again later, when we're not expecting it. We've learnt not to measure the accuracy of Thursday training so much — the test of accuracy and everything else is on Saturday.

By Friday, captain's run, the coaches don't have any say at all, it's all me and Dan and the senior guys. We're in charge and we decide what we're going to do. We'll do some lineouts and we'll go through our team patterns. How we're going to start the game, kick-offs, first lineout and defensive lineout. How we're going to get ourselves out of there. We'll go through about eight or nine starter plays from set-piece, then a little bit of broken play too, like kick retrieval, setting up the counter. Thursday is opposed and

Dan kicks a penalty goal against Wales to break the world points scoring record.

unpredicted, so you've got guys under pressure who maybe made a few mistakes. From a live scrum, maybe the pass was meant to go wide but it broke down in the middle, but we only got one crack at it. So on Friday we get a chance to go back and work out what the problem was, make sure that we've got it right. And guys can look at what they're doing and say, 'Shit, let's go through that again, we'd better just make sure.'

In Cardiff, on the Friday, just as well we're at the end of the tour and there's not a lot to be done: it's bloody snowing. We haven't always welcomed the roof at Millennium Stadium and the effect it seems to have on the grass surface, but we're grateful this time around.

We start well in front of 70,000 at the Millennium. Dan doesn't kick particularly well in this test, but early on slots the penalty he needs to take him to 1188 test points, a new world record. We get 12 points up and then start leaking penalties and points to a willing, resilient Welsh team, until midway through the second half after Stephen Jones has kicked six penalties, we're pegged back to 23–18, and in a dogfight we don't need.

Once again, our scrum's being punished, seemingly for being dominant. Things aren't going well for us, we've lost momentum, but there are no wrong pictures in my head, even though we're in the same stadium as 2007. I keep the emotion at bay, stay on task, think about which parts of our game are serving us well, what I have to do

With my cousin Alex McCaw after the 1000-kilometre challenge. Alex made it.

to get our game going, how to stop giving away penalties or at least get down their end of the field. Jerome's giving us go-forward and from a Mils chip we get the ball back, and in the seventy-third minute Brad holds a beautiful ball to put Anthony Boric into a hole and Ice scores. We go straight back down there, and Jimmy back-flips a pass to Mils who puts big John Afoa in the clear with 30 metres to the line. It's no race, and neither is the game on the scoreboard at 37–25. We know different.

My third Grand Slam in six years, 2005, 2008 and 2010. Before that, you have to go back to 1978. Ted makes the point that they shouldn't be taken for granted, that there've been 24 Grand Slam opportunities and only eight have been successful. South Africa last achieved it in 1961 and Australia won their one and only in 1984.

It's just as well there's no stone under the seat of the Discus, because Gavin suggests that a 1000-kilometre flight is the next challenge. I'm up for it, and so is my 17-year-old cousin, Alex, a glider prodigy. We get the tow out of Omarama and start just to the south of Glentanner, heading south to Waiparu, near Lumsden, then back up to Mount D'Archiac, then south again to Waikaia, near Mossburn, down past Riversdale. Coming back to the Lindis, I need to get over into the Maniototo, to fly down the eastern side of the Dunstan Range, but I get a bit low and I fall below the wave set up by the nor'-wester.

The wind has changed at low level but is still blowing up high. I try, but can't get a thermal to climb back into the wave. Alex is half a kilometre to the east and stays in the wave and is gone. I struggle for a long time. It's late evening by now and if I go any further south but don't get any lift, I might have to put down a long way from home with darkness closing in. I've been in the Discus for nine hours already. I decide to bail and then have to battle at low level from Cromwell to get home to Omarama. It takes over an hour. I'm shagged. I miss the 1000-kilometre mark by 100. Alex, the little bugger, completes the course in magnificent style and lands just before nightfall.

What the hell. It's been a great year in other respects. We've survived an earthquake, and the trophy cupboard at NZRU is full, apart from the one that really matters. On reflection, it's not the win/loss record that gives satisfaction and faith for next year's RWC, it's the tests we won that we could have lost. We were in the hole against South Africa at Soweto, against Australia in Sydney, and against Wales in Cardiff. Not once did we slip into Ceri Evans' Red Zone.

But there's a niggling question that won't go away. The only match we lost that we could and should have won was against Australia in Hong Kong. We didn't lose it through panicking. We were in a position of strength, but couldn't last 20 minutes without Dan. Can we do it without Dan? We did it in Sydney without him — just — by going back to the pick-and-gos and beating up their pack. If we had to, could we do that against the Boks? Against France?

I'm a man who likes a plan, but as gliding keeps demonstrating, you can't plan for everything. Rugby's maybe the most demanding mix of anaerobic stress and collision trauma there is. There are always injuries. Shit happens, says Bert, it's how you deal with it. Which is helpful and true, to a point. I'm not naive, though: some stuff you can't get over or around. If I was religious, I'd be praying for a smooth glide home in 2011.

Broken

On 31 December, some old mates from school and uni help me celebrate my thirtieth birthday at my just-finished home at Wanaka. As the clock ticks over to 1 January 2011, amid the hugs and kisses and tooting of horns around the town, there's a moment where I remember doing much the same thing with a group of mates at Omarama in 2007. I'd just turned 26. *Four years. It's here. I get another crack at it.*

In early January, the New Zealand Gliding Championships come to Omarama. I'm not competing but try to do some of the same tasks. On one occasion I'm in the Hunter at the northern end of Lake Hawea, and get caught down low in the valley. The airstrip I'm counting on is overgrown, and the wind is coming from the wrong direction and I think, *Shit, I'm going to have to commit to that real soon.* But I find a wee spur that's giving me a little bit of lift. I can't do a full turn in it, so I pick up 50 feet and then lose 40. I work away at it for half an hour, and finally pick up 500 feet, enough to get over into the Dingle Valley, where there's another strip where some of the other guys have landed. But I work for another hour to get myself on top of Dingle Ridge, and from there I can make a final glide for home. *That's so-o-o-o satisfying.* I get out of the glider exhausted but exhilarated.

For what seems like a long time in 2011, that's about as good as it gets.

On 9 February, training with the Crusaders, no contact, just turning during a yo-yo, f'godsake, I feel a bit of a clunk on the outside of my right foot, and suddenly I can't run or put much weight on it. I'd been feeling the foot towards the end of last year, a bit of a niggle, achy at times, but it never let go like this.

A scan shows a stress fracture of the fifth metatarsal of my right foot. My first thought is that I'm bloody lucky it's now. You start counting down to October. A knee reconstruction is nine months — that'd be me out. *Imagine if you busted your knee and it's just bang, goodbye RWC,* I tell myself. *A stress fracture can't be that big a deal.*

Celebrating my birthday at Wanaka, 31 December 2010: 'I remember doing much the same thing with a group of mates at Omarama in 2007.'

I sit down with orthopaedic surgeon Rhett Mason and All Black doctor Deb Robinson, who tell me that normally they'd rest it for six weeks and see if it came right. Trouble is, if that doesn't work, if it doesn't come right, I'd be up for an operation and a screw and then I'd be out for a further six to 12 weeks. Bugger that. We decide to go for the screw now, to make sure.

On 15 February, I spend the night in hospital and a screw is inserted under general anaesthetic, then home to Mum and Dad's in plaster on crutches. I'm looking at a rehab plan of two weeks to get the wound healed, then four weeks progressing back to walking, then running by six weeks, and playing when I can after that.

Given that I was going to sit out the first three rounds of the new Super 15 anyway, that's effectively only another month to six weeks of rugby I'll be missing. I can wear that; it's a huge year. The new Super 15 format extends the Super rugby season through three conferences, 18 rounds, then play-offs, semis and finals. In RWC year, we probably could have done without that, but now that I'm going to be missing until about Round 8, I'm happy there are going to be plenty of games left for me.

Ted's been careful not to mention any 'r' words, like recovery or rotation, this time around. Instead the key word has been 'manage' — Ted has met with the Super coaches, who've agreed to rest — manage, sorry — their All Blacks at various points during the season, and Toddy agreed to give me a late start.

On Friday, 18 February, my sister Jo marries Sam Spencer-Bower and I'm there playing the bagpipes on my crutches. It's a welcome, happy diversion, because I'm already bored stiff with rehab.

On Saturday, 19 February in Auckland, the Blues beat the Crusaders 24–22 in an error-filled opening to the New Zealand conference. It's Ali's first game back in New Zealand after two ops on his Achilles and nearly two seasons on the sidelines doing the lonely rehab thing. I'm pleased for him. He does battle with Brad, who's also been doing it hard. After enduring the earthquakes in Christchurch, Brad took his family back to Brisbane for the summer, just in time for the horrific floods which devastated Queensland during December and into January.

On Monday, I get Mum to drop me off at Rugby Park on her way to work, relief teaching at St Mark's Primary in Opawa, so I can spend the day with the boys and start doing some upper body work on the grinder. Toddy's not happy with what happened in Auckland, when the Blues pack took us on in pick-and-gos and got over the top of us. It's frustrating not being able to play. I try to help Kieran as much as I can behind the scenes.

18 February 2011: Playing the bagpipes at Jo's wedding.

On Tuesday, 22 February, I get Mum to drop me off on her way to work again, and after morning training, Kieran and I head to Merivale Mall to have some sushi and talk about how the team are going.

We're sitting there with our sushi when we're engulfed by a noise like thunder, or a train coming, just like the guys described back in September, and the floor starts heaving and shuddering and the lights go out and I slip to the floor down on one knee and grab the crutches. People start screaming, and trying to run, but you can't even stand up. I'm thinking about trying to get under the table. From where I am I can see into the supermarket that opens into the mall, and everything's being thrown off the shelves across the aisles. *When is this going to end?* I look up and there's this big steel beam rocking and rolling above us. *How is this going to end?* When it stops heaving and shuddering enough to stand up, I grab the crutches, lever myself up and Kieran and I make for the Papanui Road exit, where Kieran's parked the car.

Outside, there are a couple of older women who've lost it, so Kieran and I give them a hug — as much as I can with the crutches — and look at the liquid starting to bubble up through cracks in the concrete. I know the guy who owns the camera shop at the entrance to the mall and he tells us there's twice as much damage in his shop as there was in September. People stream past us, shocked, those glazed eyes, that Red Zone stare. I ask Kieran how that shock compares with September. 'Seems

23 February 2011: Part of Merivale Mall a day after the big one.

way worse,' he says. There's another good aftershock and we decide to get out of there. We walk under the façade and over to Kieran's car, parked against the kerb.

There's not a lot of traffic and we make it back to my place, which looks okay, and so we carry on back to Rugby Park. By the time Kieran drops me off and goes home to Bridget and the baby, the sirens are wailing all over the city and there's a pancake cloud of smoke and dust rising over towards the CBD. A few of the boys had been under the grandstand in the changing rooms and one of them was in the shower and he was like, 'Jesus, I got out of there in a hurry!' Then I get a text from my sister: 'Are you okay?'

It's only then that I think of trying to contact anyone, but all the lines are choked, you can't get through, so we stand around outside for a while knowing some serious stuff has happened but not knowing what. I get Corey to drop me home and there's nothing around my house at that stage, so I go inside to wait for Mum to come and pick me up. There's no power or internet connection, so I pull out the Meridian Energy freebie transistor I was so dismissive of and start listening to the Civil Defence bulletins, which confirm that something massive and awful has happened.

The mobile connection comes back and Dad eventually gets through to me and tells me to stay where I am until Mum gets there. She's had to stay with the kids at school until their parents can get to them. There are all these text messages from people who're watching television in Auckland and all over, asking 'Are you okay?' and 'How bad is it?' They've got more idea than me at that point, though the transistor is telling me that some buildings have collapsed and there's been some loss of life, but it's still pretty sketchy. Then people begin ringing in to the station, some really upset at what they've seen — eyewitness reports of dead bodies lying in Cashel Mall and crushed cars and buses. Smoke and dust blanketing the CBD, with choppers overhead, dumping monsoon buckets on smouldering buildings. People in sneakers and bike helmets combing through rubble, trying to help victims caught in collapsed buildings. People shocked, crying and injured, taking refuge in open spaces like Latimer Square and Hagley Park.

At one point, I think I hear running water, which is odd because the water's off. It's coming from over by the front door, and when I hobble over and open it, I see liquid bubbling up through the concrete just outside in the little courtyard. I ignore it for a while, but when I come back and have another look about half an hour later it's still coming and starting to bubble up quite a bit, so I grab a spade from the garage and I'm out there on one foot trying to dig a little trench to take it away from the house. An hour later it starts to come up everywhere. The neighbour's arrived home and I ask him if he can give me a hand, and for the next half-hour he's trying to scoop it away while I'm sticking boards in front of the door to stop it coming in. Then Dad arrives to pick me up, because Mum's tied up.

When we join the traffic heading west out of the city, Dad tells me that Jo's had a narrow escape. She was in her building by the Cashel Street Mall at the Bridge of Remembrance end luckily, and someone managed to get one car out of the car park and eight or nine of them squeezed into it and fled.

By the time we get home, Mum's there too, and over the next few hours we're joined by Jo and Sam and friends and relations, and there's power on out there and we watch the television pictures coming in and realise the extent of the unfolding disaster. Those pictures of the CTV and PGG buildings, and the Cathedral. Streets with dead bodies and badly injured survivors. The death toll going up by the hour. The heroic rescue attempts. Hundreds of people setting up camp in Hagley Park, roads out of the city jammed with fleeing people. Dozens of vehicles abandoned in the liquefaction. Pictures I'll never forget. We sit there mute with sadness watching our wrecked city, disbelieving really, though September has sort of prepared us for some version of this reality.

Jo wasn't the only lucky one. That evening, there's a sequence shown on television of a miraculous escape by a woman with a dog, running into the street as the façade behind her collapses, just about ensnaring her under a huge wave of dust and debris. I recognise the façade of Merivale Mall, the one Kieran and I walked under to get to his car. Must have been moments before.

Over the next few days, it's the stories that get me. Sad. Tragic. Heroic. Lucky. I've always been a bit fatalistic — when your number's up, that's it. What I see and

What's left of the CTV building.

hear confirms it. The sheer luck, good or bad, that means death or survival. Where you were, when. The ones in the CTV building who found a pocket of air. Those poor Japanese students so far from home. The one texting rescuers on her mobile as they tried futilely to get to her before the texts stopped. The guy from the PGG building who went for a run that lunchtime. A woman who lost her son — he was usually in one of the buildings that survived but had gone for a walk down Cashel Mall to do something and it collapsed on him. Those crushed in cars and buses because they were in the wrong place at the wrong time. My sister Jo who was at the right end of Cashel Street Mall. Me and Kieran at the Merivale Mall.

The death toll rises past 100 as rescue workers from around the country concentrate on the CTV and PGG buildings, and more are flown in from Australia and Japan and the States. The CTV building is still on fire. Sewers and water mains are severely damaged, flooding large areas of the city. The port of Lyttelton is closed, and the tunnel, and Evans Pass, the road connecting Lyttelton to Sumner. There's huge damage to houses up in the hills and on the cliff edges around Sumner. The Christchurch Hospital emergency department is still open but damaged, and four other triage centres are set up around the city . . .

Over the next few days, people come and stay, friends from town with no sewers or power, many who'd been at Jo's wedding just days before. That timing was lucky too.

However bad the pictures on television, they don't prepare me for the reality of what I eventually see in what becomes known as the Red Zone of the CBD. If I was underwhelmed in September, this is overwhelming. It's actually worse than pictures can show. It's worse than I can imagine.

In the aftermath, the Crusaders have to make a decision about something as inconsequential as a game of rugby. The guys are all affected differently and you can't tell the way any of them is going to react. Some of the toughest guys that you think will handle anything are the worst. Some of the guys who you think would be a basket case are strong. You have to be careful making any assumptions, what you say to who. It's not a case of telling people to harden up. People deal with stuff in different ways. The most predictable reaction is that some of the guys who aren't from Christchurch don't want to stay, which is understandable, but not acceptable. They take some convincing to stay.

On Wednesday we have to make a decision about whether the team should play on Saturday against the Hurricanes. Toddy says, 'What do you reckon, do we just get on with it?' But none of our boys is anywhere near in a state to play. The decision is made, and we're told to go back to our homes and do what we need to do. We'll get together next week.

I feel a bit useless, but quite a few of the guys get out with shovels and wheelbarrows. I know Brad up his street spends a lot of time on the end of a shovel.

There's liquefaction all around my place, but I can't do anything, so Mum and Dad and Jo and Sam and some mates come and dig all that out. Everyone around the place, all the neighbours, is doing the same. The upside is you get to know them and help each other out.

That sort of spirit is seen right across the city, people just pitching in, doing what they can to help those around them.

Ali, Dan and I have a water business and a few of us decide to put a couple of pallets on a trailer and drive round the bad areas, just knocking on doors, saying gidday and dropping off boxes of water. That's an eye-opener — some really sad sights, like elderly people living in tents, no water, power or sewage. After the drama and tragedy of the CBD, you realise that it's out here in the broken suburbs that the privations and suffering are going to go on for weeks and months. People living in terrible conditions, homes completely knackered, with winter coming in a month or two.

News comes through that AMI Stadium is damaged. Liquefaction has swamped the field and there are rumours about serious structural damage to the stands, even

All roads no longer lead to AMI Stadium . . .

the ones just completed for the RWC. No one says at that point that Christchurch has lost the Cup, but how can it still come? The stadium's wrecked, but even if we play somewhere else, we've seen the pictures of the leaning Grand Chancellor Hotel and heard about the damage to others, and we know that the accommodation infrastructure is pretty much stuffed. And who's going to want to come to a place where the aftershocks are still shuddering through like endless underground waves? But no one wants to say out loud that the RWC's not coming, that we've lost the chance to show off the Garden City and have some fun and celebration to look forward to, because it's almost too much to bear on top of everything else.

A week on, the Crusaders have to decide when and where to play. We can't train at Rugby Park, as the old grandstand's got to be properly assessed, so we shift out to Lincoln.

There's the question as to whether playing rugby is respectful to what's going on, bodies still being retrieved from the rubble, people who've lost their homes camping out in terrible situations, is it right to get out there and play rugby? But if we don't, what are we achieving by not doing it?

If there was something else we could be doing to help, sure. But there's not really anything we can do that makes a difference, other than play. It's not going to help anyone if we sit at home wondering what the hell we do now. We decide it's better that we get back on the horse, give people something other than their misery to look at.

Playing rugby is what we do, it's all we can do really, and in the end it's also probably the most useful thing we can do — embrace the 'new normal' and show people that you've got to get on with things at some point, somehow.

Round 3 is against the Waratahs and has been transferred to Nelson. I fly up from Dunedin, where All Black physio Pete Gallagher has been checking out the foot, giving me the okay to start on the bike.

We'd already agreed to play in the red-and-white hoops of the West Coast union, part of the Crusaders' catchment, in memory of the 29 miners lost at Pike River. I stand there in my moon boot with the team for a minute's silence for the miners and for the dead in Christchurch, the toll still rising. That weekend, all the Super rugby teams do the same.

When the whistle blows, we don't look ready to play. The Waratahs score a couple of tries and I wonder whether we've come back too soon. But Dan keeps us in touch with a couple of penalties, then in the last 10 minutes of the first half, Sonny Bill, on debut, finds his feet with his big mate Robbie Fruean, who scores twice, and we're away. In the second half, as we get out to 33 points, I almost feel sorry for the Tahs — it must be tough up against guys who aren't playing just for themselves any more.

'Hopefully, we showed the region what we're about,' Kieran says after the game. 'Everyone's been showing it the last 10 days, everyone who's been working around

On the sideline for the Crusaders against the Waratahs . . . the guys aren't just playing for themselves any more.

the city and in the suburbs. We just carried on the work that they've been doing.'

In Round 4 the guys trounce the Brumbies in Canberra, running in 46 straight points after trailing 10–6 at the end of the first quarter, and in Round 5 they cream the Highlanders 44–13 in Dunedin.

Round 6 against the Sharks is a radical departure from anything we've done before. Although we've talked about taking the Crusaders roadshow to the northern hemisphere, it's always been pie-in-the-sky stuff, but this seems like the ideal time to try it out. When it's seriously touted by the Crusaders Board that we play the Sharks at Twickenham some of the guys are a bit less than enthusiastic. But given we can't play at home and we've got to go somewhere, and this might be a big earner for the franchise and the Earthquake Appeal, they come round to getting excited about a trip to London and showcasing Super rugby in the northern hemisphere. For the Sharks, London's in the same time zone as Durban and less of a hassle.

The showpiece side of it certainly works — our scrum kills them and Dan and SBW and wingers Zac and Sean Maitland feature in a brand of high-scoring, fast-paced, high-intensity rugby that looks great on my television screen back home. Some of the English scribes are still lost in the Stone Age, though, and seem to equate pace with soft rugby — a funny equation, which isn't actually supported by physics or by the injury toll caused by the big collisions in the game.

As a fund-raiser for the Earthquake Appeal, it's not as successful as hoped. A 35,000-odd crowd isn't bad given the short lead-time, but it means the Crusaders barely break even, a tough result for the Board, not to mention the guys who travel right round the world and back in the space of a week, even if they do manage a 44–28 bonus point win.

The guys get the bye to recover in Round 7, and then stomp all over the Bulls in Timaru. The following week in Tauranga, I finally get to play rugby in 2011, albeit 30 minutes off the bench. The day before the game the foot's a bit sore, but it doesn't worry me in the game. The Chiefs haven't been going well, but, as usual, that doesn't stop them giving us grief until the last quarter, when we ease away to 34–16 and a bonus point.

My foot seems to come through the game okay, but on Monday night after a bit of a light training, I'm woken by pain — my bloody foot's just killing me. I take some painkillers, but come morning I can barely walk and have to get back on my crutches to make it to training. The head-space is not good. *This is bloody ridiculous! What's happening here?* And for the first time, *Shit, it's all going wrong.*

It's the same foot, but the pain seems to be on the inside, not where the screw is on the outside. I get an X-ray and, thank Christ, it's just deep bruising on the bone, caused by an orthotic arch I've been wearing for extra support.

I miss the next game and watch us go down 18–26 to a really committed Highlanders team. We come away with nothing.

But the big news seems to be that I've turned down an invite to Prince William and Kate's wedding. I was flattered to be asked and had I been playing Super rugby from the word go, I might have been due a rest about now. The team is off to Perth and then to South Africa, and I might have been able to scoot off to London, miss the Force game and rejoin the team in Cape Town. But once I got injured and missed so much rugby, it was never a goer — I've got other things on my mind that I need to get right.

I don't get everything right in Perth; in fact I get sin-binned for repeated infringements. Some people might regard that as a return to form! We get a bonus point win and the foot gives me no trouble. But something else does give me trouble. Head bang. Blurred vision.

I might be okay to play against the Stormers, but I decide not to. *They come in threes*, I tell myself, *I'll be right now.* And the one I told myself back in February when my foot went. *Better now, than later.* That one's wearing thin, and something else is rising up instead, a bit of despair. *Jesus, when am I going to get a break here?*

The Stormers match is one of our best wins, only their second defeat of the season. Crocky is deserved Man of the Match, bulldozing them in the scrums, big hits in defence and two tries. But it's brutally hard on us. We lose Israel after just four minutes, then Kahn Fotuali'i, then Adam Whitelock, who'd come on to replace Izzy, then Sean Maitland — by halftime we'd lost four backs, while Dan, with a hamstring strain, and I hadn't even got to the starting line.

The 20–14 scoreline means no bonus point. We're third on the points table, but in reality we're fourth in the standings, because under the new rules the top teams from each conference have preference. So the Stormers, who are one point below us, would go through before us because they top the South African conference.

I get back on the field against the Cheetahs in Bloemfontein, along with Dan and SBW, and last 80 minutes, but that's where the satisfaction ends. We get done 33–20. We lost the last time we played here in 2009 too. I don't know what it is about these guys, but they grow an extra leg when we arrive. It's annoying. It's frustrating. And I have the feeling it might cost us.

Dan basically kicks us to a win over the Chiefs when we get 'home' — this time Napier. It's a short turnaround after the flight back from Africa to Christchurch, and Sonny Bill, Izzy, Andy Ellis and Sean are all out injured. But Dan's there and boots over 20 of our 25 points — five penalties, one dropped goal and a conversion. No bonus point, so we're still two points behind the Blues, who top the New Zealand conference.

The defining event of the Crusaders' season comes in the next match, against the Reds at Suncorp, in front of an Australian record crowd of over 48,000, and unfortunately it stars me and my favourite referee, Stu Dickinson. We're up by two points in the last seconds, after a bad start and a lot of penalties from Dickinson, when a Reds attack breaks down right in front of our posts. They have one guy parked over the ball, who is bowled out of the way by Franksy as I come through the gate. The ball's just sitting there with no one over it, so I pick it up just before Dickinson says, 'Hands off, it's a ruck.' I drop the ball and look at him, still basically on my own, as he raises his arm for a penalty. I'm bewildered. A ruck has to have some participants, some people over the ball, doesn't it? Quade's kicked badly all game, but he's not going to miss one right in front. That's the game, 16–14.

And it's kind of our season too, because we know it's likely to condemn us to the long route to the finals, if we make it, via South Africa. We need another long flight from home like a hole in the head.

Meantime, I've got other worries. The foot's come back to haunt me. Before the Chiefs game I'd started to feel the outside of my foot a little bit. I didn't think too much of it, but before the Reds game it was quite sore. I got through the game, but a scan shows a stress riser down the end of the same bone. *Bloody hell, what else!*

But I'm still able to tell myself that I'm lucky, when Deb Robinson says that this new stress seems to be healing itself and won't need a moon boot. She reckons the new stress probably came about because of the screw in the bone, but that the screw was the right thing because that original stress fracture hasn't healed and the screw is holding it together. *Right.*

So it's three weeks off — we've got a bye, so that means missing only two games. I'm starting to make deals with myself. From thinking about the perfect build-up to the RWC, now just weeks away, I'm gradually trading down to, *Okay, if I can get four tests before the Cup, that's going to have to do.* Or even: *If I get no tests before the*

What's a bloody ash cloud? The Crusaders on the tarmac in Christchurch with the chartered DC-3 before taking off for Wellington.

Cup, but get to play in the Cup, I'll just deal with that too. Deb is positive, reassures me that I've still got time up my sleeve, that we'll get the foot right. That's what I need to hear, as I sit and watch the last two conference games, wins against the Blues in Timaru and Hurricanes in Wellington.

For the trip to Wellington to play the Hurricanes, an ash cloud from an erupting Chilean volcano forces the Crusaders on to a DC-3, which flies below the altitude of the dust particles. By this time, the guys have coped with fallout from earthquakes, exploding mines, floods, and have been living out of suitcases and gear bags for months — what's a bloody ash cloud? On the Monday, there's another magnitude 6, causing further damage to Kieran's place.

In the DC-3, the guys get to fly over the CBD Red Zone, and for most of them it's the first time they've seen it. The scale of the devastation is a shock, despite all the pictures they've seen.

The win against the Canes gets us into the quarter-final play-offs against the Sharks in Nelson, while the top two, the Reds and the Stormers — and me — have the luxury of a week off.

I watch the guys deal to the Sharks 36–8, lost in admiration for the guts and application of the buggers after what they've been through, then pack my mouthguard and boots — gratefully this time — to join them for the trek to the semi in Africa, where our guys get themselves up once again to blow the Stormers off Newlands 29–10 in one of the best Crusaders performances I've been part of. Crocky is huge again, and our scrum gives us go-forward and penalties. We're 23–10 up at halftime after a Sean intercept and a Sonny Bill offload for Robbie. Habana gets one back from a tap penalty, but the second half is hard, attrition rugby where we don't give an inch and keep the buffer, courtesy of huge defence and Dan's kicking.

I'm rejoicing at the win and at having got through 80 minutes on my twice-broken foot, but the trip back to Brisbane for the final proves to be an air-bridge too far.

After everything they've been through, the guys are knackered, but hugely determined to try to make a fairytale ending to a traumatic season. It's a great opportunity to sort out the Reds — we owe them one for the Stu Dickinson moment.

We need a structured game where we can exert pressure on their scrum and marshal our energies. Instead we get Bryce Lawrence who, in front of a new record 50,000-plus Australian Super rugby crowd at Suncorp, either does a Wayne Barnes freeze or is trialling a new, non-interventionist, minimalist refereeing style. Lawrence lets everything go. There's no gate at the back of the ruck, just a big welcome mat right around the tackled ball. Anyone can pile in from any angle. On your feet, off your feet, hands wherever you feel like putting them. *Come back Stu Dickinson, all is forgiven!* After five minutes of this helter-skelter headless chicken stuff, I ask Bryce what the hell's going on. 'There are players coming from everywhere at the breakdown and getting away with it.'

'It's the same for both teams,' he says.

'I don't give a damn which side you penalise,' I tell him, unused to pleading with a ref to actually blow his whistle. 'Just give us a line in the sand, f'chrissakes!'

But Bryce either can't see anything wrong with the free-for-all or he doesn't know how to get control back.

Despite Bryce's no-show, we stay in the game for a long time. After an energy-absorbing, scoreless first half-hour, Quade and Dan swap penalties, then Dan finally breaks their staunch line with a genius grubber kick, regathers and scores, and converts from wide out. Cooper cuts the margin again with a penalty in the thirty-eighth minute after Brad foot-trips him — Bryce at least saw that — and we go into halftime one point up.

But the writing's kind of on the dressing-room wall. We've managed to shut the Reds down for 40 minutes, pressured Genia and Cooper into mistakes, but it feels like we've already done 80 minutes' worth of running and the guys are close to being played out.

The tipping point comes in the forty-seventh minute when Brad crashes over in the tackle of Radike Samo. Logic says it has to be a try, the way Brad fell, where the ball was. We go back to halfway in anticipation. But instead of asking the TMO, 'Any reason I can't award the try?' Bryce asks, 'Try or no try?' When the replays can't show definitively whether or not the ball was grounded, the TMO has no choice and calls us back for the five-metre scrum.

Crocky looks unimpressed as Bryce Lawrence finally blows his whistle in the Super 15 final against the Reds in Brisbane.

Dan goals after a Reds infringement at a rare scrum, to make it 10–6 in the forty-ninth minute. But we're starting to make a lot of unforced errors, crooked lineout throws, ball spills, and give the Reds the ball back.

Digby Ioane finally breaks our line after 50 minutes, and when Cooper converts, the Reds are up 13–10. Dan brings us level with a long-range penalty in the fifty-sixth, but it's pretty clear that the longer the game stays in the balance, the less likely we are to win it. We're on our last legs, feeling every kilometre of the one hundred thousand we've travelled.

As both defences tire, the game opens up, but the Reds are the team with the energy — and the play-maker in Will Genia — to take advantage of it. From a turnover in broken play, he shapes to kick, then runs and runs and runs to score a brilliant solo try that is worthy of the first Super 15 championship.

The Crusaders' fairytale is over.

A lot of our guys are shattered after the game. Brad is as down as I've seen him. He was so determined to win his last tilt at Super rugby. The boys have travelled so far this season, sacrificed so much in terms of time with families who were often doing it tough in the Christchurch aftershocks, got to the final against all the odds, but couldn't top it off. To come so far and trip over at the last. It's a real bugger.

The way my season's been going, I'm pleased to have got through another 80 minutes, but I'm not pleased with how I played the final, nor with how I led the team in it. We were points up after 50 minutes in a final and I didn't grab it by the

For all the effort we've put in, the distance we've travelled, the sacrifices we've made . . .
Sam Whitelock and me after the final whistle in Brisbane.

scruff of the neck. And, equally worryingly, the way the match was played, it's hard to figure out even in retrospect what I might have done, apart from nobble the ref.

For all the effort we've put in, the distance we've travelled, the sacrifices we've made, the horrors we've lived through, we've lost at the final hurdle. John Smit's words come back to me from last year, after he'd cost his team in the final minutes of his 100th test: 'It's a cruel game.'

The game doesn't know the stats, or whether one team usually wins at this venue, it doesn't have a clue what's riding on the result or who the favourite might be or who might deserve what, and it doesn't care who wins and who loses.

It's a reminder, as I finally head into camp with the All Blacks for the 2011 RWC, that the game doesn't have a memory or sentiment, and that fairytales are highly improbable. You have to make it happen.

What else?

There's an inspirational sequence on high rotation on New Zealand television as the RWC gets close. Captain Kirk is holding the Webb Ellis Cup aloft in the old main stand at Eden Park back in 1987, with the cheering crowd down on the field in front of him.

I like that image. I see myself doing that. The 2011 All Backs have decided we're not going to be aw-shucks modest about our aims: we're here to win the RWC. And we're not going to be intimidated or overwhelmed by the pressure of history.

Quite a few of us were burned in Cardiff in 2007. Dan, Mils, Brad, Ma'a, Kevvy, Ali and I were also scorched in Sydney in 2003, but the whole squad and virtually the whole nation is aware of our RWC record, a record of stumbling and missing since 1987. It could be regarded as a history of failure. Our take on it is that it demonstrates just how tough and unique a challenge the RWC is, that it's like nothing else we've ever done or will do. It's different. We reckon if we acknowledge that and embrace it, rather than downplay it like we did last time, we'll be better prepared to succeed this time.

We're also going to try to enjoy every moment of what's being touted as the last time our little corner of the world gets to host the RWC. That fits with me too. The penultimate word I write down in the Warwick every game day is always: *Enjoy*.

But when I watch that footage from 1987, there's a bit of unintended consequence for me. When David Kirk holds the Cup aloft, there's a moment when he turns to the forgotten man, the original captain Andy Dalton, to come and hold it. Dalton's sort of reluctant, because he did a hammy before the tournament and couldn't play one minute of one game.

It's an image that sits in the back of my head, ready on playback every time my foot flares. *Don't let that be me.*

When the RWC circus starts rolling into town, there's a rising buzz of anticipation as the teams arrive and the civic welcomes are extended across the country and the overseas media begins to make their presence felt and cars and buildings and lampposts sprout flags.

Down south, they're doing things their own way. Mum and Dad tell me that a local farmer has upended three of those big plastic hay bales at the Kurow side of the old wooden bridge across the Waitaki leading to the Haka Valley. The hay bales are festooned with the flags of all the countries in the Cup, and on top there's a sign with a big 7 on it, and the words 'This is McCaw Country'.

It's a relief that it's finally under way — and not just for me, I reckon.

So much has happened globally and locally since 2005, when Jock Hobbs and Prime Minister Helen Clark and Tana Umaga and Pinetree and BJ went to Dublin and won the Cup for New Zealand. A lot of what's happened hasn't exactly been helpful to the prospective success of the tournament. The global financial crisis struck in 2008, and most people have been staggering into and out of recession ever since. We're so far away from the rest of the world, so expensive to get to, that there must have been the odd dark day when Martin Snedden and his administration feared we might be throwing a party that no one would be able to come to. And then this year, the February earthquake in Christchurch, which might have precipitated a crisis of confidence when it forced a huge reshuffle of venues and schedules. It must be gratifying for Martin to watch it all fire up. And for Jock, who said to me once, 'Gee, I promised everyone so much.'

For me, there's a moment when the RWC 2011 really comes alive. When the Tongan team arrives at Auckland airport and is welcomed by a huge contingent of mostly Auckland-based Tongans, and we see pictures on our screens of all those red-and-white flags and the band and the dancing, it confirms to me — and a lot of other Kiwis, I suspect — that this is going to be something special, this is going to be fantastic.

A big part of Jock's pitch in Dublin was the concept of New Zealand as 'a stadium of four million'. And Tana told them in Dublin that if we held the World Cup here, it wouldn't just be home for New Zealand, but also for the Pacific Island nations. The Tongans prove that that wasn't just PR hype, and ought to allay the fears — mainly from the English media — that New Zealanders will be one-eyed supporters of one team, and that the only celebration will be around All Black wins. That criticism betrays an ignorance of New Zealand's demographics: the various ethnic and 'expat' communities who live here were always going to ensure that the Tongan, Samoan, Fijian, Scots, Welsh, Irish, Springbok and even English teams wouldn't lack for local support.

That airport welcome also guarantees that there'll be a vibrant atmosphere at the opening match of the tournament, that the 'away' team won't lack for passionate support. It's Tonga. They're playing the All Blacks. When I watch those pictures, I'm thinking, *Shit, it's on. We'd better be ready.*

Six weeks ago, when the All Blacks first came together, things didn't look that flash.

Ted and Smithy and Shag had been keeping close tabs on us during the Super

There's a moment when the RWC really comes alive. Tongan fans at the welcome ceremony at Papakura Marae.

15, trying to be supportive, and at the same time trying to keep their distance and not betray their anxieties. It can't have been easy watching.

Some of the Crusaders were pretty much spent. They and their families had been in coping mode for four or five months during the Super 15, focused on the need to get up for the next game. When the campaign finished with that loss in Brisbane, a kind of emotional payback set in. One of Ted's first decisions after we got together was to send Brad and Kieran and Owen home to their families for a couple of weeks.

The Hurricanes also had an awful Super 15, more of their own doing. New coach Mark Hammett's attempts to change the culture there resulted in a bit of a meltdown. Core All Blacks like Horey, Ma'a and Cory lost form and confidence. Piri badly broke his leg in 2010 and struggled to get back to full fitness. Conrad lost most of the season to a badly smashed nose.

The Dan Carter Understudy auditions hadn't exactly progressed either. Aaron Cruden was dropped from the Canes after one game and took a while to regain his spot, while Colin Slade had the incredible misfortune to break his jaw twice, in different places, and was only just ready to play again.

The upside was that a lot of those guys were delighted to be back in the All Black environment. Me too: the resources; Ted and Smithy and Shag; the detailing; the sense of mission, particularly this time, when we're finally on the brink of being able to deliver on four years' preparation.

However, before we were able to get into World Cup mode, we had to survive a friendly against Fiji, and an abbreviated Tri Nations — home and away matches against Australia and South Africa.

In action in the 'friendly' against Fiji, Carisbrook, 2011.

That might have been okay for me and a couple of the others coming back from injury or needing to show some form, but it was hardly ideal preparation to have the top three ranked teams in the world bashing seven bells out of one another so close to the RWC. Except maybe for the top northern hemisphere teams, who were working their way through six uninterrupted weeks of comprehensive, concentrated preparation with the sun on their backs. In 2007 we were criticised — perhaps correctly — for not having enough tough rugby before the tournament. That's one criticism at least that won't fly this time.

But it turned out not to be the Tri Nations as we've come to know it.

The day after a preliminary run-around against Fiji at Carisbrook — the last test there — we watched a very strange Springboks team get stuffed 39–20 in Sydney. There was a reason for all the no-names on the Springbok team-sheet. No fewer than 21 of their first-choice players were injured and unable to play.

Before we got a chance to sympathise with such a dreadful run of bad luck for the poor old Bokkies, reports came through of many of those same 'injured' players training up a storm at a secret location up on the high veldt. We weren't likely to make a fuss about it, however, because we were planning to do much the same ourselves.

We decided that our main objective for the Tri Nations was not in fact the Tri Nations but the Bledisloe Cup. To retain that, we had to win one of the two tests against the Aussies. We still wanted to win both trophies, but the Bledisloe was a must-have, whereas the Tri Nations was a like-to-have. As Shag said, who remembers who won the Tri Nations in 2007?

Well, apart from us. We won it. In last place were the winners of the 2007 RWC, South Africa.

I'd like to be able to say that our concentration on the Bledisloe was due to history and tradition et cetera, but it also had a lot to do with our developing dislike of the Aussie team, and a need to get our foot back on their throat after what happened in Hong Kong last year. It wasn't just Cooper's spray-and-shove after O'Connor's winning try, and it wasn't just their prolonged celebrations after the final whistle — after all, they had just broken a losing streak of 10 tests. Nor was it just because they refused to have a beer with us — if Robbie was worried that familiarity might breed contempt, it'd be difficult to see how there could be much downside there any more. It was also because they'd developed into genuine contenders.

Happy loosies after the Eden Park Bledisloe Cup test, 6 July 2011 — Kieran Read,
Jerome Kaino, me, Liam Messam and Adam Thomson.

After Hong Kong, they went on to Europe and were frighteningly good against
France, absolutely smashing them 59–16. That backline in particular, of formerly
wayward talents like Kurtley Beale and Cooper, shred France. After seeing that,
Ma'a said they were now more dangerous than we were.

Before the Tri Nations, there'd been lots of trans-Tasman chat reported, that they
were ready, that they'd timed their rise perfectly while we were on the slide. So it was
hardly surprising that we were well primed for them after a 40–7 whacking of a Bok
team full of names we didn't expect to see in their top RWC team.

In my notes for the team leaders' meeting before the Wallaby test at Eden Park,
I wrote: *Mindset: Physically and mentally stuff them through ruthless execution.*

I wish all games were that predictable! By halftime the contest was effectively
over: we scored twice from Cooper mistakes and were 20–nil up. We pressured the
Genia–Cooper axis and closed it and Beale and the rest down. It wasn't just the
30–14 scoreline that eased the angst after Hong Kong, it was the way we unfurled
a pretty complete statement from the different components of our team: from the
scrum, from Jerome and Kieran and me, from Dan and the guys outside him.

After the game, we didn't bother having a beer with them: there was bound to be
a plane or bus they had to catch.

With the Bledisloe back in the cabinet for another year, we turned our attention
to the return games, against South Africa in Port Elizabeth and Australia in Brisbane

— although we were already looking beyond them to the beginning of the RWC, 12 days after the match in Brisbane.

Ted decided to use the trip to Africa to test-drive the younger and fringe players, and part of that entailed leaving most of the leadership group behind in order to see how they coped without us. There was some debate about whether I should go and not play. But, as Ted pointed out, if I got injured during the World Cup, then this was the way it would have to be. *Gulp.* Luckily, I hadn't seen the Andy Dalton footage at that stage.

So Brad, Kieran, Dan, Mils and I got sent home, and on television I watched an All Black team run out in Port Elizabeth which had one back who'd smashed the Boks in Wellington three weeks before, and four forwards. The Boks side was even more different, after a truly remarkable mass rehab: just two backs survived from the earlier game.

The Tri Nations championship had become an exercise in shadow-boxing.

The Boks won, but the real winners and losers were revealed after the final whistle, when the RWC teams had to be named. At least the Boks had completed their Tri Nations responsibilities — last again, just like 2007 — and the guys who missed out could slink off home to the comfort of their families. Not so the All Blacks.

Crocky hadn't made the squad for South Africa and probably expected his fate, but Liam Messam, Hosea Gear and Jarrad Hoeata had to travel back from South Africa to Sydney with the rest of the team after missing the cut. Awkward for everyone. On reaching Sydney, the RWC squad flew north to Brisbane to join Kieran, Brad, Mils, Dan and me, while the rejects flew home. That was a tough and hardly satisfactory way of doing things, one that the IRB could have avoided with a little flexibility, and it had an unsettling effect on those who made the cut as well.

We spent the first day in Brisbane doing media for the RWC, and didn't get to run together until Wednesday, not ideal for a test with the Tri Nations championship at stake.

Maybe it wouldn't have mattered what sort of preparation we'd had, because the Aussies were really bloody fired up and hit us hard for the first 20 to 30 minutes. I found myself standing under the sticks two tries down, with the score already out to 20–3. *Shit, if we ship any more points this could really blow out.* I told the guys that this was the moment where we saw what we were made of.

We'd been going side to side, too lateral, so we changed that and tightened it up, engaged them, really took them on. It was a bit wet and we started making them tackle us around the fringes. They struggled to hang in there, and we clawed our way back to 20–20 and it felt like we had the edge, had them sorted — apart from a bit of Genia brilliance which took the game and the Tri Nations away from us.

There was a bit of post-game controversy around Quade Cooper's attempt to knee me in the head as he was extricating himself from a ruck. The intent of what he was trying to do pissed me off more than the execution. Shortly after that happened, I was carrying and should have passed, but I lit up when I saw Quade standing in

'. . . but I lit up when I saw Quade standing in front of me. . .', against Australia, Brisbane, 2011.

front of me and clattered into him instead. I was disappointed in myself doing that, letting it get personal. There's no need — players like Quade get sorted. Sooner or later, they get their beans.

Of much greater importance were Kieran's high ankle injury, and Thommo's elbow damage. If either were serious, the coaches had a dilemma, thanks to the IRB. They couldn't call anyone else into the squad unless they were prepared to rule that player out for the whole tournament. Thankfully, the early indications were that Thommo's wasn't that serious and that Reado would be back before the business end of the RWC.

While it's galling seeing the Aussies as Tri Nations champions and giving them belief that they've got it over us again, there were really important things I took away from the game in Brisbane. We were in a deep hole and we got back to 20–20 and you could see it in their eyes that they were gone. Brad saw it too. He was as pissed off as I was about losing, but said it could be the best thing for us. 'It's great that they think they've got it over us,' he told me. 'We know they were there for the taking.'

While it gave me the shits that we weren't able to take advantage of it and finish them, that moment will come round again, in a much more important game. I'll be looking for it. We won't let it slip away next time.

My foot came through the Tri Nations okay, although it was aching a bit during the week before the Brisbane game. I can't risk doing the kind of training I used to lap up, road running, shuttle sprints, yo-yos, but after all I've been through,

Opening World Cup match against Tonga.

I'm grateful to be here in camp, on the cusp of the RWC. *So far, so good* — Andy Dalton stays on freeze-frame.

We watch television pictures of the build-up for the opening on a beautiful clear sunny Auckland spring afternoon — the arrival of the waka at Queens Wharf, the crowds pouring down to the waterfront, so many that it takes the organisers and the Auckland public transport system by surprise. I'm thinking about the game and trying not to get too engrossed in what's happening out there, a few hundred metres from our hotel, but I'm also thinking, *Wow, it's on.*

We see a little of the buskers and musicians on the Fan Trail along Great North Road, but don't see anything of the opening ceremony at Eden Park, because we're not allowed out on to the field to warm up, but it sounds amazing from the changing rooms.

The game itself is a bit of a one-half wonder. We play well in the first half, with structure and urgency, and go to sleep in the second. Maybe that has to do with the late start — the second half kicks off when I'd be normally doing the after-match interviews. The main thing is that it's a good competitive match for the opening of the RWC, in which the minnows aren't monstered. Tonga plays well, particularly in the second half, and 41–10 is a respectable scoreline for both sides. The other big thing is that there are no major injuries, and that includes me — I have that rare sensation this year of being on two functional pegs.

Which proves to be short-lived. I strain my calf at Thursday training in Hamilton preparing for Japan, and Dan feels his hammy tighten. When our minor injuries are announced, some in the media suspect rotation by stealth, but that's bullshit — I've already done all the media for what would have been my 100th test.

My calf isn't that bad and if it was a knockout match I might have played, but, realistically, Japan isn't worth the risk, even though Buck Shelford's on the radio saying that if we don't play our top XV we'll lose. We've come to expect that play-your-top-team-every-week stuff from elements in the media, but not from the likes of Buck and Fitzy. I hope when I'm retired, I'm able to recognise that the game will have changed since I played.

Ironically, it might be Japan who are pulling the rotation tricks. There are 10 changes to the team that did quite well against France last week, eventually going down 47–21. Their main objectives are Tonga and Canada, so coach John Kirwan might be keeping his powder dry against us.

After a minute's silence for the victims of the earthquake in Christchurch and the tsunami on the east coast of Japan, we beat them 83–7. Given Colin Slade's lack of match practice, it's another important milestone for his regaining confidence and match fitness.

Some pundits reckon every tournament needs a major upset to get it fizzing. Down in the bars of Queenstown, England are doing their best to make that unnecessary, with royal shenanigans and dwarf-throwing, but Ireland oblige anyway, by throttling Australia 15–6 at Eden Park the following day.

That really throws the seedings and tournament predictions into disarray. It means that the two halves of the draw are now divided neatly into northern and southern hemisphere battles. It also means that if we get to the final, we won't be playing Australia. They're now on our side of the draw. We'll have to beat them to make the final . . . unless we lose to France in our next pool match, which will throw all the balls into the air again and put us on the other side of the draw.

I can't say I'm fazed by all these permutations. In 2007, we constantly looked at what was happening around us in the other pools, trying to suss out who we'd be playing when. We got ahead of ourselves. This time, I don't think like that, I don't even look at what's up the road beyond the next game. My attitude is: who cares what side of the draw we're on? We'll have to play all the good bastards at some point, and whenever that is, we'll have to beat them. Next up is France.

There's no way of knowing whether France have the same attitude. If they lose to us and finish second in our pool, they'd be playing the knockout phase against teams they play regularly in the Six Nations — England or Wales or Ireland. There's a theory that they would prefer to be over there, and avoid the All Blacks, Aussies and Boks. There's another theory that France do best when they don't care. That's a theory I don't subscribe to — I think they play their best, like most teams, when they're most under the hammer and fearful of failure.

Whatever, we've just got to beat whichever French team turns up — and I reckon we've got the team to do it. Dan's back, and this is our best team, apart from Mils and Kieran who are not quite right yet. Thommo goes into No. 8 for this game, and he and I plan to swap roles a bit, with him packing 8 on defence and me on attack.

There's a bit of media talk of revenge for Cardiff, but it's not a knockout game and whoever loses will still get a second chance, perhaps even an easier road. But we're not thinking like that. We want to beat them, really make a statement, so we pull the emotional trigger with some powerful stuff from the aftermath of a France/New Zealand test some time ago.

It's also my 100th test match, the most by any All Black, one ahead of Mils, who will have to wait another week. Some stats don't matter that much, but this one does — it's an incredible honour to have gone out into battle in the black jersey a hundred times. I know that there's going to be a special presentation by Jock Hobbs after the match, a special All Black cap, and I don't want to be walking over to receive that from a great rugby man like Jock after captaining the All Blacks to their first loss in a RWC pool game.

That doesn't happen. But something else happens that from a personal point of view is almost as bad.

France start well, keeping possession, running good angles, stretching us, yes, but our defence is up to it and they don't collect any points for their efforts. It seems like it might be a Toulouse kind of day for them, rather than Biarritz, and it's certainly not the French team that turned up to Cardiff. Even Dusautoir doesn't look that interested — I can't tell that from his facial expression or anything he says or doesn't say — but he misses a tackle on Cory Jane that takes us to 12–nil.

We win comfortably 37–17 and I would have no idea whether that suits French plans or not. Smithy tells me Lievremont's been saying that France would struggle to beat the All Blacks twice at home, so they'd best make it the one that counts. Then some of their players come into our changing room for a drink after the game and a couple of them say as they're leaving, 'See you in the Final.'

The result might be the equivalent of a Gallic shrug, who'd know, but there are a lot of good things to take out of the game. We've lifted ourselves to a new level, killing them in the scrums and beating them in the collisions. Collective pace and power. And Dan is magic, right back to his best.

'The rapier came from Carter,' writes Gregor Paul. 'He played with his head up again and that calm authority that his team-mates thrive on. His passing had that easy rhythm that lets everyone know he's in the zone — ready to play and have a bit of fun. He made an electric break to set up Israel Dagg's first try, where he dummied and disappeared. He even dropped a goal for no particular reason but to show he could. Gutted by his efforts at the last Word Cup, he chose the right night to play such a big game. Dagg, Richard Kahui, Cory Jane and Sonny Bill Williams . . . all fed off Carter's energy and enterprise.'

It's not all about Dan, of course — 'this beautifully organised, dynamic machine

Dan is magic, right back to his best in the pool match against France. Morgan Parra is the Frenchman.

Jock Hobbs presents me with my 100th test cap. It was an emotional moment.

that was slick and clever' — is gratifying for the team in general. 'Favourites by reputation yesterday morning; the All Blacks were favourites by right last night.'

Which is great, except that it's also the day my foot goes bang.

Right before halftime, I take the ball up. When I step, it feels like I've been kicked in the foot or jumped on. I feel a pop or a crack. *Shit, I hope that was a kick.* When the whistle goes for halftime, I jog in and tell Doc Deb that it's a bit sore, that I heard it go. She says I'll be right, which is what I want to hear, but running back out on the field, it hits me — *Fuck, that's sore!* Then the whistle goes and I carry on and get to the end of my 100th game.

By the time the presentation is made by Jock, it takes a lot of self-control to walk over to him, rather than hobble. But, hell, in the presence of a man who's done so much to give me and the other All Blacks a career and to bring the Cup here, and who is so obviously ravaged by his illness, it's not that hard. I'm not the most emotional guy around, but that presentation really gets to me: what Jock says, the fact that it's him, huge numbers of the crowd sticking around for it and chanting my name, the cap.

The boys also have a presentation for me for my 100th. It was supposed to happen in the changing room, but they made the mistake of telling security at Eden Park they were carrying a shotgun and, even though it was broken down and in a case, there was no way. So we do it back at the hotel — a beautiful under-and-over with my name engraved on the butt. Something I'll always treasure.

I have a beer and enjoy the moment and the performance by the team and try not to think about the foot too much, and keep those pictures of Andy Dalton at bay. The odd time the foot's been sore after a game, it's been fine again the next day, so Deb and I are hopeful that it's just that.

That night, though, it swells up. Next day, when we fly down to Wellington, I feel like I'm walking on a lump. *That's different. I've never had this before.*

I ice it and swallow anti-inflammatories, but it's sore walking. I'm down to play against Canada and we're trying to be positive, but as the week goes on there's some debate over whether I should play. Deb says wait and see, reckons if it's anything drastic it's not going to improve a whole lot. I don't train on Tuesday and we have a day off on Thursday, and by that time it's feeling heaps better, the swelling's gone down a bit.

That night, I go out with the physio and try to run, and it's not feeling too bad, so I do quite a bit, because I haven't trained at all, and I'm surprised how much I can do on it. At that point, I tell the coaches, 'Yeah, I think I'll be all right to play on Sunday.'

But next day we're at Westpac Stadium training and as soon as I start running on it, the foot is really sore again. I get through training, just, but then it swells up again. Suddenly, I'm seeing those pictures of Andy Dalton. *It's going to be me.*

It's not a good situation for Deb. Her medical instincts and training must be telling her to get an X-ray or scan, find out what's wrong, get an accurate diagnosis, put a proper rehab plan in place. But I don't want an X-ray or a scan. All that's going to do is show that something's wrong. That would mess with my head, let alone Deb's and the coaches'. If they know for sure it's serious, I won't be allowed to play. I need to be able to keep telling myself that it's just one of those things, a bit of stress, it'll be fine. If it's something worse than that, I don't want to know. Deep down I know that whatever it is, it's not good.

On Saturday morning before the media conference and captain's run, we sit down, the coaches, me and Deb, and try to look at the cards we've been dealt. We know the foot improved when I rested it between Saturday and Thursday, that's a positive. If I don't play against Canada tomorrow, that'll give me another 10 days effectively until I play in the quarter-final, and if I don't train too much up until that point then hopefully I'll be able to get into that game and get going. Then, if we win that, we'll have another week to the semi-final. We decide to play it by ear. We're worried about the media and hysteria if I pull out of a game that I'm set down to play in, but what the hell, that's the only thing we can do.

Dan and I at the fateful conference to announce his captaincy against Canada and my 'precautionary withdrawal' from the match.

Ted tells Dan that he'll captain the side tomorrow, and he's delighted. At the media conference that morning, I sit beside Dan and Ted and play down the 'niggle' in my foot, call my withdrawal precautionary, give Dan a chance to say how excited he is to be leading the team, and that it's an important game in the context of being able to get through to the last three weeks. And the really good news is that Kieran is back from his ankle injury and is down to start.

The media safely negotiated, we go to lunch and then in the afternoon head to Rugby League Park for the captain's run. It's Dan's show, and I just hang around the edges, watching.

We've finished the run and the forwards are doing lineouts. I'm standing on the far side of the field and Dan's down the other end, practising his kicking.

I don't hear him scream, don't see him go down.

It's only when I'm wandering back towards the changing rooms that I notice he's no longer out there. One of the management team is standing outside the changing room, ashen-faced.

'DC's wrecked,' he says.

When I get inside Dan's with Deb, in agony. Ted's hovering, stricken. I can see he's having one of those *This can't be happening* moments.

I put a hand on Dan and say, 'You poor bugger,' then Ted tells me that Deb reckons he's probably out of the Cup. Dan's taken away for a scan which confirms

DC's wrecked!

Deb's initial diagnosis that Dan's pulled a tendon in his groin right off the bone.

That evening after dinner, Ted and I try to work through next week's plan, but it's overwhelmed by what's happened to Dan. When do we say what to the media? How do we handle this? You just know that the words 'worst nightmare' and 'national disaster' are going to get a trot. Dan's arguably the most difficult player in the side to replace, demonstrated by the endless and pretty much unresolved attempts over the last four years to find a back-up. But the most important element is the team. We need to be positive around the team and not let on that we're thrown by this. We've always told them to expect the unexpected, and now it's happened. We've got to make adjustments and move on — nothing's changed in terms of our objectives. We won't be using Dan's absence as an excuse for not doing what we set out to do. It's definitely going to be tougher from here on in, but we've just got to box on.

All that stuff, while behind the eyes both of us are probably wondering how the hell we're going to win without Dan.

When I go to Dan's room that evening and sit beside his bed, Smithy's already there. He was going to go to see France versus Tonga but is too depressed. He was catching while Dan was kicking. Dan was only going to do four. The first one flew like a wounded duck and so did the next two. Smithy was thinking that this was bloody strange — he'd caught a lot of Dan's practice kicks when Mick Byrne wasn't around, and could almost point Dan to either shoulder and Dan would hit it.

JK's become a massive, bullying presence in the middle of the park.

Three duds in a row was really odd. The fourth one was worse, a duck hook that almost took out the corner post. And Dan went down in a screaming heap. Smithy said he thought Dan was joking, throwing a wobbly after missing so badly.

I don't know what to say to Dan, neither does Smithy. Here's a guy, a decent humble man, acknowledged to be the best of his generation, perhaps of any generation, who's been crocked at the top of his game just when he's about to perform on the biggest stage. He'd played at Cardiff but hadn't been right. Now he's missed what is probably his last shot at RWC glory. I guess I could say that there are other great players in his position, like Barry John and Jackie Kyle and Cliff Morgan, who never got to play in a Rugby World Cup either, yet are still regarded as the among the greatest. I don't think that would be any consolation right now.

After Smithy goes, Dan asks questions to which there are no answers. 'Why? Why me? How did this happen? I was just kicking the ball, the same ball we used in the Super 15, the same routine I've done a thousand times.' There's bugger all to say, except, 'Oh, mate, I have no idea. I'm so sorry.' Then he tells me that he used to think everything happened for a reason, but he can't believe that any more.

That Dalton image from '87. I've had the odd moment since Dan went down this afternoon where I thought, *Jesus, it could be the two of us.* But sitting with Dan, I know that it can't be me now. Can't happen. No moaning about my foot. Unlike Dan, I've still got a chance of playing and somehow, any old how, that's what I've got to do.

The game against Canada passes in a bit of a blur. The boys do really well to put 79 points on them, and Kieran manages 50 minutes before Jerome Kaino switches to No. 8 and just carries on doing what he's been doing the whole tournament, the whole year — dominating the opposition in attack and defence. JK's become a massive bullying presence in the middle of the park, and jeez, I so want to play with him and Kieran, with us all at the top of our games. Colin Slade, taking Dan's place, slots five goals from nine, but looks like a man who hasn't had a lot of game time and is down on confidence. The other worrying thing is that he comes off with some sort of leg strain, and Piri finishes as first-five.

The same day we play Canada, there's an amazing spectacle at Eden Park, where 50,000 people turn out in the rain to watch the pool match between Samoa and Fiji. It makes us proud to be Kiwis — where else in the world could that possibly happen?

We head back to Auckland for the quarter-final against Argentina and, for me anyway, it's like going into a bubble of hotel-bus-training ground that might last the next three weeks. We see a fantastic RWC festival unfolding around us on television. This week we're at Spencer on Byron at Takapuna, but even when we're at the Heritage, a few hundred metres from the Cloud and Queens Wharf, there's no chance of me going there. Apart from the attention I'd attract, I can't walk properly most of the time and I've got to be careful to mask the worst effects of the injury not just from the media but also from all the people constantly coming and going from the hotel. Not to mention the team and the coaches.

Ted overseeing Aaron Cruden's kicking technique.

Dan's injury really reinforces my determination to play, but more than that, to be really positive around the team. I don't want people worrying about me; I want to give the impression I'm always going to play, and keep my down times to myself. I don't let on to the coaches too much, there's no point in freaking them. I just keep telling them I'll be right, I'm good to go, that I'm confident that even if I don't train at all, I can still go out and perform. I don't know how much they know, how much Deb is telling them. They just accept that that's the way it's got to be if I'm going to be able to get on the field.

It gets no easier for Deb, sitting with me in this medical netherworld, not knowing how bad it might be. As hard as that is, it's better than the alternative. If we know for sure it's broken, then it's going to be much more difficult for both of us and everyone around us to keep me on the field. Because whatever the ramifications, I'm going to keep playing on it as long as I can stand up and do my job.

But I do confide in Bert and Ceri Evans. Both are really helpful. Ceri chats with me about how I manage the week, where and how I direct my thoughts with not being able to train, and how I can put the consequential fears and worries to one side so I can still get out there and perform the way I need to. Bert suggests I break it down into 240 minutes. Three games. 240 minutes doesn't sound that much. 240 minutes sounds manageable. Getting through those 240 minutes has got to be my focus.

The media conferences are a trial. Getting in and out without limping and giving it away, for a start. They can see I'm not taking much part in training, so I'm constantly being asked how bad it is. As long as I don't get it X-rayed, I can just about get away with telling them it's just 'a niggle'. I don't know any different. I'm asked if I'm having injections and can honestly say that I'm not. A needle might get me through one game, but it would probably wreck me for the next two. I've got to be optimistic. And sometimes, towards the end of the week, when the oral anti-inflams and Panadols and a lot of rest have done their work, I can almost convince myself it's just a soft-tissue injury. 'Nah, I'll be fine,' I keep telling anyone who'll listen, media, team-mates, coaches, myself. 'Just can't train because it'll get a bit sore, but I'm ready to go. I'm good to go.' And I am. I believe it.

Aaron Cruden's been called up in place of Dan, who's being operated on, and I spend a lot of time at training staying close to him and Colin Slade, making

Kieran Read thunders it up against Argentina in the quarter-final.

sure they're on the same page as me. I'm not doing much running, but mentally I'm completely engaged with the team, helping prioritise, liaising between the unit leaders and the coaches.

Two days out from the quarter-final, I manage to do a bit of training at North Harbour Stadium, a bit of a run-around, and it feels not too bad — it's had 10 days to settle. Next day, Saturday, I manage to run around a bit during the captain's run, although I'm really careful about what I do.

On Saturday night we watch France deal to England 19–12. France are better than the score indicates. I don't care who we play, but France are so difficult to read: they've metamorphosed from the almost pathetically unmotivated wretches who lost to Tonga last week in pool play to a driven, skilful top international side. I remember what those guys said to me after our pool game, and get a feeling that they'll be the ones who'll win the semi, even though their opponents, Wales, are expansive and efficient in knocking out Ireland 22–10. But whatever, whoever.

Next day, I get through the warm-up okay and play most of a tough uncompromising quarter-final without having to think about the foot. The Pumas score a great try from a simple move off the back of the scrum which does no credit to Kieran or me, while we bash and crash away without breaching them. We do apply

Piri was the star against Los Pumas.

enough pressure for Piri to slot four penalties and we go into halftime with the lead. It's brutally tough attrition, knockout rugby, and there are casualties. Colin Slade only lasts 30 minutes before being replaced by Aaron Cruden, who's wearing a heavy knee bandage and gets whacked across the mouth almost as soon as he gets on. Mils, who's finally got on the field for his 100th test, cracks his shoulder blade and doesn't come out for the second half. That looks like his tournament over. *Jesus, what else?*

The answer doesn't take long in coming.

I go close to scoring our first try against the padding of the posts, but the TMO rules it out and Piri kicks his sixth penalty. But we're getting on top of them, buckling their scrum even, and we know the win will come.

Almost in that moment of revelation, about 60 minutes in, I feel it, the foot. It goes again. Clunk. Just like against France.

Then it gets very sore again, almost immediately. When the ball's in play, I'm okay. But as soon as the whistle goes and I stop, it hurts. If I have to jump or run or push or tackle, I can do it — adrenalin's a great painkiller. But when play stops and I have to walk or jog to a lineout or scrum 20 metres away, I'm really struggling.

I watch from the bench as Brad scores against Argentina.

I tell Deb when she comes out with the water. She says they'll get me off when they can.

With 15 to go, Kieran goes over and the game's safe.

I watch the rest from the bench — Brad scoring and a sideline conversion from Aaron.

When the whistle blows for fulltime and we get around Mils and Jock for his presentation, I have to make an effort not to limp. Once again, it's moving — this time to see my old mate who's been there with me through so many battles, all the ups and all the downs, get honoured with his 100th cap.

I've played with Mils since the New Zealand Under 19s, then the Under 21s and all those test matches. He's a great man to have in the team and I have a huge amount of respect for how he plays the game and also how he handles himself as a person. He's been a valuable member of the leadership group for a long time, helping the All Blacks function. The bitter-sweet is that it looks like his tournament is over. After playing in three World Cups, perhaps his best chance to play in the winning side is gone.

Milsy is clapped from the field by the Argentinians and the All Blacks after receiving his 100th test cap. The bitter-sweet is that it looks like his tournament is over.

There's no justice for him or Dan. This game has no memory or sentiment.

We're into the semis. That's a step up from Cardiff. The solid lump of pain in my foot is back, I can feel the swelling already. But I'm still in there with a chance, so much luckier than Dan and Mils.

The same day, Australia are lucky to beat South Africa in Wellington, after Bryce Lawrence does what he did in Brisbane in the Super 15 final — freezes, and forgets to blow his whistle.

Which means we play Australia in the semi. Somehow, I always knew we would.

Eighty minutes down, 160 to go.

Semi tough

There's a thought I'm struggling to get out of my head. *We played our final last week.* It's the ritual game-day coffee with Mum and Dad and Jo and Sam in a little café just round the corner from the Heritage before the biggest game of my life: the 2011 RWC final.

Last week, we beat Australia in the semi. We played as well as we've ever played, while France narrowly, luckily, beat Wales in the other semi, after the Welsh captain was sent off for a tip-tackle quite early in the game.

Last week the whole of New Zealand was anguishing about the prospect of losing to the Aussies, including the old man. He was jumpy, up and down, up and down, couldn't drink his coffee. He couldn't understand why I was so calm.

I wasn't that calm, but I knew the team was ready. There's a feeling you get sometimes. I could see it in our guys' eyes. When Australia was beating the All Blacks pretty regularly back at the turn of the century, I remember the great Australian No. 8 Toutai Kefu saying, 'We know how to beat these blokes.' That's what I felt last week in the build-up to the game. *We know how to beat these blokes.*

This week, I don't feel that. This week there's been media speculation about how much we're going to beat France by. The whole of New Zealand, it seems, thinks the Webb Ellis Cup is as good as won. Even Dad's relaxed about France, can't understand why I'm so subdued.

In the knockout phase of the RWC, you have to win every game, obviously, but you have to bring your best game to the final.

My fear is that we played our best game last week.

My foot wasn't pretty after the Argentinian game. During the build-up to Australia, in my mind I kept going back to the week before, when it had improved enough to train after four days of rest and anti-inflams. But this time, after four days I still couldn't train, I couldn't risk it. I went out in my gym shoes and stood beside Aaron and Beaver, who Ted had found whitebaiting somewhere. Beaver dropped his net and picked up the ball and ran with it, keen as. He's a good bugger.

Out at training, there were three of us standing round in our gym shoes, all leaders of our mini units, all crocked. Mils, with his cracked shoulder and Dan, back after his op. The guys in their respective units asked if Dan and Mils could come back to keep leading them, and they did. Dan's bloody amazing — no one would have begrudged his right to stay home and cry into his beer, but he came straight back to help as soon as he got out of hospital. Mils too, stranded on his 100th game and invalided out of his chance, after three RWCs, to play for the Cup.

The 'what else?' feeling had gone. We'd got used to the new normal. All that preparation for the unexpected seemed to have worked. Rather than thinking, *Shit, why is all this happening to us*, we're thinking, *Bring it on*. We even said, 'There'll be something else happen, there will be more things happen, just expect it and deal with it.' In a funny sort of way, everything that'd gone wrong was keeping our feet on the ground, reinforced by my meetings with Bert and Ceri. Even the foot. Ceri was telling me that this was the challenge that's been given me; it was about how I dealt with it.

Other teams were having their challenges. Australia had lost Kurtley Beale.

When training was over on the Tuesday, I went to the pool and did 40 minutes aqua jogging just to get things going. I still couldn't train on the Thursday, so I did a light bike to make sure I was okay, then I managed to get through the captain's run on the Saturday, still in gym shoes. Just enough to feel like I had it sorted. The physios were trying things like whether strapping helped or different things in my boots helped. But nothing seemed to make much of a difference.

We heard during the week that the Aussie camp was pretty confident. I'm not sure where this information came from, but there are people in and out of the teams' hotels all the time, and secrets are hard to keep. I know that — trying to get around the hotel without limping on my 'niggle'. However accurate the rumour might have been, it was great to hear that they were confident. I don't go along with most people who say the Wallabies are more dangerous when they're confident. I reckon they're more vulnerable.

I don't know whether the Aussies heard any rumours about us, but if they'd heard the truth, they would have been alarmed: that was the best-prepared All Black team I've ever been a part of. I knew the Aussies were going to get it. Part of it was an address on Thursday evening from Willie Apiata. He may not be a great public speaker, but he carried an aura. He talked about what he did when he won the VC, and why he did what he did, what drove him. As much as he fought for his country and his family, the main driver was his mates, the ones who stood at his shoulder, upon whom he depended for his life. I could see from the rapt faces around me that his words were sinking in. We were mates. We didn't have to face live rounds, but we were in this together and we'd get it done.

On the way to the ground on the bus, I looked out on the Great North Road part of the Fan Trail and saw a sign on one of the car yards.

Izzy Dagg's moment of genius against Australia in the semi-final.

I HOPE YOU'RE READY QUADE. RICHIE IS.

I wondered whether Cooper had seen it when the Aussie bus went by.

I went into that game looking for the moment we'd let slip in Brisbane. It came a lot sooner than I thought it would. As early as the 20-minute mark, I could see the inevitability in their eyes. They knew this day wasn't going to go that good for them.

James Horwill had won the toss and chose to kick off, to put pressure on us. Which Quade immediately blew by kicking it out on the full.

Cory won Man of the Match by defusing all their bombs and looking tricky every time he got the ball, but Israel could have got it too. From his first touch, he beat four tacklers, then a couple of minutes later, after we'd punched it up midfield, Piri threw it right to Aaron, who found Izzy carving right, inside Anthony Fainga'a and on the outside of Rocky Elsom. Electric Izzy broke Elsom's tackle — second time in five minutes — this time with a fend, then body-swerved Quade on the cover. Cooper tried to hang on and it looked like he might have got Izzy across the touchline, but Izzy served up a brilliant one-handed flip off the turf as he rolled out, collected by Ma'a on the inside, and we were over in the corner.

Five–nil, only seven minutes gone.

Piri missed the conversion and then a relatively easy penalty, after Brad had timed his jump brilliantly on their throw, got in front of Elsom and swatted it back our side. I took a wide pass on the charge, and saw Radike Samo and David Pocock in front

Cory Jane won Man of the Match by defusing all their bombs.

of me. The plan was to make Pocock tackle, stop him lurking around the tackle as the second man in, so I veered right to try to find his shoulder. I got a bit of him — and a lot of Samo, who smashed me from the left — but it was enough. Pocock got himself over the ball, but only by bridging with both hands on the ground. Penalty, just to the right of the posts. Perfectly to plan, except that Piri bounced it off the posts.

At that point, the Aussies looked shell-shocked, but not beaten. They kept going to the high ball, but Cory and Izzy defused those brilliantly, and we were getting quick recycled ball and finding overlaps wide and holes in the middle.

Shortly after, JK plundered a ball at the back of their ruck and we got in behind them again. From the recycle, Ma'a was at first receiver and found Aaron on the drift outside him. Taking the space, Aaron broke the line outside Ben Alexander, was half-checked by Genia on the cover, and Pocock was caught again, down on one knee trying to pinch it. This time Piri nailed it.

There must be an easier way to win a turnover.

Eight–nil was a great start, but it didn't necessarily reflect the dominance we had. For the first 13 minutes, we'd played the game with pace and power, had most of the possession, almost all the territory. Then came the play that broke them.

Piri cleared from a ruck on our 22, failed to find touch. O'Connor collected, found Digby Ioane on his inside. Digby showed how dangerous he was by beating Sam Whitelock, stepping Piri, fending Kevvy and charging for the line, dragging Izzy with him. Digby had Ben Alexander and James Horwill in behind him and it looked like he'd be driven over. Somehow JK just picked him up ball and all and carried him sideways away from the momentum. It was an extraordinary piece of defence.

A few plays later, after desperate D by us, they got an easy penalty in front when I was pinged for not releasing. I wasn't actually the tackler, but three points was a hell of a lot better than seven.

Shortly after, Izzy decided to give them a bit of their own medicine and hoisted one. Quade, self-styled Public Enemy No. 1, closed his eyes as he was taking it and knocked it on. Our pressure brought another penalty, but Piri missed again. We regrouped and had them under the hammer for some phases, before Aaron stayed back in the pocket after a JK midfield charge over the gain-line and dropped the goal.

That put us out to an eight-point lead again, but Cooper returned the favour, and they got back to 11–6. Although they never stopped trying and were able to get some territory and possession and put some phases together at various stages, they

Fulltime against Australia.

never looked like breaching our try-line. The JK moment with Ioane was the one that defined the game in the end, mostly because it epitomised the intensity and commitment of the whole team.

Once again, the only spoiler of a great night was my foot.

During the warm-up I didn't feel it too much, but five minutes into the game I felt it again. Something letting go. A clunk or pop or crack. The pain came back.

Again, when the ball was in play, I could get through and not think about it. It didn't inhibit me actually running around and doing things. I could put it to the side. But as soon as the whistle went and there was a lineout 30 metres away, jogging over there was bloody sore. I'd told Deb that I'd play as long as I could do my job without thinking about the pain, but as soon as I started thinking about the foot while the ball was actually in play, and the pain started affecting the decisions I was making about what I would do, that would be the time to quit.

It was sore all the way through the semi, but only really sore when the whistle went. One of the most challenging bits was running up the tunnel at halftime. Getting on and off the field was complete agony.

But when the final whistle went, the score was 20 points to 6, and we were into the final of the RWC.

I've got cabin fever. We've been three weeks in the hotel, watching this rugby festival go on around us, at the centre of it, but also remote from it. My foot hasn't helped.

It's worse, taking longer to come right. I have to rest it, choose when and where I want to walk. How far. Who might see me if I limp.

I'm sick of the bloody foot. It's like stepping on a red-hot lump of coal. I have to change my gait slightly and then other parts of my foot get sore, but it kind of doesn't matter any more, because I got through the semi and I know I can play in the final. I tell myself that if it's like that for this week, I'm sweet. I can get through. If you're ever going to be a bit tough, if ever you're going to grit your teeth and get on with it, this is the time. If it had been another week after this one, I don't think I could get there. Knowing there's only one more. I keep talking to Bert. We're down to 80 minutes. That doesn't sound a lot. I can do that.

The hardest bit is around the team and around the media, particularly. I have to really grit my teeth and try to walk normally. The worst thing would be if it got out, and we lost. If it's seen as an excuse.

I've got plenty to distract me from my bloody foot.

Jock comes to talk to us about the work and inspiration that went into bringing the World Cup to New Zealand, the approach he took, the promises he made about what the rugby world could expect from us. I'm so glad he's still round to see it come to fruition.

A lot of my efforts go into making sure that the guys are on the job. We had a hell of a good game in the semi and my biggest concern is getting ourselves back to that state again. I'm having to think about all that with the coaches and leadership group. The mindset meeting on Monday. Getting us ready for a war against France, because I'm convinced that's what they'll bring.

We don't use the emotional trigger we used in the pool game against France. Instead, different players talk about their experiences of the French. Woody talks about Paris in 2004, Conrad about Lyon in 2006, I talk about Marseilles in 2009. How we attacked and beat them then. How we took their heart away from them. We talk about them being most dangerous when they're scared and don't expect to win. That's when they die for the jersey. Like 1999, like 2007. That's what we can expect.

We hear through the grapevine that their team meeting room is plastered with newspapers, full of headlines which accuse them of cowardice, of being failures, of being an embarrassment to La France. We know that's going to get them fizzing.

I go through the familiar names. Their front row, Mas, Servat, Barcella, might be one of the few in world rugby to equal ours. Their second row of big mean lumps. Their loosies, Bonnaire, Harinordoquy and Dusautoir, the guys who did us at Cardiff, on paper the equal of JK, Reado and me. If there's a question mark over their halves, there's got to be one over ours too, without Dan. Their centres: Aurelien Rougerie would be one of the few guys who measures up to Ma'a in power and speed. The French back three — tricky bastards, fast — when are they ever weak there? I keep going through those names. *Any team with these guys in it has at least one great match in them and they haven't played it yet.*

Ma'a doing his best to cheer up
Dan at training.

Whereas we might have.

At training, DC, Mils and I do our best out there in our gym shoes, staying close to Aaron and Beaver. The wisdom of taking Beaver on the end-of-year tour last year becomes apparent. He has the calls, knows what it's about, fits in easily.

Inside them, Piri's become a national folk hero in the space of two weeks. There are T-shirts everywhere of Piri with a Superman cape — *Leave it to me* and *Chill out, I've Got This* — and viral emails — *Do I need to do everything around here?* He was Man of the Match against Argentina, and, despite attending his grandfather's tangi in the week leading up to the semi, has really stepped up and shouldered a huge workload. Since Dan went down, he's become our main play-maker, and now he's also kicking for goal and taking restarts, to take the pressure off Aaron.

I try not to think too much about the Dan what-ifs. We left quite a lot of points out on the park against Australia: a missed conversion and several penalties by Piri and a penalty by Aaron. Dan would have nailed most of them, perhaps all of them. Ten or a dozen points. It didn't hurt us in that game, but it might if it happens again. Luke McAlister missed a bread-and-butter conversion in Cardiff that turned out to be the difference. But so did the French. Mind games. I try not to think about it, but logic says losing the best play-maker and kicker in the world is surely going to count sooner or later. Sooner is over: it's later already.

We all know that as much as we have to believe that our fate is in our hands, history says we also have to survive one of those tipping moments, on which winning and losing the World Cup turns. We know there'll be a moment when the next minute, the next play, the next second, will decide who wins and who loses. We know to expect it and be ready for it. We know we've got to execute in that moment, rather than freeze or worry about what will happen if we don't.

The 1987 All Blacks were the only ones who didn't need to survive such a moment. Grant Fox and John Kirwan come to talk to us about that tournament. Foxy's pretty phlegmatic in the way he describes it, while JK's quite emotional. It's a good mix and gives the guys an inkling of how long and strong their memories will be of Sunday's game, if we can pull it off, if we can survive that moment.

In 1991, eventual champions Australia had their tipping moment in the quarter-final against Ireland. In 1995, champions South Africa were lucky to have made it to the final — if there'd been today's video technology available, France's last-minute

I've just got to get through it . . . At the end of a shortened captain's run on the eve of the final.

try, ruled out by the ref, would have won them the semi. In the 1999 semi, Stephen Larkham drop-kicked a goal from 48 metres in extra time to beat South Africa. Larkham had never once drop-kicked in a long test career, and was reportedly so blind he could barely see the posts from that far out. Australia went on to win the final against France, whose path was made easier courtesy of a dreadful refereeing performance by Paddy O'Brien in the pool match against Fiji, which, to his credit, he owned up to. In 2003, eventual winners England were fortunate to win against Wales and Samoa. In 2007, eventual champions South Africa had a close shave against Fiji.

You could look at some of those moments and blame fate, chance, rub of the green, bounce of the ball, sheer luck. Whatever, that moment hasn't come for us, yet. You could argue that the French have had several already. When the Welsh captain, Sam Warburton, was sent off early in their semi. And then later, when Stephen Jones missed a penalty he would have thrown over on any other day.

You could also argue that France have already lost against Tonga — they don't deserve to win. But I know that the game doesn't care who deserves what. No memory, no sentiment, no history, no fairytales. You have to believe that you can go out there and make it happen.

George Gregan brings me a bottle of Dom Pérignon for my 100th test. The last thing he says to me is, 'It won't fall in your lap, you know.'

On Saturday, I get through my last captain's run, but cut it short.

On the afternoon of the game, still worried at how relaxed and expectant Dad was at this morning's coffee, I take out the Warwick and go through my visualisations. Usually, on the facing page, I would have already listed my tick-offs for the week: weights, pad work, clean-outs, ball skills, evading, fending. This week that page is blank, and when I write down my mantras, they seem pared down to bedrock. No wonder. This is our twelfth test in 14 weeks.

> *Start again, get involved early.*
> *Work rate. Keep getting up, make it count.*
> *DMJ — tackle, hit with shoulders, bounce up*
> *clean — ID threat, effective, ID early and remove*
> *steal — pick my time, make it count, fully committed*
> *run, link, demand ball, run hard, expect to bust*
> *Just play, back my gut*
> *Be calm, clear and decisive*
> *Enjoy*
> *GAB*

The toughest one to deliver on might be the second-last one. Enjoy. I'm struggling to live that part of it any more. I've just got to get through it.

Eighty minutes to go.

The right picture

I*'m looking for that moment.* If I stay in the present, I'm pretty sure I'll know it when I see it. Unless it's already been and gone. We're five points up at halftime, but we've left another eight out on the field, lost points that we can't get back, which may bite us in the arse.

Woody's try might have been the moment, but I suspect it was too early in the game. The Teabag move, resurrected from 2008. Our video analysis was right. We knew the French would contest that lineout, fancy their chances, try to disrupt us early in the game. But it was so easy, so perfectly executed that maybe we thought that's the way the rest of the game was going to go for us. It hasn't.

Piri missed the conversion — and two penalties which were pretty handy. I don't want the defining moment of this final to be the one when Dan went down screaming, but we'd probably be 13 points up if he was here. Aaron's gone too now, with a bent knee. *Was that the moment?* Beaver's there, though, so reassuring and assertive that it's easy to just get on with it. Their response to the haka didn't throw us. In Cardiff they did the red, white and blue tricolour thing. This time, in white, against the dark mass of the black-clad crowd, they formed an arrowhead with Dusautoir at the point, and everyone linking hands behind him. As we belted into 'Kapa o Pango' —

Kapa o Pango kia whakawhenua au i ahau!
All Blacks, let us become one with the land

Hī auē, hī! Ko Aotearoa e ngunguru nei!
This is our land that rumbles

— the French walked forward and fanned out along their 10-metre line, then advanced again, to the halfway line, trying to take some of the visual focus away from us.

It's my time! It's my moment!

> *Au, au, auē hā!*
> It's my time! It's my moment!
>
> *Ko Kapa o Pango e ngunguru nei!*
> This defines us as the All Blacks
>
> *Au, au, auē hā!*
> It's my time! It's my moment!

We expected they'd bring something. That was fine. *Bring it on. Give us what you've got.*

They did. We thought the opening exchanges would show which style they were bringing, Biarritz or Toulouse. As they went wide early instead of kicking, it was clear that they'd left Biarritz at home. But there was nothing mad-headed or desperate in the way they attacked. They punched it close, setting narrow targets, trying to get us to commit numbers in there, before going wide. Punch, punch, go. As I reacted to what they were doing, it suddenly hit me how familiar this pattern was. The sequences they were putting together, the way they were trying to manipulate us in defence, the pace, the power. *They're playing like us.*

We're surrounded by the familiar. That's good. On the bus to Eden Park, sitting out there in the Mount Eden darkness like a spaceship, I was thinking if there's one game you want to be playing for the All Blacks, it would be the RWC final at home,

The 'Teabag' move comes off and Woody is on his way to the line in the final.

surrounded by the familiar. *This is what I play the game for, this moment. Don't be scared of it, embrace it.*

That was better than what I was thinking this morning as I sat on my bed. *If we don't win today, this could be my last game as an All Black.* Ceri keeps telling me to imagine the worst that could happen and say, Okay, I can handle that. I'm not sure if that's true this time, if we don't win this game. It's my third attempt to win the RWC, my second as captain. *Three-time loser.* I don't want to find out whether I can handle that.

It's not about the past or the future, it's about the present. There'll be a moment.

Ted comes over and tells me Beaver's taking the shots now, not Piri. Piri's still got the restarts. Trainer Nic Gill gives us the call to get back on the track. *Keep getting up.*

The most painful part is getting down the players' tunnel and back out on the field. Once I'm there, and into it again, the foot's irrelevant.

Start again.

We're almost immediately under the hammer after the restart. After a desperate scramble, we're penalised. It's just outside the 22, about 10 in from touch, infinitely kickable. Dimitri Yachvili's kick looks like it's going over from where I'm standing, but keeps sliding across the face of the posts and away. *Is that the moment?*

Shortly after, our chance comes, when referee Craig Joubert's arm goes up.

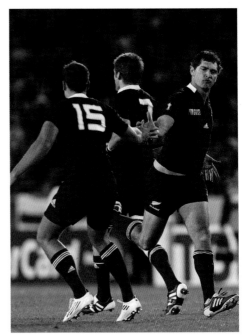

Beaver belts it . . . He's never in doubt.

Penalty. Beaver quickly grabs the ball in case anyone has second thoughts. He's right in front, midway 22 and 10-metre mark. Almost exactly the position he missed from against the Aussies in Hong Kong last year, when he could have put us eight points up with four minutes to go. He seems to have no doubts, walks in, belts it.

This time, from where I'm standing it looks like it might have shaved the outside of the right-hand post. The assistant referee on that side hesitates, then raises his flag. Beaver's never in doubt, puffing his cheeks, pulling the number 21 jersey down over his love handles and sprinting back to halfway: 8–0.

With 35 minutes to go, it's not likely to be his last clutch kick in the game.

From the French restart, JK crunches forward, Piri hoists one over the top. It's a bit shallow, and I'm challenging for it among a pod of their loosies. I get shoved aside by Dusautoir but do enough to put Harinordoquy off and — he sprays the ball forward. As I pick myself off the turf, I see Izzy latch on to the loose ball and strike off upfield. It's the perfect counter opportunity — the suddenness of the turnover has got them at sixes and sevens, and Izzy's got two on one outside him, Conrad and Kakas — Richard Kahui — covered by one defender. Instead of passing, Izzy has a rush of blood, tries to step inside and is hammered by three defenders as Kakas throws his head back in frustration.

Bugger!

It quickly goes bad. They've got numbers over the ball, so Conrad has to go in to clean, supported by Beaver and Brad and Piri, but it's all pretty desperate and when they go to ground, the ball's sitting behind them. Rougerie steps through and gets a toe to it. The ball goes through Ma'a's grasp and Piri, who's just picked himself up, and with time to do any number of things with his hands, decides to pass it with his foot, chipping it gently towards Reado standing wide left. Instead, the ball lobs perfectly into Francois Trinh-Duc's hands and he beats Piri's tackle and hares off downfield.

Shit! Now we're the ones terribly exposed on the counter, they're in behind us and the bells are ringing. As Kakas and JK get back to Trinh-Duc, he lobs it infield to Yachvili, who has to check to collect it, giving us crucial moments to scramble.

I'm still way out wide on the right, but as Yachvili flips it left to Rougerie on the charge, I come tearing in and try to crash him high with my left shoulder to stop him moving the ball to the space and numbers behind me. Too high — my left shoulder bounces off his and he charges on to five metres out from our posts, dragged down by Reado. France recycle quickly and have big numbers left — four on two — but great scrambling defence by Cory and Kevvy and Ma'a takes Servat to ground one metre out.

Thierry Dusautoir is congratulated after scoring by Aurelien Rougerie. I feel prepared for exactly this.

We put numbers into the maul — there's no option — but when they win it and go back right, it's like watching their first try at Cardiff: that mathematician Dusautoir out there counting the numbers and finding the ghost of a hole outside Ma'a. He slides in against the right-hand post.

It's not the only parallel with Cardiff. Poor choices when we had them on the ropes. Izzy's choice not to pass. Piri's choice to audition for Man United. And this moment, standing under our own posts shell-shocked. Those pictures from '99. From 2007, after the Traille try.

This time it's different. I feel prepared for exactly this. It was always going to be this way. Instead of feeling shocked, I feel as if it's playing out exactly the way I always knew it would. The guys are all around me. I'm talking, they're listening, Conrad's chipping in. There are no glazed eyes, no one in the Red Zone. *Don't panic. We knew it was going to be like this. We're ready for it.*

Easy conversion.

8–7, with 48 gone, 32 minutes to go. *That's a goddamn age.*

Horey on for Kevvy, who's been really nervous all night on the lineout throws, and Ali for Sam.

Back to halfway for the restart. I see Reado and Ali out right, with none of their big men opposing. I indicate the space to Piri and yell at him — 'Go go go!'

Piri goes all right — drop-kicks it out on the full. Scrum back.

My mistake. I did what I told the team not to do. Panicked. Lost it.

Horey must see the wild look in my eyes. He cuffs me as he comes back for the scrum. 'Oi! Calm down!'

That's all I need. That's my last slip. This game is going to come down to who holds their nerve and finds a way to win. This is the place I've visualised over and over leading up to the Cup. How I was going to act in this situation, what I was going to do.

No bad pictures, past or future. Stay in the present. What do we need to do now? And now? And now? *Let's get this done.*

That's Piri's last act — he's pulled for Andy Ellis.

Unsurprisingly, France have lifted. From the scrum, Harinordoquy punches close off the back, then they go wide right, making inroads now. Confident. They kick behind us, forcing Cory to retrieve a couple of metres from our goal-line. Cory throws it wide across our line to Izzy. Where last week he carved, this week he slips over into Dusautoir's hungry hands. We recycle under pressure, and Kakas rakes it back to halfway.

Their lineout, but Mas makes us wait. Joubert gives Dusautoir the chat for wasting time and a bent arm. I opt for the scrum. We need close targets, to work them over.

Cory comes in off the blindside wing as first receiver, gets smacked by Bonnaire, I clean Bonnaire out. Andy clears to JK who makes the gain-line, with Ali and Brad in the van. Then left again with Franksy, then back right to Beaver, who does that thing, sticks the ball under one arm, puffs his cheeks and charges through a pod of their front-rowers.

Rougerie and Bonnaire nail him, but we're on the front foot, go right to Ali, crunch, then back left to Izzy. No holes this week, only Franksy plodding outside him. When it comes back right, I charge it up, set it midfield, then Ma'a takes it right and Woody bunts it up on the 10-metre line. *Nine phases and we've gone 10 metres.*

We pick and go. Brad punches, Dusautoir nearly steals it, Horey goes again. *Twelve phases.* We're still on the 10-metre mark. *This is hard yakker!* But we have possession and a little bit of territory, keeping it out of kicking range at least. Crunch it up again. At the back of the ruck, Woody has a brain fade, heaves it back blind between his legs. Andy scrambles back, shapes to kick but the French are all over him. We only just save it. We're back on halfway, go left, Ma'a tries to crash, loses it forward in a heavy crunch.

Shit! Fifteen phases over four minutes and we're back where we started, but this time it's their ball. I can see the French bench, jumping up; they think they've got us.

24 minutes to go.

Mind on the job. Start again.

It's a war of attrition played out between the 10-metre lines. France running at us now, punching close until they think they have the numbers, then coming wide. We keep our line, keep knocking them over, but they're mixing it up nicely, punching us close, stretching us wide, drawing us up, then sliding a kick through to touch or popping one over the top. Our defence is right on. The guys are fantastic. But we can't get the ball back. There's a fatal rhythm developing.

I can feel the change in the crowd. They sense it too. The air of expectation has gone. They're not making much noise any more. Watching. Waiting. At this level it's about sequences and momentum. France are pulling the sequences, getting the momentum. We're holding on. Just.

I slip off Maxime Mermoz as they drive him up to 15 metres out from our line, then redeem myself by getting a hand in as JK and Ma'a wrestle Lionel Nallet to the ground and he loses it forward.

Our scrum. Horey slaps me on the back, and we put on a good scrum. Jean-Baptiste Poux folds in and we get the penalty.

Back on halfway again. Our throw.

20 to go. *It feels like we've been out here forever.*

We desperately need to keep the pill, but Harinordoquy gets a mitt in front of Brad and swats it back to his side, Dusautoir crunches it up and sets it midfield and we're back in that fatal sequence, defending desperately, on our own 10-metre line, knowing that one mistake and a penalty goal will put them in front.

Trinh-Duc grubbers it through. Out. Our throw.

This time Ali claims it, Andy hoists it, but it bounces for Harinordoquy and he rumbles it back up. Horey and I get a rare turnover, Izzy goes right, but Beaver and Reado run out of room and it's their lineout.

From the next ruck Ali gets penalised for playing it on the ground. Trinh-Duc misses touch, Izzy hoists but too far and Harinordoquy gets to run it back at us again. JK hits him brutally hard and he knocks on.

Scrum halfway. *It's groundhog day.* We're going in circles within the 10-metre marks, always ending up back here. But this time, it's our ball.

Just as we threaten to finally break out of those fatal sequences, stopping their momentum, get back to parity, France kill our scrum. Mas and Servat bore in on Horey and pop him. Penalty, two metres our side of halfway. *Shit.*

As Trinh-Duc lines it up with what looks like a smile on his face, I'm doing Ceri's worst-case scenario. *They'd be two up, still 15 to go, there'll be time to come back.* But I know from Cardiff, even exercising the strongest will in the world to keep the bad pictures at bay, what difference being behind by two points, rather than ahead by one, will make to that last 15 minutes.

Trinh-Duc blocks it right. *Maybe that's the moment, the bit of luck we need.*

But minutes later, we might have blown it. Trinh-Duc hoists it and Izzy is robbed by Traille in mid-air, and they're rucking it outside our 22, and it's desperate defence until Yachvili fumbles it at the base.

Keep defending, keep believing . . . A massive hit on Damien Traille by Brad Thorn, assisted by Jerome Kaino.

We put down a better scrum. They've got dominance there now, but we manage to clear it as we go down and Andy kicks deep right. Traille takes it and puts up a high ball, too shallow but they're winning everything in the air, and they take it wide left, straight back into our half with numbers. We scramble well, and Trinh-Duc hoists it again — too far and Izzy punishes them with a huge punt which takes us down to midway their 10 metres and 22.

The relief as we march forward into their half. *Gotta stay down here, their turn to be under the hammer.*

12 minutes to go.

The French lineout is immaculate. Harinordoquy is impregnable in the middle and they drive it forward before Yachvili puts one over the top, brilliantly taken by Kakas who makes good metres. Andy clears it to Beaver, who sees space behind them and finds touch on their 22 with a beautifully weighted ball.

That's more like it.

We walk forward again. We've been under the pump for the best part of 20 minutes, but we're finally getting some territory, getting some control, some leverage on them.

10 to go. *We can do this.*

But Harinordoquy pulls it in again, and they set up a rolling maul. We go for the ball instead of stopping the drive. When it collapses, Joubert calls the penalty.

How can they be this good for this long? I realise that was a question I was asking myself in Cardiff too. This time I know it's not worth asking. *Expect it.*

Back at halfway, their throw.

They get another go.

Start again.

They go wide and there's big danger. Ma'a shows their left winger the touchline and he takes it, goes round Ma'a. I only just get across to him, take his legs away into touch. I'm sure he's out, but the touchie's flag stays down and I get up and throw myself into trying to stop the French rolling maul. It's a desperate wrestle as we try to hold them. We can't do it, but pull them sideways so that when we collapse, the ball is out. I'm flat on my back at the bottom, when I see the touchie's flag go up. Our ball.

I'm stuffed. The desperate sprint across the width of the field. The desperate tackle. The desperate wrestle. *Was that the moment?*

Keep getting up.

Our throw-in. Horey to Brad, this time hits him bang on.

Andy hoists it again, perfect kick, but as brilliant as we were aerially last week, this week we can't get our bloody hands on it.

France come wide right, big blond Rougerie slams into Conrad, who hangs on. We put numbers in, try to slow it, which means when they get it and come back left, they've got huge numbers. This time Dusautoir's calculator lets him down. The hole's not there: I am. I drag him down, but they get quick ball again, and this time they've got numbers right. Ma'a takes Mermoz down, but we can't stop the recycle or even slow it and Nallet charges it up when they come back midfield.

8 to go. France have the momentum, they're putting together the sequences. How to change it. *Get the ball.* Keep defending, keep believing. *But look for the moment. Break the cycle.*

They keep coming left, towards me and Reado and Cory, with numbers massing behind Yachvili, who gets smashed by Reado, but gets it away to Dusautoir, who's stopped by Conrad. I see a moment, try to steal, get blown off it and they're away again, wide right. Numbers again out there, three on two.

Rougerie does brilliantly to commit Ma'a to the tackle and lure in Beaver before getting it wide to Mermoz, who's hit by Kakas and a recovering Beaver. Great defence.

7 to go.

They've still got it, coming back left. Szarzewski drives short right, smashing over the gain-line. Every time they do that, our defence has to run backwards to a new offside line. I can see they're getting buggered. *I'm buggered.*

We've retreated to midway between our 10-metre line and 22.

I'm hanging out, calling the D, thinking if they get another penalty here, we're gone. *No panic.* We're trying to police ourselves, stay calm, as they pick and go again, pile drive another two metres on the short blind, forcing our string of defence to back up another two metres across the field.

I can see it unfolding in slow-mo, there's a dreadful inevitability about what they're doing: picking their time, making us commit numbers to stop the close drives, while out in the centre they're organising themselves for the quick ball that'll enable them to take advantage of the holes. Part of me can appreciate the brutal logic and brilliant execution of what they're doing. It's what we would do.

Now they come left — *Is this it, the moment?*

No, Harinordoquy crunches it up again, taken down by Beaver. JK's in there too, but can't stop the quick ball.

Now they've got what they want. It comes quickly left to Yachvili, to Mermoz. To Alexis Palisson on the cut, hammered by Reado and Brad, who drive over him.

Is this it? I see the ghost of a chance, a sliver of space, drive in there to steal, but lose my feet and the ball flips out their side. We appeal for the knock-on but Joubert holds his hands wide — play on.

Ali gets a toe to it and chases, but Dusautoir really shows his class, somehow scooping the ball into his mitt off the ground while running backwards, then turning and charging it back up at us.

Chance gone.

6 to go. *We can't get the pill. Don't panic. Don't force it. Keep doing what we're doing and the opportunity must come.*

Dusautoir is hammered by Woody and Brad, but it's quick ball, coming right, and we're back to square one, defending desperately in our own territory as they come back left and we're calling to each other to not give away the penalty, to trust each other.

Nallet hammers into Ma'a and I see another false moment, get a hand to it, before I'm hit by Mas and cleaned out.

Harinordoquy crunches it up close right, forcing us to put in numbers to stop the drive and it's all happening again, and we can't seem to stop it.

I keep thinking, though, that there's pressure on them too, because this time we're one point up, not two points down, and the longer this lasts, the more the screw will turn on them. That's one picture from the last 10 minutes at Cardiff that's helpful.

They crunch it up short right again, waiting for the perfect ball to go wide left.

This time, Bonnaire drives it up, and I have a look at going for it, but decide not to. Then they come left, with Harinordoquy, and I look again to steal it, but I'm belted off it.

Trench warfare. France has gone 16 phases. We're still hanging in there. The penalty is the danger. Andy's trying to referee us, I hear him screaming at us — Hands off! Get out of there!

JK has a dab at the next ruck, is blown away, too late, we think, appealing. Joubert holds his hands wide again — play on.

We're trying to pressure them at the breakdown, and almost turn it over when the ball goes loose behind them and we think we might have the knock-on when Joubert whistles. It's a scrum, yes, but their ball.

Shit. They get another go. When will this end?

5 to go.

We're all out on our feet. I can't feel my foot any more; I can't feel anything.

The coaches put out Sonny Bill for Ma'a, who's defended brilliantly and is shattered. *That makes sense.*

What Lievremont does makes no sense. Yachvili's off for Jean-Marc Doussain, on debut. You put a guy out there at halfback for the last five minutes of a World Cup final who's never played a test before? Only the French would see any logic in that. Maybe he's got a play we haven't seen before.

Start again.

Scrum just outside our 10-metre line. France is aligned wide left. It's a better scrum from us but still good ball for them.

I track across as Doussain clears to Trinh-Duc who throws a miss-ball past Maxime Medard to Rougerie, who is so strong he drops his shoulder into Conrad and spins him off, then shrugs off Sonny Bill and is finally dragged down by Beaver, right in front of me. *Is this it?*

Rougerie's pace and strength has taken him too far ahead of his support, only a couple of backs around him, too slow . . . *This is it!*

As Rougerie goes to ground, I drive forward over him, get under his support, see the ball loose in front of me, get another two steps towards it before I get hit. There's someone on my back and I'm falling, can't play it, but I just about get over it as Reado cleans out the guy on me a split second before we both get monstered by the heavy cavalry. But we've done enough to put the new halfback off and he fumbles it under intense pressure.

Keep getting up. Get up. After the gouging, with Dr Deb by my side and Dusautoir looking on.

I'm flat on my back on the grass under some bodies when I hear the whistle go and Joubert call 'Knock on', but I can't see anything, got both hands to my eyes because in the washing machine of bodies there was a hand like a half-closed fist or claw banging across my face, looking for my eyes.

I'm still down as everyone gets up, and Joubert calls time out, and Deb gets there as I rise to one knee. She looks at my left eye. I can't see out of it and I'm bleeding from my nose and ear. She asks me if I want to come off. *Shit no!*

We've got the ball. Four minutes to go.

This is it. We've got to do this right.

Deb's got a message from the coaches, probably Smithy. There's space deep left. Beaver should kick for it. Beaver comes over to me while I'm on the ground. 'What do you reckon?' I tell him I think we should get it down there.

Keep getting up. Get up.

I get up. I blink the eye and it sort of clears. I tell Joubert I've been gouged, but what can he do?

Dusautoir has been named Man of the Match while I've been lying there. When the scrums line up, he's got a look in his eyes that I've seen before, but not in his eyes. Desperation. Last throw of the dice. This time, they're behind.

While I've been down, Beaver's taken the message back to the boys — 'Right, we're kicking it.' But when Conrad looks out to where the space was, it's gone: the French fullback has sensed it and moved across.

We're ready to pack the most important scrum we've ever put down, when Andy comes back. 'We can't kick it,' he tells me. I go, 'Righto' — that's what we have a leadership group for — they're seeing better than me now. Andy tells Reado, 'You're taking it up.'

Four years into four minutes.

Start again.

Our scrum holds. Reado takes it off the back and punches up the blind, over the gain-line into Dusautoir and Harinordoquy and we smash in behind him. Franksy drives it, makes no real progress. Doesn't matter. We hold the ball at the back, static. Counting down. *Three minutes is a bloody long time to keep this going!*

I'm over it at the back of the ruck, keeping my hands off it, looking across to Joubert, checking we don't have to play it.

I sense that Joubert's not going to do anything rash. There'll be no penalties unless it's obvious.

I finally pick and go, get smashed down, but we've got numbers in there and we keep it at the back again.

Static. Franksy goes again. Andy's talking us through it. He's great. No panic. Job to do, boys.

2 to go.

We crunch it up again. It's sitting at the back of the ruck again at my feet. Just as I reach for it, someone gets a toe to it and it goes back between my feet. I only just pick it up without fumbling — *Shit!* — and go, get smashed down again, but there's desperate support behind me, over me and we work it to the back of the ruck again.

1.30 to go.

Ali goes the other way, but when he goes down, it's an almighty fight to get numbers over it this time. France force the issue — penalty.

Too far out to kick for goal. What if we miss? What if it falls short? We can't give France the ball back. We can't give them a sniff. What was that try called they scored to win a test back in the 1990s right here at Eden Park? The try from the end of the world. *It would be the end of the bloody world if they did it here!*

Beaver makes sure it goes out.

1 minute to go.

France line up while we consult. What call? The most secure. Brad. We've lost one there already, but it's the safest option. Brad's temperament. Horey's. If there was one lineout in the last four years we needed to win, this is it. Just need everyone to do the job they've done hundreds of times. *Can't lose this one.*

Horey hits a soaring Brad, lifted by Ali. Huge take. We pile into the drive.

30 seconds to kill or be killed.

France are fringing now, desperate to get a sniff at the ball, so we drive it and make some progress.

Same image, different result. Ali and me, four years on.

It's finished. Me and Shag.

10 seconds.

They try to hold us up, get the turnover, but finally we get it to ground and Andy's clever and composed enough not to panic, not to make the pass. Lets it sit there, harangues the pack to get round it once again.

There's a constant wall of sound. I'm under a heap of bodies. Andy's waiting for the ball. *How long? How fucking long?* Somehow, I hear the hooter. Time is up. I start yelling from down under all the bodies. Get it out! Get it out! As I try and get out from under, Conrad comes sprinting in from centre, yelling at Andy. 'Time's up! The hooter's sounded! Put the fucking thing out!'

Szarzewski must have heard the hooter, or heard Conrad. He comes flying round our side of the ruck, knows it's all or nothing. Joubert blasts his whistle over the roar.

Offside! Penalty.

The crowd is off its head. I see our bench jumping in the air, but I can't believe it's over. Our guys are celebrating. I grab Andy by the shoulder.

Stop everything. Slow it down. *Is it over if we put the ball out? Is it finished?* Andy says it is.

He hoofs it into the tiers of the stand, where everyone's on their feet, arms raised.

I raise mine as Joubert blows for fulltime.

Ali hugs me. Someone else.

I bend over, hands on knees. Then sink to one knee. *We've won.* I should be happy. All I feel is relief.

It's finished. I can stop. I don't have to do this any more.

The guys are jumping around, the crowd is so loud I can't hear what they're saying. Someone pulls me up, hugs me.

I do the after-match on auto-pilot. Get my medal from dear old Jock. Lift the Webb Ellis Cup. The moment I've been waiting four years for. I thought I'd feel more. It's like I'm seeing it all through someone else's eyes. The welling emotion of the crowd rolling over me, too mentally and physically shot to really respond. I try to remember what needs to be said, to thank those who need to be thanked.

The right picture.

I feel cold, bloody awful . . .

We're out there so long I get cold.

Sometime later, I'm in the changing room, sitting by myself with my winner's medal around my neck, a beer in my hand, still in my gear. Ted's standing in front of me, patting me on the head, saying something, probably that we've still got to do the media conference, and I start shivering. I feel cold, bloody awful. Someone gets me some Powerade and lollies to get my sugar up, so I can do media.

I get through that, still shaking, so I get in the spa to warm up. At one stage I'm sitting in the spa feeding myself lollies and I look up and someone says hello, and there's John Key sitting on the side of the spa. So I chat to the Prime Minister, still sitting in the spa swallowing lollies.

It takes me quite a long time, even once we get back to the hotel and I see everyone around, so happy, to begin to feel it myself, to get past the relief that it is truly finished, that I don't have to get up tomorrow and start again.

It's over. We've won. Believe it.

Enjoy

Gratification doesn't have to be instant. The further I get from that final whistle on 23 October 2011, the more I enjoy it. I realise I've been in a tunnel for four years, enjoying my life, but pushing away anything and anyone who wasn't going to help me get to that point of light at the end. Now that I'm there, with the sun on my face, it feels bloody fantastic.

France was superb, the perfect adversary. If we'd won by 20 points, we still wouldn't know if we'd learnt anything from Cardiff. That last 30 minutes of the final was exactly the physical and psychological test we'd prepared for.

We parade the Cup down Queen Street, then in Christchurch and Wellington. Christchurch did it so tough. The city is at the centre of the national rugby community and would have given so much to the Cup, but missed out on everything. Yet they still turn out in their thousands.

Sometimes you need other people to show you the true meaning of what has happened. The parades — seeing the pleasure in all those beaming faces — helps my understanding of the significance of what we've done. People telling me that they felt like part of a national community that embraced pretty much everyone, whether or not you were a rugby fan.

We all made it happen, what most people consider to be the best festival of rugby ever. Jock's stadium of four million realised. I'm glad he's still here to enjoy the moment, along with Martin Snedden and all the people who volunteered or who supported teams from around the world and made them and their fans welcome. I didn't actually see that much of it from my tunnel, so it's special now to share the enjoyment of this moment, when New Zealand seems like a happy, seamless community. Okay, it's just a moment in time, but to see it and feel it gives me a pleasure and sense of fulfilment that's hard to describe. It will stay with me forever.

But, even now, I'm determined to carry those memories without living in the past. I can enjoy them, reflect on them, but I can't live there. To try would set me up for failure in the future. It's been such a privilege to be involved in the team

After the gold rush — a successful day's fishing with, from left, Woody, Ali, Ted, Horey and AB (Anthony Boric).

with Ted in charge. He created an environment that I and the others all loved and bought into, and he was determined to do everything we could every day to get the results we desired. I learnt so much over the time Ted and Smithy and Shag were coaching us, and I'm grateful to have had the opportunity to be part of it.

But the All Blacks go on, and are bigger than any of us. Back in May, long before the RWC, I re-signed with the NZRU for a further four years. I decided back then that, win or lose, I wanted to stay involved with New Zealand rugby. Winning the World Cup is both a huge bonus and challenge. History shows that very few winners of the World Cup have been able to live up to the world champion tag in subsequent years. I'd like us to try. To carry that title with pride and live up to what it means. There are no guarantees that we can. The game has no memory or sentiment. But a big part of what I love about the game is the obstacles you have to overcome to achieve anything. And, as the adage goes, whether you think you can or you think you can't, either way you're probably right. I choose to believe that we can.

But first I've got to recover. There's the foot, of course.

In Auckland, a couple of days after the final, Ted, Ali, Woody, Horey, DC, Anthony Boric and I go fishing in the Gulf. I'm in bare feet, rod in hand, resting my bad foot up on the side.

Ted looks at the foot, 'That doesn't look too flash.'

It doesn't. It's a horrible-looking object, swollen, red and purple. Munted. Since

I caught up with the family in the early hours of the morning following the final. Jo's got the champagne and Mum's got the Cup. Sam and Dad just look content.

the final, I've pretty much ignored it, and while the alcoholic intake might have helped with the pain, it's done bugger all to improve the condition of the foot.

When I finally get it X-rayed, it's found to have three fracture lines — effectively three breaks. That same metatarsal. The screw went in longitudinally down the bone to hold the original stress fracture together, and that's fine. But at the point where the screw ends, the breaks begin — looking back, probably one for each clunk I felt in the pool game against France, the quarter-final against Argentina, and the semi against Australia.

In late November I finally have the foot operated on. There's no pressure on me any more, but I still want a rehab plan. Crutches for four weeks, then two in a moon boot. I've got things I want to do. A certain beautiful carbon fibre and Kevlar bird is waiting for me.

When I'm down in Omarama, on a beautiful late January day, Dad and Mum and I drive over the big hill and down the valley to Kurow. The hay bales at the beginning of the wooden bridge now sport a metre-high replica of 'Old Bill', made out of a milk barrow and irrigation sprinklers. Barney McCone is there with his wife Gill, and lots of other locals I know. It's the first time I've seen my old coach since the Cup. Barney looks me in the eyes as he shakes my hand and says, 'Good on you, Richard. We're very proud of you.'

Then we do the parade down the main street, Bledisloe Street, the full Kurow ticker-tape, with the fire engine, the cop car and ambulance, all with their sirens going. The parade's been kept under the covers, so that it's a local show and no media, but through word of mouth everyone in the district turns up.

From the top of the fire engine, I can look south-east over the town towards the fields where I trained and played with the Kurow Under 9s, 10s, 11s, 12s and 13s. For a sense of completion and of coming full circle, it's hard to beat. I'm enjoying every second.

Me and Barney McCone in front of Kurow's Old Bill.

Statistics
(to 31 July 2012)

FIRST CLASS CAREER

Team	Period	Games	Tries	Points
Canterbury	2000–09	34	10	50
New Zealand	2001–12	107	20*	100
NZ Colts	2000–01	5	3	15
Invitation XV	2008	1	-	-
Crusaders	2001–12	120	26	130
Totals		267	59	295

*Includes a penalty try

ALL BLACKS TEST CAREER

Opponent	Played	Won	Drew	Lost	Tries	Points
Argentina	3	3	-	-	-	-
Australia	26	21	-	5	8	40
British & Irish Lions	2	2	-	-	1	5
Canada	2	2	-	-	-	-
England	8	7	-	1	-	-
Fiji	2	2	-	-	-	-
France	11	10	-	1	1	5
Ireland	13	13	-	-	1	5
Italy	3	3	-	-	4	20
Romania	1	1	-	-	-	-
Scotland	5	5	-	-	1	5
South Africa	19	14	-	5	4	20
Tonga	2	2	-	-	-	-
Wales	9	9	-	-	-	-
Totals	106	94	0	12	20	100

Statistics compiled by Geoff Miller

Acknowledgements

When I started giving serious thought to doing a book late last year, Greg McGee's name was one that immediately sprang to mind as a possible writer. While I didn't know Greg well, I knew he was originally from my neck of the woods and that he was highly regarded as a writer. I knew, too, from people close to me that he was a decent bloke. Now, after the work has been done, I can look back on a thoroughly memorable experience. Greg has been great to work with and has made the job of telling my story not feel like a chore. I hope he's as proud of the book as I am. Thanks, Greg.

Richie McCaw, July 2012

Being part of Richie's world for six months or so has been a privilege, not just for the insights it's given me as to how he does what he does, and why, but also for the opportunity it's given me to meet and talk to some of the people who are important to him, particularly his mother and father, Margaret and Don, and his sister Jo, who are never far from his side or his thoughts. Margaret and Richie's uncle, John McCaw, went to a lot of trouble to locate family photographs.

In late summer, 2012, I drove up the Waitaki Valley to Domett Downs to share tea and scones with Barney McCone and his wife, Gill, in a house that my father painted decades ago when it was built. Our local hero, All Black Phil Gard, ran onto halfback Barney's passes when he was playing first-five for Kurow. Barney was the first in a line of superlative coaches who have blessed Richie's career, and he showed me the meticulously kept exercise books where 'Richard's' progress was recorded week by week — a practice repeated by his pupil to this day.

From there I drove up through Kurow and over the big hill to Omarama, where my sister used to teach school, to spend an hour with Gavin Wills at the laid-back Kahu Café right by the airfield. Gavin kindly offered to take me up in a glider, but I managed to persuade him to make do with some photographs.

The book is very much Richie's story, from Richie's point of view, so I didn't speak to any of Richie's current playing colleagues or coaches, apart from Wayne Smith, who gave me a valuable perspective on some critical moments.

My thanks to them all for so generously making time for me. And to others who have supplied material for this book: Brian Ashwin, Richie's teacher and coach at Otago Boys' High School, still dedicated to the boys there; Derek Lardelli, the composer of 'Kapa o Pango'; all the sports journalists I have quoted; and to Geoff Miller and Lindsay Knight for checking the accuracy of the material.

I also want to thank Eric Young, editor of *Sky Sport* magazine back in 2006, who had a rush of blood and decided I was the man to interview Richie McCaw before the 2007 RWC. I'm not sure how these things work, but I suspect that interview set off a chain reaction that culminated in my writing this book. Certainly, I was still sufficiently intrigued by him four years later to devote one of my RWC columns in *Le Monde* to him.

Nevertheless, when I received an email from Warren Adler, Editorial Director of Hachette, in mid-December asking me if I was interested in writing sports biographies, I thought it was just a generic enquiry, and was about to write back, saying, *No, not really*, when I had a second thought. Could it possibly be Richie he wanted me to write about? Probably not, but no harm in keeping my options open: *Depends who it is*, I replied.

Soon after I got a phone call from Warren, saying that the chap he and Kevin Chapman, Managing Director of Hachette, had in mind was 'from further up the Waitaki'.

Thanks for thinking of me, Warren and Kevin, in respect of the chap from further up the Waitaki, and for your wholehearted support during the writing process. Even though deadlines were tight, you never once passed the pressure on down to me and Richie.

Speaking of pressure, it's hard to imagine what Richie's degree of fame actually means, until you're out in the world with him. You can't be a minute late picking him up, because he'll be surrounded by people wanting his autograph and photos by the time you get there. You might be sitting in a car with him outside an office block wondering — because after three hours with him, you've forgotten for a moment or two who he is — why those women have suddenly appeared at the entrance and are giggling and waving, or why that jaywalker in Queen Street has stopped in front of you and is jumping up and down and pointing. If the kids at the school next to our home had spotted his comings and goings there'd have been a mini riot. While Richie accepts that fame is a tap that can't be turned off when he's had enough, I'm pretty sure he wishes it could be. He's got an awful lot of life left to live, and I hope he's able to do that according to his own lights, without letting others' perceptions of what he should be inhibit or constrain him.

Thanks, Richie. As you say about other men you respect enormously, you're a good bugger.

Greg McGee, July 2012

Index of names

Bold page numbers refer to photographs.

Index of names

Index of names